The Complete Ninja Dual Zone Air Fryer

Cookbook

365

Effortless and Delicious Air Fryer Recipes for the Whole Family, Including Inspirations for Breakfast, Lunch, Dinner, Desserts & More.

Marie Tanner

Ninja Dual Zone Air Fryer

Table of Contents

Beef, pork&Lamb Recipes 41

Fish And Seafood Recipes 55

Poultry Recipes 67

Vegetarians Recipes 77

Desserts And Sweets 87

RECIPE INDEX 97

Introduction

The Ninja Foodi Dual Zone Air Fryer has revolutionized kitchen technology to the point where users can now enjoy fresh, crispy food in no time. It's a dual-zone air fryer that combines six culinary functions: Air Broil, Air Fry, Roast, Bake, Dehydrate, and Reheat into one device. This equipment is ideal for those who enjoy baking and cooking crispy foods. The air fryer comes with two fryer baskets labelled "1" and "2," which should be inserted into their corresponding parts.

The Ninja Foodi Dual Zone Air Fryer is an advanced and multifunctional air fryer from the Ninja Foodi family. The beautiful dark grey stainless steel air fryer comes with an 8-quart cooking capacity, which is enough for the whole family. The cooking basket comes with non-stick ceramic coatings and long handles for easy hold. Ninja Foodi invented this unique air fryer with two separate cooking baskets to work both the cooking zones independently.

The Ninja Foodi Dual Zone Air Fryer works on dual-zone technology. It allows you to cook multiple dishes at the same time in two different cooking baskets. It also allows you to customize the time and temperature for both cooking zones as per your need. The cooking zones have their separate temperature controller unit and cyclonic fan to distribute heat evenly into the cooking basket. The smart finish feature ensures that both zones complete their cooking at the same time. The Ninja Foodi Dual Zone Air Fryer cooks your favourite fried food using 75 to 80% less fat and oil than the traditional method. It makes your food crispy without changing the taste and texture.

The Ninja Foodi Dual Zone Air Fryer comes with 6 customizable program settings. These functions include air fry, air broil, roast, bake, reheat and dehydrate. The air fryer works on 1690 watt power to cook your food rapidly. It allows you to cook your main meal with a side meal simultaneously between a temperature range of 105 °F to 450 °F. The air fryer comes with a non-stick interior for effortless cleaning.

Prepare for Your Ninja Foodi Dual Zone Air Fryer Journey

What the Ninja Foodi Dual Zone Air Fryer is

The Ninja Foodi Dual Zone Air Fryer is the next revolutionary appliance coming from the awesome folks working at Ninja Kitchen! No matter how unbelievable the concept might sound, Ninja Kitchen has put on countless hours of engineering into crafting this meticulously designed appliance that takes the Air Frying game to a whole different level.

At its heart, the Ninja Foodi Dual Zone Air Fryer is a simple and exceedingly effective Air Fryer that gives you all the basic functions that you would expect from an Air Fryer. With this appliance, you can Air Frye, Bake, Broil, Dehydrate, Air Crisp, and more! You know, the usual Air Fryer stuffs.

However, what makes this unique is the super cool "Dual Zone" technology that completely flips the game in the Air Frying market.

If you are looking to cut down your cooking to half, or you want to make two different meals at the same time. The same appliance, then the Ninja Foodi Dual Zone Air Fryer is exactly what you need!

Simply put, the Dual Zone technology allows the appliance to be put on either single cook mode or multi cook mode. Single cook mode works as usual; you cook using just a single basket. However, with the Dual Cook mode, you can seamlessly set the different timer, mode, and temperature for both of the zones individually and cook the meals you require. Alternatively, you may give the same settings to both of the zones and cook the same meal in a doubled portion without spending any more time than you would need when making just a single portion.

While handling two Air Fryer baskets might sound a little bit complicated at first, the way how Ninja Kitchen has engineered this appliance has made it extremely accessible and easy to handle.

The Smart Features of the Ninja Foodi Dual Zone Air Fryers

The Ninja Foodi Dual Zone Air Fryer is one of the innovative product designs manufactured. If you are looking for a perfect air fryer for your family, then the Ninja Foodi Dual Zone Air Fryer is one of the best options available for you. Some of the important features of the Ninja Foodi Dual Zone Air Fryer are mentioned as follows.

1.   Large Capacity

The Ninja Foodi Dual Zone Air Fryer has a total of 8-qt capacity, which is divided into two 4-qt cooking zones-Zone 1 and Zone 2. The number of the zone is given on the crisper plate so you could easily detect them. Each zone has a portion in the display, and it shows their respective settings. You can use the respective keys to set the time and temperature for each zone.

2.   Multifunctional Air Fryer

The Ninja Foodi Dual Zone Air Fryer comes with 6 preset functions. These easily customizable functions include max crisp, air fry, roast, bake, reheat and dehydrate. You never need to buy separate appliances for a single cooking function.

3.   Smart Finish Technology

The smart finish function can help you cook different things in each cooking zone at different temperatures and times. When you press the SYNC button, you can sync the cook times for both zones to finish at the same time. These functions will allow both of the cooking zones to complete their cooking simultaneously, even if both of the zones have completely different cook settings.

4.   Match Cook

This feature allows you to cook meals in both of drawers at the same temperature and for the same time duration. If you want to cook a large amount of the same food, or you want to cook two different foods at the same time, you can then use the MATCH button. Select the cooking mode, temperature, and time for Zone 1. Then press the MATCH button to copy these settings for zone 2. Now both zones will have the same settings. After pressing the START/STOP button, they will start cooking the food in their respective chambers.

The Functions and Buttons of the Ninja Foodi Dual Zone Air Fryers

The Ninja Foodi Dual Zone Air Fryer comes with 6 in 1 cooking functions and different operating buttons which are mentioned as follows.

Functions

1.   **Max Crisp:** This function is ideal for frozen food like chicken nuggets and French fries. Using this function, you can add extra crispiness and crunch into your food.

2.   **Air Fry:** This function allows you to air fry your favourite food using minimal fats and oil compared with the traditional cooking method. Air frying makes your food crunchy, crisper from the outside and juicy tender from the inside. Using the air fry function, you can air fry your favourite food without changing the taste and texture of deep-fried food.

3.   **Roast:** Using this function, you can convert your air fryer into a roaster oven which helps to tender your favourite meat, vegetables and more. It is one of the dry cooking

methods that gives a nice brown texture to the food and enhances the flavor of your food.

4. **Reheat:** This function is ideal for reheating your leftover food. It makes your food warm and also makes it crispier as it was yesterday.

5. **Dehydrate:** This function is used to reduce the moisture content of food and is ideal for dehydrating your favourite vegetables, fruits, and meat slices. Using this method can also preserve your favourite food for a long time.

6. **Bake:** This function converts your air fryer into a convection oven. It is ideal for baking your favourite cakes, cookies, and desserts.

Operation Buttons

1. **Time Arrow Buttons:** Using up and down arrow keys, you can easily adjust the time settings as per your recipe needs.

2. **Temp Arrow Buttons:** Using up and down arrow keys, you can easily change the temperature settings as per your recipe needs.

3. **Sync Button:** This function is used to sync the cooking time automatically and ensures that both the cooking zones finish their cooking simultaneously, even if there is a difference between their cooking times.

4. **Match Button:** This function is used to match the cooking zone 2 settings with cooking zone 1 setting on a large quantity of the same food or different food cooking at the same function, temperature, and time.

5. **Start/Stop Button:** Use this button to start the cooking process after selecting the time and temperature settings as per your recipe needs.

6. **Standby Mode:** This equipment goes into standby mode when it is powered on but not in use for more than 10 minutes.

7. **Hold Mode:** When the time setting for both zones doesn't match but you want both zones to finish cooking at the same time, the zone with the lesser time will be on hold but when the time becomes equal the hold mode will disappear and the zone on hold will start cooking. This will also show during SYNC mode if the other zone takes too long to synchronize with the rest of the zone.

Maintaining and Cleaning the Appliance

The interior parts of the Ninja Foodi Dual Zone Air Fryer are made of non-stick coating, so you can easily clean it. Here is how to clean and maintain your Ninja Foodi Dual Zone Air Fryer after cooking:

1. Unplug your appliance before cleaning it and allow it to cool completely.
2. Remove the air fryer baskets from the unit and let them cool.
3. When cooled, remove their crispier plates and wash them in the dishwasher.
4. Clean the baskets with soapy water and but don't use hard scrubbing; otherwise, it will damage the surface.
5. Wipe the main unit with a clean piece of cloth or damp cloth.
6. When all parts of the air fryer dried, return to the unit.
7. Now, you can use it again for cooking

Hearty Tips for Using the Appliance

Since this is a relatively new appliance to hit the market, people are still beginning to grasp this amazing appliance's full potential. They are exploring how to properly use this product. The following tips will greatly enhance your cooking experience with this appliance and make everything a breeze.

1. It's always suggested that you collect all of the ingredients you require before starting your cooking session. If you are unable to find a specific ingredient, then make sure to find an alternative beforehand. The recipes in this book already have the best ingredients chosen to provide the best flavor. Still, since different people have different taste buds, you might consider altering a few if you feel like it.

2. Make sure to read the recipes thoroughly before you start cooking; if you find any step confusing, then do a simple google search to properly understand the steps.

3. Before starting your cooking session, make sure that your appliance to clean and free from any dirt or debris. Follow the steps provided in the section above if you are confused about how to do it.

4. The air fryer location is extremely important if you want your meals to cook evenly since it relies heavily on the airflow. Therefore, make sure to keep it in a space where it has enough space to "Breath" in Air and cook the meals properly.

5. If you are using frozen food, you should consider thawing them before putting them in your air fryer basket.

6. Since the air fryer relies on Superheated Air to do the cooking, make sure to never overcrowd the cooking baskets. Always keep space in between heavy ingredients.

Now that you have two zones to work with, this shouldn't be a problem at all!

7. When cooking with the air fryer, it is always advised that you opt for organic ingredients. Try to find the freshest ones possible as they will give you the best flavors.

8. When choosing a baking tray for your air fryer, try to go for lighter color trays/dishes. Dark colors such as black ones would absorb more heat that might result in uneven cooking.

It's about time that you give this appliance a try and do some cooking!

Appetizers And Snacks

Sweet Potato Fries With Sweet And Spicy Dipping Sauce

Servings:2
Cooking Time:20 Minutes
Ingredients:
- 1 large sweet potato(about 1 pound)
- 1 teaspoon vegetable or canola oil
- salt
- Sweet&Spicy Dipping Sauce
- ¼cup light mayonnaise
- 1 tablespoon spicy brown mustard
- 1 tablespoon sweet Thai chili sauce
- ½teaspoon sriracha sauce

Directions:
1. Scrub the sweet potato well and then cut it into¼-inch French fries.(A mandolin slicer can really help with this.)
2. Preheat the air fryer to 200°F(95°C).
3. Toss the sweet potato sticks with the oil and transfer them to the air fryer basket.Air-fry at 200°F(95°C)for 10 minutes,shaking the basket several times during the cooking process for even cooking.Toss the fries with salt,increase the air fryer temperature to 400°F(205°C)and air-fry for another 10 minutes,shaking the basket several times during the cooking process.
4. To make the dipping sauce,combine all the ingredients in a small bowl and stir until combined.
5. Serve the sweet potato fries warm with the dipping sauce on the side.

Buffalo French Fries

Servings:6
Cooking Time:35 Minutes
Ingredients:
- 3 large russet potatoes
- 2 tbsp buffalo sauce
- 2 tbsp extra-virgin olive oil
- Salt and pepper to taste

Directions:
1. Preheat air fryer to 380°F(195°C).Peel and cut potatoes lengthwise into French fries.Place them in a bowl,then coat with olive oil,salt and pepper.Air Fry them for 10 minutes.Shake the basket,then cook for five minutes.Serve drizzled with Buffalo sauce immediately.

Okra Chips

Servings:4
Cooking Time:16 Minutes
Ingredients:
- 1¼pounds Thin fresh okra pods,cut into 1-inch pieces
- 1½tablespoons Vegetable or canola oil
- ¾teaspoon Coarse sea salt or kosher salt

Directions:
1. Preheat the air fryer to 400°F(205°C).
2. Toss the okra,oil,and salt in a large bowl until the pieces are well and evenly coated.
3. When the machine is at temperature,pour the contents of the bowl into the basket.Air-fry,tossing several times,for 16 minutes,or until crisp and quite brown(maybe even a little blackened on the thin bits).
4. Pour the contents of the basket onto a wire rack.Cool for a couple of minutes before serving.

Potato Chips

Servings:2
Cooking Time:15 Minutes
Ingredients:
- 2 medium potatoes
- 2 teaspoons extra-light olive oil
- oil for misting or cooking spray
- salt and pepper

Directions:
1. Peel the potatoes.
2. Using a mandoline or paring knife,shave potatoes into thin slices,dropping them into a bowl of water as you cut them.
3. Dry potatoes as thoroughly as possible with paper towels or a clean dish towel.Toss potato slices with the oil to coat completely.
4. Spray air fryer basket with cooking spray and add potato slices.
5. Stir and separate with a fork.
6. Cook 390°F(200°C)for 5minutes.Stir and separate potato slices.Cook 5 more minutes.Stir and separate potatoes again.Cook another 5minutes.
7. Season to taste.

Roasted Jalapeño Salsa Verde

Servings:4
Cooking Time:20 Minutes
Ingredients:
- ¾lb fresh tomatillos,husked
- 1 jalapeño,stem removed
- 4 green onions,sliced
- 3 garlic cloves,peeled
- ½tsp salt
- 1 tsp lime juice
- ¼tsp apple cider vinegar
- ¼cup cilantro leaves

Directions:
1. Preheat air fryer to 400ºF.Add tomatillos and jalapeño to the frying basket and Bake for 5 minutes.Put in green onions and garlic and Bake for 5 more minutes.Transfer it into a food processor along with salt,lime juice,vinegar and cilantro and blend until the sauce is finely chopped.Pour it into a small sealable container and refrigerate it until ready to use up to five days.

Sweet And Salty Snack Mix

Servings:10
Cooking Time:12 Minutes
Ingredients:
- ½cup honey
- 3 tablespoons butter,melted
- 1 teaspoon salt
- 2 cups sesame sticks

- 1 cup pepitas(pumpkin seeds)
- 2 cups granola
- 1 cup cashews
- 2 cups crispy corn puff cereal(Kix® or Corn Pops®)
- 2 cups mini pretzel crisps
- 1 cup dried cherries

Directions:

1. Combine the honey,butter and salt in a small bowl or measuring cup and stir until combined.
2. Combine the sesame sticks,pepitas,granola,cashews,corn puff cereal and pretzel crisps in a large bowl.Pour the honey mixture over the top and toss to combine.
3. Preheat air fryer to 370°F(185°C).
4. Air-fry the snack mix in two batches.Place half the mixture in the air fryer basket and air-fry for 12 minutes,or until the snack mix is lightly toasted.Toss the basket several times throughout the process so that the mix cooks evenly and doesn't get too dark on top.
5. Transfer the snack mix to a cookie sheet and let it cool completely.Mix in the dried cherries and store the mix in an airtight container for up to a week or two.

Spicy Pearl Onion Dip

Servings:4
Cooking Time:20 Minutes+chilling Time
Ingredients:

- 2 cups peeled pearl onions
- 3 garlic cloves
- 3 tbsp olive oil
- Salt and pepper to taste
- 1 cup Greek yogurt
- ¼tsp Worcestershire sauce
- 1 tbsp lemon juice
- ⅛tsp red pepper flakes
- 1 tbsp chives,chopped

Directions:

1. Preheat air fryer to 360°F(180°C).Place the onions,garlic,and 2 tbsp of olive oil in a bowl and combine until the onions are well coated.Pour the mixture into the frying basket and Roast for 11-13 minutes.Transfer the garlic and onions to your food processor.Pulse the vegetables several times until the onions are minced but still have some chunks.
2. Combine the garlic and onions and the remaining olive oil,along with the salt,yogurt,Worcestershire sauce,lemon juice,black pepper,chives and red pepper flakes in a bowl.Cover and chill for at least 1 hour.Serve with toasted bread if desired.

Bacon&Blue Cheese Tartlets

Servings:6
Cooking Time:30 Minutes
Ingredients:

- 6 bacon slices
- 16 phyllo tartlet shells
- ½cup diced blue cheese
- 3 tbsp apple jelly

Directions:

1. Preheat the air fryer to 400°F(205°C).Put the bacon in a single layer in the frying basket and Air Fry for 14 minutes,turning once halfway through.Remove and drain on paper towels,then crumble when cool.Wipe the fryer clean.Fill the tartlet shells with bacon and the blue cheese cubes and add a dab of apple jelly on top of the filling.Lower the temperature to 350°F(175°C),then put the shells in the frying basket.Air Fry until the cheese melts and the shells brown,about 5-6 minutes.Remove and serve.

Bacon Candy

Servings:6
Cooking Time:6 Minutes
Ingredients:

- 1½tablespoons Honey
- 1 teaspoon White wine vinegar
- 3 Extra thick–cut bacon strips,halved widthwise(gluten-free,if a concern)
- ½teaspoon Ground black pepper

Directions:

1. Preheat the air fryer to 350°F(175°C).
2. Whisk the honey and vinegar in a small bowl until incorporated.
3. When the machine is at temperature,remove the basket.Lay the bacon strip halves in the basket in one layer.Brush the tops with the honey mixture;sprinkle each bacon strip evenly with black pepper.
4. Return the basket to the machine and air-fry undisturbed for 6 minutes,or until the bacon is crunchy.Or a little less time if you prefer bacon that's still pliable,an extra minute if you want the bacon super crunchy.Take care that the honey coating doesn't burn.Remove the basket from the machine and set aside for 5 minutes.Use kitchen tongs to transfer the bacon strips to a serving plate.

Grilled Ham&Muenster Cheese On Raisin Bread

Servings:1
Cooking Time:10 Minutes
Ingredients:

- 2 slices raisin bread
- 2 tablespoons butter,softened
- 2 teaspoons honey mustard
- 3 slices thinly sliced honey ham(about 3 ounces)
- 4 slices Muenster cheese(about 3 ounces)
- 2 toothpicks

Directions:

1. Preheat the air fryer to 370°F(185°C).
2. Spread the softened butter on one side of both slices of raisin bread and place the bread,buttered side down on the counter.Spread the honey mustard on the other side of each slice of bread.Layer 2 slices of cheese,the ham and the remaining 2 slices of cheese on one slice of bread and top with the other slice of bread.Remember to leave the buttered side of the bread on the outside.
3. Transfer the sandwich to the air fryer basket and secure the sandwich with toothpicks.
4. Air-fry at 370°F(185°C)for 5 minutes.Flip the sandwich over,remove the toothpicks and air-fry for another 5 minutes.Cut the sandwich in half and enjoy!!

Cinnamon Pita Chips

Servings:4
Cooking Time:6 Minutes
Ingredients:
- 2 tablespoons sugar
- 2 teaspoons cinnamon
- 2 whole 6-inch pitas,whole grain or white
- oil for misting or cooking spray

Directions:
1. Mix sugar and cinnamon together.
2. Cut each pita in half and each half into 4 wedges.Break apart each wedge at the fold.
3. Mist one side of pita wedges with oil or cooking spray.Sprinkle them all with half of the cinnamon sugar.
4. Turn the wedges over,mist the other side with oil or cooking spray,and sprinkle with the remaining cinnamon sugar.
5. Place pita wedges in air fryer basket and cook at 330°F(165°C)for 2minutes.
6. Shake basket and cook 2 more minutes.Shake again,and if needed cook 2 more minutes,until crisp.Watch carefully because at this point they will cook very quickly.

Jalapeño&Mozzarella Stuffed Mushrooms

Servings:4
Cooking Time:30 Minutes
Ingredients:
- 16 button mushrooms
- 1/3 cup salsa
- 3 garlic cloves,minced
- 1 onion,finely chopped
- 1 jalapeño pepper,minced
- ⅛tsp cayenne pepper
- 3 tbsp shredded mozzarella
- 2 tsp olive oil

Directions:
1. Preheat air fryer to 350°F(175°C).Cut the stem off the mushrooms,then slice them finely.Set the caps aside.Combine the salsa,garlic,onion,jalapeño,cayenne,and mozzarella cheese in a bowl,then add the stems.Fill the mushroom caps with the mixture,making sure to overfill so the mix is coming out of the top.Drizzle with olive oil.Place the caps in the air fryer and Bake for 8-12 minutes.The filling should be hot and the mushrooms soft.Serve warm.

Zucchini Fritters

Servings:8
Cooking Time:10 Minutes
Ingredients:
- 2 cups grated zucchini
- ½teaspoon sea salt
- 1 egg
- ½teaspoon garlic powder
- ¼teaspoon onion powder
- ¼cup grated Parmesan cheese
- ½cup all-purpose flour
- ¼teaspoon baking powder
- ½cup Greek yogurt or sour cream
- ½lime,juiced

- ¼cup chopped cilantro
- ¼teaspoon ground cumin
- ¼teaspoon salt

Directions:
1. Preheat the air fryer to 360°F(180°C).
2. In a large colander,place a kitchen towel.Inside the towel,place the grated zucchini and sprinkle the sea salt over the top.Let the zucchini sit for 5 minutes;then,using the towel,squeeze dry the zucchini.
3. In a medium bowl,mix together the egg,garlic powder,onion powder,Parmesan cheese,flour,and baking powder.Add in the grated zucchini,and stir until completely combined.
4. Pierce a piece of parchment paper with a fork 4 to 6 times.Place the parchment paper into the air fryer basket.Using a tablespoon,place 6 to 8 heaping tablespoons of fritter batter onto the parchment paper.Spray the fritters with cooking spray and cook for 5 minutes,turn the fritters over,and cook another 5 minutes.
5. Meanwhile,while the fritters are cooking,make the sauce.In a small bowl,whisk together the Greek yogurt or sour cream,lime juice,cilantro,cumin,and salt.
6. Repeat Steps 2–4 with the remaining batter.

Cherry Chipotle Bbq Chicken Wings

Servings:2
Cooking Time:12 Minutes
Ingredients:
- 1 teaspoon smoked paprika
- ½teaspoon dry mustard powder
- 1 teaspoon dried oregano
- 1 teaspoon dried thyme
- ½teaspoon chili powder
- 1 teaspoon salt
- 2 pounds chicken wings
- vegetable oil or spray
- salt and freshly ground black pepper
- 1 to 2 tablespoons chopped chipotle peppers in adobo sauce
- ⅓cup cherry preserves¼cup tomato ketchup

Directions:
1. Combine the first six ingredients in a large bowl.Prepare the chicken wings by cutting off the wing tips and discarding(or freezing for chicken stock).Divide the drumettes from the win-gettes by cutting through the joint.Place the chicken wing pieces in the bowl with the spice mix.Toss or shake well to coat.
2. Preheat the air fryer to 400°F(205°C).
3. Spray the wings lightly with the vegetable oil and air-fry the wings in two batches for 10 minutes per batch,shaking the basket halfway through the cooking process.When both batches are done,toss all the wings back into the basket for another 2 minutes to heat through and finish cooking.
4. While the wings are air-frying,combine the chopped chipotle peppers,cherry preserves and ketchup in a bowl.
5. Remove the wings from the air fryer,toss them in the cherry chipotle BBQ sauce and serve with napkins!

Fried Olives

Servings:5
Cooking Time:10 Minutes
Ingredients:
- ⅓cup All-purpose flour or tapioca flour
- 1 Large egg white(s)
- 1 tablespoon Brine from the olive jar
- ⅔cup Plain dried bread crumbs(gluten-free,if a concern)
- 15 Large pimiento-stuffed green olives
- Olive oil spray

Directions:
1. Preheat the air fryer to 400°F(205°C).
2. Pour the flour in a medium-size zip-closed plastic bag.Whisk the egg white and pickle brine in a medium bowl until foamy.Spread out the bread crumbs on a dinner plate.
3. Pour all the olives into the bag with the flour,seal,and shake to coat the olives.Remove a couple of olives,shake off any excess flour,and drop them into the egg white mixture.Toss gently but well to coat.Pick them up one at a time and roll each in the bread crumbs until well coated on all sides,even the ends.Set them aside on a cutting board as you finish the rest.When done,coat the olives with olive oil spray on all sides.
4. Place the olives in the basket in one layer.Air-fry for 8 minutes,gently shaking the basket once halfway through the cooking process to rearrange the olives,until lightly browned.
5. Gently pour the olives onto a wire rack and cool for at least 10 minutes before serving.Once cooled,the olives may be stored in a sealed container in the fridge for up to 2 days.To rewarm them,set them in the basket of a heated 400°F(205°C)air fryer undisturbed for 2 minutes.

Five Spice Fries

Servings:2
Cooking Time:30 Minutes
Ingredients:
- 1 Yukon Gold potato,cut into fries
- 1 tbsp coconut oil
- 1 tsp coconut sugar
- 1 tsp garlic powder
- ½tsp Chinese five-spice
- Salt to taste
- ¼tsp turmeric
- ¼tsp paprika

Directions:
1. Preheat air fryer to 390°F(200°C).Toss the potato pieces with coconut oil,sugar,garlic,Chinese five-spice,salt,turmeric,and paprika in a bowl and stir well.Place in the greased frying basket and Air Fry for 18-25 minutes,tossing twice until softened and golden.Serve warm.

Crispy Tofu Bites

Servings:4
Cooking Time:20 Minutes
Ingredients:
- 1 pound Extra firm unflavored tofu
- Vegetable oil spray

Directions:

1. Wrap the piece of tofu in a triple layer of paper towels.Place it on a wooden cutting board and set a large pot on top of it to press out excess moisture.Set aside for 10 minutes.
2. Preheat the air fryer to 400°F(205°C).
3. Remove the pot and unwrap the tofu.Cut it into 1-inch cubes.Place these in a bowl and coat them generously with vegetable oil spray.Toss gently,then spray generously again before tossing,until all are glistening.
4. Gently pour the tofu pieces into the basket,spread them into as close to one layer as possible,and air-fry for 20 minutes,using kitchen tongs to gently rearrange the pieces at the 7-and 14-minute marks,until light brown and crisp.
5. Gently pour the tofu pieces onto a wire rack.Cool for 5 minutes before serving warm.

Marmalade-almond Topped Brie

Servings:6
Cooking Time:35 Minutes
Ingredients:
- 1 cup almonds
- 1 egg white,beaten
- ⅛tsp ground cumin
- ⅛tsp cayenne pepper
- 1 tsp ground cinnamon
- ¼tsp powdered sugar
- 1 round Brie cheese
- 2 tbsp orange marmalade

Directions:
1. Preheat air fryer to 325ºF.In a bowl,mix the beaten egg white and almonds.In another bowl,mix the spices and sugar.Stir in almonds,drained of excess egg white.Transfer the almonds to the frying basket and Bake for 12 minutes,tossing once.Let cool for 5 minutes.When cooled,chop into smaller bits.Adjust the air fryer temperature to 400°F(205°C).Place the Brie on a parchment-lined pizza pan and Bake for 10 minutes.Transfer the Brie to a serving plate,spread orange marmalade on top,and garnish with spiced walnuts.Serve and enjoy!

Cocktail Beef Bites

Servings:4
Cooking Time:30 Minutes
Ingredients:
- 1 lb sirloin tip,cubed
- 1 cup cheese pasta sauce
- 1½cups soft bread crumbs
- 2 tbsp olive oil
- ½tsp garlic powder
- ½tsp dried thyme

Directions:
1. Preheat air fryer to 360°F(180°C).Toss the beef and the pasta sauce in a medium bowl.Set aside.In a shallow bowl,mix bread crumbs,oil,garlic,and thyme until well combined.Drop the cubes in the crumb mixture to coat.Place them in the greased frying basket and Bake for 6-8 minutes,shaking once until the beef is crisp and browned.Serve warm with cocktail forks or toothpicks.

Curly Kale Chips With Greek Sauce

Servings:4
Cooking Time:15 Minutes
Ingredients:
- 1 cup Greek yogurt
- 3 tbsp lemon juice
- ½tsp mustard powder
- ½tsp dried dill
- 1 tbsp ground walnuts
- 1 bunch curly kale
- 2 tbsp olive oil
- Salt and pepper to taste

Directions:
1. Preheat air fryer to 390°F(200°C).Mix together yogurt,lemon juice,mustard powder,ground walnuts,and dill until well blended.Set aside.Cut off the stems and ribs from the kale,then cut the leaves into 3-inch pieces.
2. In a bowl,toss the kale with olive oil,salt and pepper.Arrange the kale in the fryer and Air Fry for 2-3 minutes.Shake the basket,then cook for another 2-3 minutes or until the kale is crisp.Serve the chips with Greek sauce.

Homemade Pretzel Bites

Servings:8
Cooking Time:6 Minutes
Ingredients:
- 4¾cups filtered water,divided
- 1 tablespoon butter
- 1 package fast-rising yeast
- ½teaspoon salt
- 2⅓cups bread flour
- 2 tablespoons baking soda
- 2 egg whites
- 1 teaspoon kosher salt

Directions:
1. Preheat the air fryer to 370°F(185°C).
2. In a large microwave-safe bowl,add¾cup of the water.Heat for 40 seconds in the microwave.Remove and whisk in the butter;then mix in the yeast and salt.Let sit 5 minutes.
3. Using a stand mixer with a dough hook attachment,add the yeast liquid and mix in the bread flour⅓cup at a time until all the flour is added and a dough is formed.
4. Remove the bowl from the stand;then let the dough rise 1 hour in a warm space,covered with a kitchen towel.
5. After the dough has doubled in size,remove from the bowl and punch down a few times on a lightly floured flat surface.
6. Divide the dough into 4 balls;then roll each ball out into a long,skinny,sticklike shape.Using a sharp knife,cut each dough stick into 6 pieces.
7. Repeat Step 6 for the remaining dough balls until you have about 24 bites formed.
8. Heat the remaining 4 cups of water over the stovetop in a medium pot with the baking soda stirred in.
9. Drop the pretzel bite dough into the hot water and let boil for 60 seconds,remove,and let slightly cool.
10. Lightly brush the top of each bite with the egg whites,and then cover with a pinch of kosher salt.
11. Spray the air fryer basket with olive oil spray and place the pretzel bites on top.Cook for 6 to 8 minutes,or until lightly browned.Remove and keep warm.
12. Repeat until all pretzel bites are cooked.
13. Serve warm.

Onion Ring Nachos

Servings:3
Cooking Time:8 Minutes
Ingredients:
- ¾pound Frozen breaded(not battered)onion rings(do not thaw)
- 1½cups(about 6 ounces)Shredded Cheddar,Monterey Jack,or Swiss cheese,or a purchased Tex-Mex blend
- Up to 12 Pickled jalapeño rings

Directions:
1. Preheat the air fryer to 400°F(205°C).
2. When the machine is at temperature,spread the onion rings in the basket in a fairly even layer.Air-fry undisturbed for 6 minutes,or until crisp.Remove the basket from the machine.
3. Cut a circle of parchment paper to line a 6-inch round cake pan for a small air fryer,a 7-inch round cake pan for a medium air fryer,or an 8-inch round cake pan for a large machine.
4. Pour the onion rings into a fairly even layer in the cake pan,then sprinkle the cheese evenly over them.Dot with the jalapeño rings.
5. Set the pan in the basket and air-fry undisturbed for 2 minutes,until the cheese has melted and is bubbling.
6. Remove the pan from the basket.Cool for 5 minutes before serving.

Root Vegetable Crisps

Servings:4
Cooking Time:8 Minutes
Ingredients:
- 1 small taro root,peeled and washed
- 1 small yucca root,peeled and washed
- 1 small purple sweet potato,washed
- 2 cups filtered water
- 2 teaspoons extra-virgin olive oil
- ½teaspoon salt

Directions:
1. Using a mandolin,slice the taro root,yucca root,and purple sweet potato into⅛-inch slices.
2. Add the water to a large bowl.Add the sliced vegetables and soak for at least 30 minutes.
3. Preheat the air fryer to 370°F(185°C).
4. Drain the water and pat the vegetables dry with a paper towel or kitchen cloth.Toss the vegetables with the olive oil and sprinkle with salt.Liberally spray the air fryer basket with olive oil mist.
5. Place the vegetables into the air fryer basket,making sure not to overlap the pieces.
6. Cook for 8 minutes,shaking the basket every 2 minutes,until the outer edges start to turn up and the vegetables start to brown.Remove from the basket and serve warm.Repeat with the remaining vegetable slices until all are cooked.

Asian Five-spice Wings

Servings:4
Cooking Time:15 Minutes
Ingredients:
- 2 pounds chicken wings
- ½cup Asian-style salad dressing
- 2 tablespoons Chinese five-spice powder

Directions:
1. Cut off wing tips and discard or freeze for stock.Cut remaining wing pieces in two at the joint.
2. Place wing pieces in a large sealable plastic bag.Pour in the Asian dressing,seal bag,and massage the marinade into the wings until well coated.Refrigerate for at least an hour.
3. Remove wings from bag,drain off excess marinade,and place wings in air fryer basket.
4. Cook at 360°F(180°C)for 15minutes or until juices run clear.About halfway through cooking time,shake the basket or stir wings for more even cooking.
5. Transfer cooked wings to plate in a single layer.Sprinkle half of the Chinese five-spice powder on the wings,turn,and sprinkle other side with remaining seasoning.

Cheesy Green Wonton Triangles

Servings:20 Wontons
Cooking Time:55 Minutes
Ingredients:
- 6 oz marinated artichoke hearts
- 6 oz cream cheese
- ¼cup sour cream
- ¼cup grated Parmesan
- ¼cup grated cheddar
- 5 oz chopped kale
- 2 garlic cloves,chopped
- Salt and pepper to taste
- 20 wonton wrappers

Directions:
1. Microwave cream cheese in a bowl for 20 seconds.Combine with sour cream,Parmesan,cheddar,kale,artichoke hearts,garlic,salt,and pepper.Lay out the wrappers on a cutting board.Scoop 1½tsp of cream cheese mixture on top of the wrapper.Fold up diagonally to form a triangle.Bring together the two bottom corners.Squeeze out any air and press together to seal the edges.
2. Preheat air fryer to 375°F(190°C).Place a batch of wonton in the greased frying basket and Bake for 10 minutes.Flip them and cook for 5-8 minutes until crisp and golden.Serve.

Crispy Ravioli Bites

Servings:5
Cooking Time:7 Minutes
Ingredients:
- ⅓cup All-purpose flour
- 1 Large egg(s),well beaten
- ⅔cup Seasoned Italian-style dried bread crumbs
- 10 ounces(about 20)Frozen mini ravioli,meat or cheese,thawed
- Olive oil spray

Directions:
1. Preheat the air fryer to 400°F(205°C).

2. Pour the flour into a medium bowl.Set up and fill two shallow soup plates or small pie plates on your counter:one with the beaten egg(s)and one with the bread crumbs.
3. Pour all the ravioli into the flour and toss well to coat.Pick up 1 ravioli,gently shake off any excess flour,and dip the ravioli in the egg(s),coating both sides.Let any excess egg slip back into the rest,then set the ravioli in the bread crumbs,turning it several times until lightly and evenly coated on all sides.Set aside on a cutting board and continue on with the remaining ravioli.
4. Lightly coat the ravioli on both sides with olive oil spray,then set them in the basket in as close to a single layer as you can.Some can lean up against the side of the basket.Air-fry for 7 minutes,tossing the basket at the 4-minute mark to rearrange the pieces,until brown and crisp.
5. Pour the contents of the basket onto a wire rack.Cool for 5 minutes before serving.

Sweet Plantain Chips

Servings:4
Cooking Time:11 Minutes
Ingredients:
- 2 Very ripe plantain(s),peeled and sliced into 1-inch pieces
- Vegetable oil spray
- 3 tablespoons Maple syrup
- For garnishing Coarse sea salt or kosher salt

Directions:
1. Pour about½cup water into the bottom of your air fryer basket or into a metal tray on a lower rack in some models.Preheat the air fryer to 400°F(205°C).
2. Put the plantain pieces in a bowl,coat them with vegetable oil spray,and toss gently,spraying at least one more time and tossing repeatedly,until the pieces are well coated.
3. When the machine is at temperature,arrange the plantain pieces in the basket in one layer.Air-fry undisturbed for 5 minutes.
4. Remove the basket from the machine and spray the back of a metal spatula with vegetable oil spray.Use the spatula to press down on the plantain pieces,spraying it again as needed,to flatten the pieces to about half their original height.Brush the plantain pieces with maple syrup,then return the basket to the machine and continue air-frying undisturbed for 6 minutes,or until the plantain pieces are soft and caramelized.
5. Use kitchen tongs to transfer the pieces to a serving platter.Sprinkle the pieces with salt and cool for a couple of minutes before serving.Or cool to room temperature before serving,about 1 hour.

Spicy Sweet Potato Tater-tots

Servings:6
Cooking Time:10 Minutes
Ingredients:
- 6 cups filtered water
- 2 medium sweet potatoes,peeled and cut in half
- 1 teaspoon garlic powder
- ½teaspoon black pepper,divided
- ½teaspoon salt,divided
- 1 cup panko breadcrumbs
- 1 teaspoon blackened seasoning

Directions:
1. In a large stovetop pot,bring the water to a boil.Add the sweet potatoes and let boil about 10 minutes,until a metal fork prong can be inserted but the potatoes still have a slight give(not completely mashed).
2. Carefully remove the potatoes from the pot and let cool.
3. When you're able to touch them,grate the potatoes into a large bowl.Mix the garlic powder,¼teaspoon of the black pepper,and¼teaspoon of the salt into the potatoes.Place the mixture in the refrigerator and let set at least 45 minutes(if you're leaving them longer than 45 minutes,cover the bowl).
4. Before assembling,mix the breadcrumbs and blackened seasoning in a small bowl.
5. Remove the sweet potatoes from the refrigerator and preheat the air fryer to 400°F(205°C).
6. Assemble the tater-tots by using a teaspoon to portion batter evenly and form into a tater-tot shape.Roll each tater-tot in the breadcrumb mixture.Then carefully place the tater-tots in the air fryer basket.Be sure that you've liberally sprayed the air fryer basket with an olive oil mist.Repeat until tater-tots fill the basket without touching one another.You'll need to do multiple batches,depending on the size of your air fryer.
7. Cook the tater-tots for 3 to 6 minutes,flip,and cook another 3 to 6 minutes.
8. Remove from the air fryer carefully and keep warm until ready to serve.

Roasted Chickpeas

Servings:1
Cooking Time:15 Minutes
Ingredients:
- 1 15-ounce can chickpeas,drained
- 2 teaspoons curry powder
- ¼teaspoon salt
- 1 tablespoon olive oil

Directions:
1. Drain chickpeas thoroughly and spread in a single layer on paper towels.Cover with another paper towel and press gently to remove extra moisture.Don't press too hard or you'll crush the chickpeas.
2. Mix curry powder and salt together.
3. Place chickpeas in a medium bowl and sprinkle with seasonings.Stir well to coat.
4. Add olive oil and stir again to distribute oil.
5. Cook at 390°F(200°C)for 15minutes,stopping to shake basket about halfway through cooking time.
6. Cool completely and store in airtight container.

Artichoke Samosas

Servings:6
Cooking Time:25 Minutes
Ingredients:
- ½cup minced artichoke hearts
- ¼cup ricotta cheese
- 1 egg white
- 3 tbsp grated mozzarella
- ½tsp dried thyme
- 6 phyllo dough sheets
- 2 tbsp melted butter
- 1 cup mango chutney

Directions:

1. Preheat air fryer to 400°F(205°C).Mix together ricotta cheese,egg white,artichoke hearts,mozzarella cheese,and thyme in a small bowl until well blended.When you bring out the phyllo dough,cover it with a damp kitchen towel so that it doesn't dry out while you are working with it.Take one sheet of phyllo and place it on the work surface.
2. Cut it into thirds lengthwise.At the base of each strip,place about 1½tsp of filling.Fold the bottom right-hand tip of the strip over to the left-hand side to make a triangle.Continue flipping and folding triangles along the strip.Brush the triangle with butter to seal the edges.Place triangles in the greased frying basket and Bake until golden and crisp,4 minutes.Serve with mango chutney.

Zucchini Boats With Bacon

Servings:4
Cooking Time:35 Minutes
Ingredients:
- 1¼cups shredded Havarti cheese
- 3 bacon slices
- 2 large zucchini
- Salt and pepper to taste
- ¼tsp garlic powder
- ¼tsp sweet paprika
- 8 tsp buttermilk
- 2 tbsp chives,chopped

Directions:
1. Preheat air fryer to 350°F(175°C).Place the bacon in the frying basket and Air Fry it for 10 minutes,flipping once until crisp.Chop the bacon and set aside.Cut zucchini in half lengthwise and then crosswise so that you have 8 pieces.Scoop out the pulp.Sprinkle with salt,garlic,paprika,and black pepper.Place the zucchini skins in the greased frying basket.Air Fry until crisp-tender,8-10 minutes.Remove the basket and add the Havarti inside each boat and top with bacon.Return stuffed boats to the air fryer and fry for 2 minutes or until the cheese has melted.Top with buttermilk and chives before serving immediately.

Prosciutto Polenta Rounds

Servings:6
Cooking Time:40 Minutes+10 Minutes To Cool
Ingredients:
- 1 tube precooked polenta
- 1 tbsp garlic oil
- 4 oz cream cheese,softened
- 3 tbsp mayonnaise
- 2 scallions,sliced
- 1 tbsp minced fresh chives
- 6 prosciutto slices,chopped

Directions:
1. Preheat the air fryer to 400°F(205°C).Slice the polenta crosswise into 12 rounds.Brush both sides of each round with garlic oil and put 6 of them in the frying basket.Put a rack in the basket over the polenta and add the other 6 rounds.Bake for 15 minutes,flip,and cook for 10-15 more minutes or until the polenta is crispy and golden.While the polenta is cooking,beat the cream cheese and mayo and stir in the scallions,chives,and prosciutto.When the polenta is cooked,lay out on a wire rack to cool for 15 minutes.Top with the cream cheese mix and serve.

Muffuletta Sliders

Servings:8
Cooking Time:7 Minutes
Ingredients:
- ¼pound thin-sliced deli ham
- ¼pound thin-sliced pastrami
- 4 ounces low-fat mozzarella cheese,grated or sliced thin
- 8 slider buns
- olive oil for misting
- 1 tablespoon sesame seeds
- Olive Mix
- ¼cup sliced black olives
- ½cup sliced green olives with pimentos
- ¼cup chopped kalamata olives
- 1 teaspoon red wine vinegar
- ¼teaspoon basil
- ⅛teaspoon garlic powder

Directions:
1. In a small bowl,stir together all the Olive Mix ingredients.
2. Divide the meats and cheese into 8 equal portions.To assemble sliders,stack in this order:bottom bun,ham,pastrami,2 tablespoons olive mix,cheese,top bun.
3. Mist tops of sliders lightly with oil.Sprinkle with sesame seeds.
4. Cooking 4 at a time,place sliders in air fryer basket and cook at 360°F(180°C)for 7 minutes to melt cheese and heat through.

Sweet Apple Fries

Servings:3
Cooking Time:8 Minutes
Ingredients:
- 2 Medium-size sweet apple(s),such as Gala or Fuji
- 1 Large egg white(s)
- 2 tablespoons Water
- 1½cups Finely ground gingersnap crumbs(gluten-free,if a concern)
- Vegetable oil spray

Directions:
1. Preheat the air fryer to 375°F(190°C).
2. Peel and core an apple,then cut it into 12 slices(see the headnote for more information).Repeat with more apples as necessary.
3. Whisk the egg white(s)and water in a medium bowl until foamy.Add the apple slices and toss well to coat.
4. Spread the gingersnap crumbs across a dinner plate.Using clean hands,pick up an apple slice,let any excess egg white mixture slip back into the rest,and dredge the slice in the crumbs,coating it lightly but evenly on all sides.Set it aside and continue coating the remaining apple slices.
5. Lightly coat the slices on all sides with vegetable oil spray,then set them curved side down in the basket in one layer.Air-fry undisturbed for 6 minutes,or until browned and crisp.You may need to air-fry the slices for 2 minutes longer if the temperature is at 360°F(180°C).
6. Use kitchen tongs to transfer the slices to a wire rack.Cool for 2 to 3 minutes before serving.

Hungarian Spiralized Fries

Servings:4
Cooking Time:30 Minutes
Ingredients:
- 2 russet potatoes,peeled
- 1 tbsp olive oil
- ½tsp chili powder
- ½tsp garlic powder
- ½tsp Hungarian paprika
- Salt and pepper to taste

Directions:
1. Preheat the air fryer to 400°F(205°C).Using the spiralizer,cut the potatoes into 5-inch lengths and add them to a large bowl.Pour cold water,cover,and set aside for 30 minutes.Drain and dry with a kitchen towel,then toss back in the bowl.Drizzle the potatoes with olive oil and season with salt,pepper,chili,garlic,and paprika.Toss well.Put the potatoes in the frying basket and Air Fry for 10-12 minutes,shaking the basket once until the potatoes are golden and crispy.Serve warm and enjoy!

Cheese Straws

Servings:8
Cooking Time:7 Minutes
Ingredients:
- For dusting All-purpose flour
- Two quarters of one thawed sheet(that is,a half of the sheet cut into two even pieces;wrap and refreeze the remainder)A 17.25-ounce box frozen puff pastry
- 1 Large egg(s)
- 2 tablespoons Water
- ¼cup(about¾ounce)Finely grated Parmesan cheese
- up to 1 teaspoon Ground black pepper

Directions:
1. Preheat the air fryer to 400°F(205°C).
2. Dust a clean,dry work surface with flour.Set one of the pieces of puff pastry on top,dust the pastry lightly with flour,and roll with a rolling pin to a 6-inch square.
3. Whisk the egg(s)and water in a small or medium bowl until uniform.Brush the pastry square(s)generously with this mixture.Sprinkle each square with 2 tablespoons grated cheese and up to½teaspoon ground black pepper.
4. Cut each square into 4 even strips.Grasp each end of 1 strip with clean,dry hands;twist it into a cheese straw.Place the twisted straws on a baking sheet.
5. Lay as many straws as will fit in the air-fryer basket—as a general rule,4 of them in a small machine,5 in a medium model,or 6 in a large.There should be space for air to circulate around the straws.Set the baking sheet with any remaining straws in the fridge.
6. Air-fry undisturbed for 7 minutes,or until puffed and crisp.Use tongs to transfer the cheese straws to a wire rack,then make subsequent batches in the same way(keeping the baking sheet with the remaining straws in the fridge as each batch cooks).Serve warm.

String Bean Fries

Servings:4
Cooking Time:6 Minutes
Ingredients:

- ½pound fresh string beans
- 2 eggs
- 4 teaspoons water
- ½cup white flour
- ½cup breadcrumbs
- ¼teaspoon salt
- ¼teaspoon ground black pepper
- ¼teaspoon dry mustard(optional)
- oil for misting or cooking spray

Directions:

1. Preheat air fryer to 360°F(180°C).
2. Trim stem ends from string beans,wash,and pat dry.
3. In a shallow dish,beat eggs and water together until well blended.
4. Place flour in a second shallow dish.
5. In a third shallow dish,stir together the breadcrumbs,salt,pepper,and dry mustard if using.
6. Dip each string bean in egg mixture,flour,egg mixture again,then breadcrumbs.
7. When you finish coating all the string beans,open air fryer and place them in basket.
8. Cook for 3minutes.
9. Stop and mist string beans with oil or cooking spray.
10. Cook for 3 moreminutes or until string beans are crispy and nicely browned.

Crab Rangoon

Servings:18
Cooking Time:6 Minutes
Ingredients:

- 4½tablespoons(a little more than¼pound)Crabmeat,preferably backfin or claw,picked over for shells and cartilage
- 1½ounces(3 tablespoons)Regular or low-fat cream cheese(not fat-free),softened to room temperature
- 1½tablespoons Minced scallion
- 1½teaspoons Minced garlic
- 1½teaspoons Worcestershire sauce
- 18 Wonton wrappers(thawed,if necessary)
- Vegetable oil spray

Directions:

1. Preheat the air fryer to 400°F(205°C).
2. Gently stir the crab,cream cheese,scallion,garlic,and Worcestershire sauce in a medium bowl until well combined.
3. Set a bowl of water on a clean,dry work surface or next to a large cutting board.Set one wonton wrapper on the surface,then put a teaspoonful of the crab mixture in the center of the wrapper.Dip your clean finger in the water and run it around the edge of the wrapper.Bring all four sides up to the center and over the filling,and pinch them together in the middle to seal without covering all of the filling.The traditional look is for the corners of the filled wonton to become four open"flower petals"radiating out from the filled center.Set the filled wonton aside and continue making more as needed.(If you want a video tutorial on filling these,see ours at our YouTube channel,Cooking with Bruce and Mark.)
4. Generously coat the filled wontons with vegetable oil spray.Set them sealed side up in the basket with a little room among them.Air-fry undisturbed for 6 minutes,or until golden brown and crisp.
5. Use a nonstick-safe spatula to gently transfer the wontons to a wire rack.Cool for 5 minutes before serving warm.

Basil Feta Crostini

Servings:4
Cooking Time:10 Minutes
Ingredients:

- 1 baguette,sliced
- ¼cup olive oil
- 2 garlic cloves,minced
- 4 oz feta cheese
- 2 tbsp basil,minced

Directions:

1. Preheat air fryer to 380°F(195°C).Combine together the olive oil and garlic in a bowl.Brush it over one side of each slice of bread.Put the bread in a single layer in the frying basket and Bake for 5 minutes.In a small bowl,mix together the feta cheese and basil.Remove the toast from the air fryer,then spread a thin layer of the goat cheese mixture over the top of each piece.Serve.

Mustard Greens Chips With Curried Sauce

Servings:4
Cooking Time:20 Minutes
Ingredients:

- 1 cup plain yogurt
- 1 tbsp lemon juice
- 1 tbsp curry powder
- 1 bunch of mustard greens
- 2 tsp olive oil
- Sea salt to taste

Directions:

1. Preheat air fryer to 390°F(200°C).Using a sharp knife,remove and discard the ribs from the mustard greens.Slice the leaves into 2-3-inch pieces.Transfer them to a large bowl,then pour in olive oil and toss to coat.Air Fry for 5-6 minutes.Shake at least once.The chips should be crispy when finished.Sprinkle with a little bit of sea salt.Mix the yogurt,lemon juice,salt,and curry in a small bowl.Serve the greens with the sauce.

Crunchy Spicy Chickpeas

Servings:6
Cooking Time:12 Minutes
Ingredients:

- 2½cups Canned chickpeas,drained and rinsed
- 2½tablespoons Vegetable or canola oil
- up to 1 tablespoon Cajun or jerk dried seasoning blend(see here for a Cajun blend,here for a jerk blend)

- up to ¾teaspoon Table salt(optional)

Directions:

1. Preheat the air fryer to 400°F(205°C).
2. Toss the chickpeas,oil,seasoning blend,and salt(if using)in a large bowl until the chickpeas are evenly coated.
3. When the machine is at temperature,pour the chickpeas into the basket.Air-fry for 12 minutes,removing the basket at the 4-and 8-minute marks to toss and rearrange the chickpeas,until very aromatic and perhaps sizzling but not burned.
4. Pour the chickpeas into a large serving bowl.Cool for a couple of minutes,gently stirring once,before you dive in.

Cheesy Green Pitas

Servings:4
Cooking Time:15 Minutes
Ingredients:

- ½cup canned artichoke hearts,sliced
- 2 whole-wheat pitas
- 2 tbsp olive oil,divided
- 2 garlic cloves,minced
- ¼tsp salt
- ¼cup green olives
- ¼cup grated Pecorino
- ¼cup crumbled feta
- 2 tbsp chopped chervil

Directions:

1. Preheat air fryer to 380°F(195°C).Lightly brush each pita with some olive oil,then top with garlic and salt.Divide the artichoke hearts,green olives,and cheeses evenly between the two pitas,and put both into the air fryer.Bake for 10 minutes.Remove the pitas and cut them into 4 pieces each before serving.Top with chervil.Enjoy!
2. Roast the shrimp for 4 minutes,then open the air fryer and place the ramekin with oil and garlic in the basket beside the shrimp packet.Cook for 2 more minutes.Place the shrimp on a serving plate or platter with the ramekin of garlic olive oil on the side for dipping.

Crispy Chicken Bites With Gorgonzola Sauce

Servings:4
Cooking Time:30 Minutes
Ingredients:

- ¼cup crumbled Gorgonzola cheese
- ¼cup creamy blue cheese salad dressing
- 1 lb chicken tenders,cut into thirds crosswise
- ½cup sour cream
- 1 celery stalk,chopped
- 3 tbsp buffalo chicken sauce
- 1 cup panko bread crumbs
- 2 tbsp olive oil

Directions:

1. Preheat air fryer to 350°F(175°C).Blend together sour cream,salad dressing,Gorgonzola cheese,and celery in a bowl.Set aside.Combine chicken pieces and Buffalo wing sauce in another bowl until the chicken is coated.

2. In a shallow bowl or pie plate,mix the bread crumbs and olive oil.Dip the chicken into the bread crumb mixture,patting the crumbs to keep them in place.Arrange the chicken in the greased frying basket and Air Fry for 8-9 minutes,shaking once halfway through cooking until the chicken is golden.Serve with the blue cheese sauce.

Balsamic Grape Dip

Servings:6
Cooking Time:25 Minutes
Ingredients:

- 2 cups seedless red grapes
- 1 tbsp balsamic vinegar
- 1 tbsp honey
- 1 cup Greek yogurt
- 2 tbsp milk
- 2 tbsp minced fresh basil

Directions:

1. Preheat air fryer to 380°F(195°C).Add the grapes and balsamic vinegar to the frying basket,then pour honey over and toss to coat.Roast for 8-12 minutes,shriveling the grapes,and take them out of the air fryer.Mix the milk and yogurt together,then gently stir in the grapes and basil.Serve and enjoy!

Homemade French Fries

Servings:2
Cooking Time:25 Minutes
Ingredients:

- 2 to 3 russet potatoes,peeled and cut into½-inch sticks
- 2 to 3 teaspoons olive or vegetable oil
- salt

Directions:

1. Bring a large saucepan of salted water to a boil on the stovetop while you peel and cut the potatoes.Blanch the potatoes in the boiling salted water for 4 minutes while you Preheat the air fryer to 400°F(205°C).Strain the potatoes and rinse them with cold water.Dry them well with a clean kitchen towel.
2. Toss the dried potato sticks gently with the oil and place them in the air fryer basket.Air-fry for 25 minutes,shaking the basket a few times while the fries cook to help them brown evenly.Season the fries with salt mid-way through cooking and serve them warm with tomato ketchup,Sriracha mayonnaise or a mix of lemon zest,Parmesan cheese and parsley.

Plantain Chips

Servings:2
Cooking Time:14 Minutes
Ingredients:

- 1 large green plantain
- 2½cups filtered water,divided
- 2 teaspoons sea salt,divided

Directions:

1. Slice the plantain into 1-inch pieces.Place the plantains into a large bowl,cover with 2 cups water and 1 teaspoon

salt.Soak the plantains for 30 minutes;then remove and pat dry.

2. Preheat the air fryer to 390°F(200°C).

3. Place the plantain pieces into the air fryer basket,leaving space between the plantain rounds.Cook the plantains for 5 minutes,and carefully remove them from the air fryer basket.

4. Add the remaining water to a small bowl.

5. Using a small drinking glass,dip the bottom of the glass into the water and mash the warm plantains until they're¼-inch thick.Return the plantains to the air fryer basket,sprinkle with the remaining sea salt,and spray lightly with cooking spray.

6. Cook for another 6 to 8 minutes,or until lightly golden brown edges appear.

Spicy Chicken And Pepper Jack Cheese Bites

Servings:8
Cooking Time:8 Minutes
Ingredients:
- 8 ounces cream cheese,softened
- 2 cups grated pepper jack cheese
- 1 Jalapeño pepper,diced
- 2 scallions,minced
- 1 teaspoon paprika
- 2 teaspoons salt,divided
- 3 cups shredded cooked chicken
- ¼cup all-purpose flour*
- 2 eggs,lightly beaten
- 1 cup panko breadcrumbs*
- olive oil,in a spray bottle
- salsa

Directions:
1. Beat the cream cheese in a bowl until it is smooth and easy to stir.Add the pepper jack cheese,Jalapeño pepper,scallions,paprika and 1 teaspoon of salt.Fold in the shredded cooked chicken and combine well.Roll this mixture into 1-inch balls.

2. Set up a dredging station with three shallow dishes.Place the flour into one shallow dish.Place the eggs into a second shallow dish.Finally,combine the panko breadcrumbs and remaining teaspoon of salt in a third dish.

3. Coat the chicken cheese balls by rolling each ball in the flour first,then dip them into the eggs and finally roll them in the panko breadcrumbs to coat all sides.Refrigerate for at least 30 minutes.

4. Preheat the air fryer to 400°F(205°C).

5. Spray the chicken cheese balls with oil and air-fry in batches for 8 minutes.Shake the basket a few times throughout the cooking process to help the balls brown evenly.

6. Serve hot with salsa on the side.

Vegetarian Fritters With Green Dip

Servings:6
Cooking Time:40 Minutes
Ingredients:
- ½cup grated carrots
- ½cup grated zucchini
- ¼cup minced yellow onion
- 1 garlic clove,minced
- 1 large egg
- ¼cup flour
- ¼cup bread crumbs
- Salt and pepper to taste
- ½tsp ground cumin
- ½avocado,peeled and pitted
- ½cup plain Greek yogurt
- 1 tsp lime juice
- 1 tbsp white vinegar
- ¼cup chopped cilantro

Directions:
1. Preheat air fryer to 375°F(190°C).Combine carrots,zucchini,onion,garlic,egg,flour,bread crumbs,salt,pepper,and cumin in a large bowl.Scoop out 12 equal portions of the vegetables and form them into patties.Arrange the patties on the greased basket.Air Fry for 5 minutes,then flip the patties.Air Fry for another 5 minutes.Check if the fritters are golden and cooked through.If more time is needed,cook for another 3-5 minutes.

2. While the fritters are cooking,prepare the avocado sauce.Mash the avocado in a small bowl to the desired texture.Stir in yogurt,white vinegar,chopped cilantro,lime juice,and salt.When the fritter is done,transfer to a serving plate along with the avocado sauce for dipping.Serve warm and enjoy.

Bagel Chips

Servings:2
Cooking Time:4 Minutes
Ingredients:
- Sweet
- 1 large plain bagel
- 2 teaspoons sugar
- 1 teaspoon ground cinnamon
- butter-flavored cooking spray
- Savory
- 1 large plain bagel
- 1 teaspoon Italian seasoning
- ½teaspoon garlic powder
- oil for misting or cooking spray

Directions:
1. Preheat air fryer to 390°F(200°C).

2. Cut bagel into¼-inch slices or thinner.

3. Mix the seasonings together.

4. Spread out the slices,mist with oil or cooking spray,and sprinkle with half of the seasonings.

5. Turn over and repeat to coat the other side with oil or cooking spray and seasonings.

6. Place in air fryer basket and cook for 2minutes.Shake basket or stir a little and continue cooking for 2 minutes or until toasty brown and crispy.

Shrimp Egg Rolls

Servings:8
Cooking Time:10 Minutes

Ingredients:

- 1 tablespoon vegetable oil
- ½head green or savoy cabbage,finely shredded
- 1 cup shredded carrots
- 1 cup canned bean sprouts,drained
- 1 tablespoon soy sauce
- ½teaspoon sugar
- 1 teaspoon sesame oil
- ¼cup hoisin sauce
- freshly ground black pepper
- 1 pound cooked shrimp,diced
- ¼cup scallions
- 8 egg roll wrappers
- vegetable oil
- duck sauce

Directions:

1. Preheat a large sautépan over medium-high heat.Add the oil and cook the cabbage,carrots and bean sprouts until they start to wilt–about 3 minutes.Add the soy sauce,sugar,sesame oil,hoisin sauce and black pepper.Sautéfor a few more minutes.Stir in the shrimp and scallions and cook until the vegetables are just tender.Transfer the mixture to a colander in a bowl to cool.Press or squeeze out any excess water from the filling so that you don't end up with soggy egg rolls.
2. To make the egg rolls,place the egg roll wrappers on a flat surface with one of the points facing towards you so they look like diamonds.Dividing the filling evenly between the eight wrappers,spoon the mixture onto the center of the egg roll wrappers.Spread the filling across the center of the wrappers from the left corner to the right corner,but leave 2 inches from each corner empty.Brush the empty sides of the wrapper with a little water.Fold the bottom corner of the wrapper tightly up over the filling,trying to avoid making any air pockets.Fold the left corner in toward the center and then the right corner toward the center.It should now look like an envelope.Tightly roll the egg roll from the bottom to the top open corner.Press to seal the egg roll together,brushing with a little extra water if need be.Repeat this technique with all 8 egg rolls.
3. Preheat the air fryer to 370°F(185°C).
4. Spray or brush all sides of the egg rolls with vegetable oil.Air-fry four egg rolls at a time for 10 minutes,turning them over halfway through the cooking time.
5. Serve hot with duck sauce or your favorite dipping sauce.

Bread And Breakfast

French Toast And Turkey Sausage Roll-ups

Servings:3
Cooking Time:24 Minutes
Ingredients:
- 6 links turkey sausage
- 6 slices of white bread,crusts removed*
- 2 eggs
- ½cup milk
- ½teaspoon ground cinnamon
- ½teaspoon vanilla extract
- 1 tablespoon butter,melted
- powdered sugar(optional)
- maple syrup

Directions:
1. Preheat the air fryer to 380°F(195°C)and pour a little water into the bottom of the air fryer drawer.(This will help prevent the grease that drips into the bottom drawer from burning and smoking.)
2. Air-fry the sausage links at 380°F(195°C)for 8 to 10 minutes,turning them a couple of times during the cooking process.(If you have pre-cooked sausage links,omit this step.)
3. Roll each sausage link in a piece of bread,pressing the finished seam tightly to seal shut.
4. Preheat the air fryer to 370°F(185°C).
5. Combine the eggs,milk,cinnamon,and vanilla in a shallow dish.Dip the sausage rolls in the egg mixture and let them soak in the egg for 30 seconds.Spray or brush the bottom of the air fryer basket with oil and transfer the sausage rolls to the basket,seam side down.
6. Air-fry the rolls at 370°F(185°C)for 9 minutes.Brush melted butter over the bread,flip the rolls over and air-fry for an additional 5 minutes.Remove the French toast roll-ups from the basket and dust with powdered sugar,if using.Serve with maple syrup and enjoy.

Apple-cinnamon-walnut Muffins

Servings:8
Cooking Time:11 Minutes
Ingredients:
- 1 cup flour
- ⅓cup sugar
- 1 teaspoon baking powder
- ¼teaspoon baking soda
- ¼teaspoon salt
- 1 teaspoon cinnamon
- ¼teaspoon ginger
- ¼teaspoon nutmeg
- 1 egg
- 2 tablespoons pancake syrup,plus 2 teaspoons
- 2 tablespoons melted butter,plus 2 teaspoons
- ¾cup unsweetened applesauce
- ½teaspoon vanilla extract
- ¼cup chopped walnuts
- ¼cup diced apple
- 8 foil muffin cups,liners removed and sprayed with cooking spray

Directions:

1. Preheat air fryer to 330°F(165°C).
2. In a large bowl,stir together flour,sugar,baking powder,baking soda,salt,cinnamon,ginger,and nutmeg.
3. In a small bowl,beat egg until frothy.Add syrup,butter,applesauce,and vanilla and mix well.
4. Pour egg mixture into dry ingredients and stir just until moistened.
5. Gently stir in nuts and diced apple.
6. Divide batter among the 8 muffin cups.
7. Place 4 muffin cups in air fryer basket and cook at 330°F(165°C)for 11minutes.
8. Repeat with remaining 4 muffins or until toothpick inserted in center comes out clean.

Smooth Walnut-banana Loaf

Servings:4
Cooking Time:40 Minutes
Ingredients:
- 1/3 cup peanut butter,melted
- 2 tbsp butter,melted and cooled
- ¾cup flour
- ½tsp salt
- ¼tsp baking soda
- 2 ripe bananas
- 2 eggs
- 1 tsp lemon juice
- ½cup evaporated cane sugar
- ½cup ground walnuts
- 1 tbsp blackstrap molasses
- 1 tsp vanilla extract

Directions:
1. Preheat air fryer to 310°F(155°C).Mix flour,salt,and baking soda in a small bowl.Mash together bananas and eggs in a large bowl,then stir in sugar,peanut butter,lemon juice,butter,walnuts,molasses,and vanilla.When it is well incorporated,stir in the flour mixture until just combined.Transfer the batter to a parchment-lined baking dish and make sure it is even.Bake in the air fryer for 30 to 35 minutes until a toothpick in the middle comes out clean,and the top is golden.Serve and enjoy.

Crunchy French Toast Sticks

Servings:2
Cooking Time:9 Minutes
Ingredients:
- 2 eggs,beaten
- ¾cup milk
- ½teaspoon vanilla extract
- ½teaspoon ground cinnamon
- 1½cups crushed crunchy cinnamon cereal,or any cereal flakes
- 4 slices Texas Toast(or other bread that you can slice into 1-inch thick slices)
- maple syrup,for serving
- vegetable oil or melted butter

Directions:
1. Combine the eggs,milk,vanilla and cinnamon in a shallow bowl.Place the crushed cereal in a second shallow bowl.

2. Trim the crusts off the slices of bread and cut each slice into 3 sticks.Dip the sticks of bread into the egg mixture,turning them over to coat all sides.Let the bread sticks absorb the egg mixture for ten seconds or so,but don't let them get too wet.Roll the bread sticks in the cereal crumbs,pressing the cereal gently onto all sides so that it adheres to the bread.

3. Preheat the air fryer to 400°F(205°C).

4. Spray or brush the air fryer basket with oil or melted butter.Place the coated sticks in the basket.It's ok to stack a few on top of the others in the opposite direction.

5. Air-fry for 9 minutes.Turn the sticks over a couple of times during the cooking process so that the sticks crisp evenly.Serve warm with the maple syrup or some berries.

Effortless Toffee Zucchini Bread

Servings:6
Cooking Time:30 Minutes
Ingredients:

- 1 cup flour
- ½tsp baking soda
- ½cup granulated sugar
- ¼tsp ground cinnamon
- ¼tsp nutmeg
- ¼tsp salt
- 1/3 cup grated zucchini
- 1 egg
- 1 tbsp olive oil
- 1 tsp vanilla extract
- 2 tbsp English toffee bits
- 2 tbsp mini chocolate chips
- 1/2 cup chopped walnuts

Directions:

1. Preheat air fryer at 375ºF.Combine the flour,baking soda,toffee bits,sugar,cinnamon,nutmeg,salt,zucchini,egg,olive oil,vanilla and chocolate chips in a bowl.Add the walnuts to the batter and mix until evenly distributed.

2. Pour the mixture into a greased cake pan.Place the pan in the fryer and Bake for 20 minutes.Let sit for 10 minutes until slightly cooled before slicing.Serve immediately.

Southwest Cornbread

Servings:6
Cooking Time:18 Minutes
Ingredients:

- cooking spray
- ½cup yellow cornmeal
- ½cup flour
- 2 teaspoons baking powder
- ½teaspoon salt
- ½cup frozen corn kernels,thawed and drained
- ¼cup finely chopped onion
- 1 or 2 small jalapeño peppers,seeded and chopped
- 1 egg
- ½cup milk
- 2 tablespoons melted butter
- 2 ounces sharp Cheddar cheese,grated

Directions:

1. Preheat air fryer to 360°F(180°C).

2. Spray air fryer baking pan with nonstick cooking spray.

3. In a medium bowl,stir together the cornmeal,flour,baking powder,and salt.

4. Stir in the corn,onion,and peppers.

5. In a small bowl,beat together the egg,milk,and butter.Stir into dry ingredients until well combined.

6. Spoon half the batter into prepared baking pan,spreading to edges.Top with grated cheese.Spoon remaining batter on top of cheese and gently spread to edges of pan so it completely covers the cheese.

7. Cook at 360°F(180°C)for 18 minutes,until cornbread is done and top is crispy brown.

Banana Bread

Servings:6
Cooking Time:20 Minutes
Ingredients:

- cooking spray
- 1 cup white wheat flour
- ½teaspoon baking powder
- ¼teaspoon salt
- ¼teaspoon baking soda
- 1 egg
- ½cup mashed ripe banana
- ¼cup plain yogurt
- ¼cup pure maple syrup
- 2 tablespoons coconut oil
- ½teaspoon pure vanilla extract

Directions:

1. Preheat air fryer to 330°F(165°C).

2. Lightly spray 6 x 6-inch baking dish with cooking spray.

3. In a medium bowl,mix together the flour,baking powder,salt,and soda.

4. In a separate bowl,beat the egg and add the mashed banana,yogurt,syrup,oil,and vanilla.Mix until well combined.

5. Pour liquid mixture into dry ingredients and stir gently to blend.Do not beat.Batter may be slightly lumpy.

6. Pour batter into baking dish and cook at 330°F(165°C)for 20 minutes or until toothpick inserted in center of loaf comes out clean.

American Biscuits

Servings:4
Cooking Time:30 Minutes
Ingredients:

- 2 cups all-purpose flour
- 1 tbsp baking powder
- ½tsp baking soda
- ½tsp cornstarch
- ½tsp salt
- ½tsp sugar
- 4 tbsp cold butter,cubed
- 1¼cups buttermilk
- 1/2 tsp vanilla extract
- 1 tsp finely crushed walnuts

Directions:

1. Preheat air fryer at 350ºF.Combine dry ingredients in a bowl.Stir in the remaining ingredients gradually until a sticky dough forms.Using your floured hands,form dough into 8 balls.Place them into a greased pizza pan.Place pizza pan in the frying basket and Bake for 8 minutes.Serve immediately.

Carrot Orange Muffins

Servings:12
Cooking Time:12 Minutes
Ingredients:
- 1½cups all-purpose flour
- ½cup granulated sugar
- ½teaspoon ground cinnamon
- 2 teaspoons baking powder
- ¼teaspoon baking soda
- ½teaspoon salt
- 2 large eggs
- ¼cup vegetable oil
- ⅓cup orange marmalade
- 2 cups grated carrots

Directions:
1. Preheat the air fryer to 320°F(160°C).
2. In a large bowl,whisk together the flour,sugar,cinnamon,baking powder,baking soda,and salt;set aside.
3. In a separate bowl,whisk together the eggs,vegetable oil,orange marmalade,and grated carrots.
4. Make a well in the dry ingredients;then pour the wet ingredients into the well of the dry ingredients.Using a rubber spatula,mix the ingredients for 1 minute or until slightly lumpy.
5. Using silicone muffin liners,fill 6 muffin liners two-thirds full.
6. Carefully place the muffin liners in the air fryer basket and bake for 12 minutes(or until the tops are browned and a toothpick inserted in the center comes out clean).Carefully remove the muffins from the basket and repeat with remaining batter.
7. Serve warm.

Morning Potato Cakes

Servings:6
Cooking Time:50 Minutes
Ingredients:
- 4 Yukon Gold potatoes
- 2 cups kale,chopped
- 1 cup rice flour
- ¼cup cornstarch
- ¾cup milk
- 2 tbsp lemon juice
- 2 tsp dried rosemary
- 2 tsp shallot powder
- Salt and pepper to taste
- ½tsp turmeric powder

Directions:
1. Preheat air fryer to 390°F(200°C).Scrub the potatoes and put them in the air fryer.Bake for 30 minutes or until soft.When cool,chop them into small pieces and place them in a bowl.Mash with a potato masher or fork.Add kale,rice flour,cornstarch,milk,lemon juice,rosemary,shallot powder,salt,pepper,and turmeric.Stir well.
2. Make 12 balls out of the mixture and smash them lightly with your hands to make patties.Place them in the greased frying basket,and Air Fry for 10-12 minutes,flipping once,until golden and cooked through.Serve.

Sweet Potato&Mushroom Hash

Servings:6
Cooking Time:35 Minutes
Ingredients:
- 2 peeled sweet potatoes,cubed
- 4 oz baby Bella mushrooms,diced
- ½red bell pepper,diced
- ½red onion,diced
- 2 tbsp olive oil
- 1 garlic clove,minced
- Salt and pepper to taste
- ½tbsp chopped marjoram

Directions:
1. Preheat air fryer to 380°F(195°C).Place all ingredients in a large bowl and toss until the vegetables are well coated.Pour the vegetables into the frying basket.Bake for 8-10 minutes,then shake the vegetables.Cook for 8-10 more minutes.Serve and enjoy!

Quiche Cups

Servings:10
Cooking Time:16 Minutes
Ingredients:
- ¼pound all-natural ground pork sausage
- 3 eggs
- ¾cup milk
- 20 foil muffin cups
- cooking spray
- 4 ounces sharp Cheddar cheese,grated

Directions:
1. Divide sausage into 3 portions and shape each into a thin patty.
2. Place patties in air fryer basket and cook 390°F(200°C)for 6minutes.
3. While sausage is cooking,prepare the egg mixture.A large measuring cup or bowl with a pouring lip works best.Combine the eggs and milk and whisk until well blended.Set aside.
4. When sausage has cooked fully,remove patties from basket,drain well,and use a fork to crumble the meat into small pieces.
5. Double the foil cups into 10 sets.Remove paper liners from the top muffin cups and spray the foil cups lightly with cooking spray.
6. Divide crumbled sausage among the 10 muffin cup sets.
7. Top each with grated cheese,divided evenly among the cups.
8. Place 5 cups in air fryer basket.
9. Pour egg mixture into each cup,filling until each cup is at least⅔full.
10. Cook for 8 minutes and test for doneness.A knife inserted into the center shouldn't have any raw egg on it when removed.
11. If needed,cook 2 more minutes,until egg completely sets.
12. Repeat steps 8 through 11 for the remaining quiches.

Chili Hash Browns

Servings:4
Cooking Time:45 Minutes
Ingredients:
- 1 tbsp ancho chili powder
- 1 tbsp chipotle powder
- 2 tsp ground cumin
- 2 tsp smoked paprika
- 1 tsp garlic powder
- 1 tsp cayenne pepper
- Salt and pepper to taste
- 2 peeled russet potatoes,grated
- 2 tbsp olive oil
- 1/3 cup chopped onion
- 3 garlic cloves,minced

Directions:
1. Preheat the air fryer to 400°F(205°C).Combine chili powder,cumin,paprika,garlic powder,chipotle,cayenne,and black pepper in a small bowl,then pour into a glass jar with a lid and store in a cool,dry place.Add the olive oil,onion,and garlic to a cake pan,put it in the air fryer,and Bake for 3 minutes.Put the grated potatoes in a bowl and sprinkle with 2 tsp of the spice mixture,toss and add them to the cake pan along with the onion mix.Bake for 20-23 minutes,stirring once or until the potatoes are crispy and golden.Season with salt and serve.

Easy Corn Dog Cupcakes

Servings:6
Cooking Time:30 Minutes
Ingredients:
- 1 cup cornbread Mix
- 2 tsp granulated sugar
- Salt to taste
- 3/4 cup cream cheese
- 3 tbsp butter,melted
- 1 egg
- ¼cup minced onions
- 1 tsp dried parsley
- 2 beef hot dogs,sliced and cut into half-moons

Directions:
1. Preheat air fryer at 350ºF.Combine cornbread,sugar,and salt in a bowl.In another bowl,whisk cream cheese,parsley,butter,and egg.Pour wet ingredients to dry ingredients and toss to combine.Fold in onion and hot dog pieces.Transfer it into 8 greased silicone cupcake liners.Place it in the frying basket and Bake for 8-10 minutes.Serve right away.

Southern Sweet Cornbread

Servings:6
Cooking Time:17 Minutes
Ingredients:
- cooking spray
- ½cup white cornmeal
- ½cup flour
- 2 teaspoons baking powder
- ½teaspoon salt
- 4 teaspoons sugar
- 1 egg

- 2 tablespoons oil
- ½cup milk

Directions:
1. Preheat air fryer to 360°F(180°C).
2. Spray air fryer baking pan with nonstick cooking spray.
3. In a medium bowl,stir together the cornmeal,flour,baking powder,salt,and sugar.
4. In a small bowl,beat together the egg,oil,and milk.Stir into dry ingredients until well combined.
5. Pour batter into prepared baking pan.
6. Cook at 360°F(180°C)for 17 minutes or until toothpick inserted in center comes out clean or with crumbs clinging.

Egg Muffins

Servings:4
Cooking Time:11 Minutes
Ingredients:
- 4 eggs
- salt and pepper
- olive oil
- 4 English muffins,split
- 1 cup shredded Colby Jack cheese
- 4 slices ham or Canadian bacon

Directions:
1. Preheat air fryer to 390°F(200°C).
2. Beat together eggs and add salt and pepper to taste.Spray air fryer baking pan lightly with oil and add eggs.Cook for 2minutes,stir,and continue cooking for 4minutes,stirring every minute,until eggs are scrambled to your preference.Remove pan from air fryer.
3. Place bottom halves of English muffins in air fryer basket.Take half of the shredded cheese and divide it among the muffins.Top each with a slice of ham and one-quarter of the eggs.Sprinkle remaining cheese on top of the eggs.Use a fork to press the cheese into the egg a little so it doesn't slip off before it melts.
4. Cook at 360°F(180°C)for 1 minute.Add English muffin tops and cook for 4minutes to heat through and toast the muffins.

Roasted Tomato And Cheddar Rolls

Servings:12
Cooking Time:55 Minutes
Ingredients:
- 4 Roma tomatoes
- ½clove garlic,minced
- 1 tablespoon olive oil
- ¼teaspoon dried thyme
- salt and freshly ground black pepper
- 4 cups all-purpose flour
- 1 teaspoon active dry yeast
- 2 teaspoons sugar
- 2 teaspoons salt
- 1 tablespoon olive oil
- 1 cup grated Cheddar cheese,plus more for sprinkling at the end
- 1½cups water

Directions:

1. Cut the Roma tomatoes in half,remove the seeds with your fingers and transfer to a bowl.Add the garlic,olive oil,dried thyme,salt and freshly ground black pepper and toss well.
2. Preheat the air fryer to 390°F(200°C).
3. Place the tomatoes,cut side up in the air fryer basket and air-fry for 10 minutes.The tomatoes should just start to brown.Shake the basket to redistribute the tomatoes,and air-fry for another 5 to 10 minutes at 330°F(165°C)until the tomatoes are no longer juicy.Let the tomatoes cool and then rough chop them.
4. Combine the flour,yeast,sugar and salt in the bowl of a stand mixer.Add the olive oil,chopped roasted tomatoes and Cheddar cheese to the flour mixture and start to mix using the dough hook attachment.As you're mixing,add 1¼cups of the water,mixing until the dough comes together.Continue to knead the dough with the dough hook for another 10 minutes,adding enough water to the dough to get it to the right consistency.
5. Transfer the dough to an oiled bowl,cover with a clean kitchen towel and let it rest and rise until it has doubled in volume–about 1 to 2 hours.Then,divide the dough into 12 equal portions.Roll each portion of dough into a ball.Lightly coat each dough ball with oil and let the dough balls rest and rise a second time,covered lightly with plastic wrap for 45 minutes.(Alternately,you can place the rolls in the refrigerator overnight and take them out 2 hours before you bake them.)
6. Preheat the air fryer to 360°F(180°C).
7. Spray the dough balls and the air fryer basket with a little olive oil.Place three rolls at a time in the basket and bake for 10 minutes.Add a little grated Cheddar cheese on top of the rolls for the last 2 minutes of air frying for an attractive finish.

Aromatic Mushroom Omelet
Servings:4
Cooking Time:30 Minutes
Ingredients:
- 6 eggs
- 2 tbsp milk
- ½yellow onion,diced
- ½cup diced mushrooms
- 2 tbsp chopped parsley
- 1 tsp dried oregano
- 1 tbsp chopped chives
- ½tbsp chopped dill
- ½cup grated Gruyère cheese

Directions:
1. Preheat air fryer to 350°F(175°C).Beat eggs in a medium bowl,then add the rest of the ingredients,except for the parsley.Stir until completely combined.Pour the mixture into a greased pan and bake in the air fryer for 18-20 minutes until the eggs are set.Top with parsley and serve.

Ham&Cheese Sandwiches
Servings:2
Cooking Time:15 Minutes
Ingredients:
- 1 tsp butter
- 4 bread slices
- 4 deli ham slices
- 4 Cheddar cheese slices
- 4 thick tomato slices
- 1 tsp dried oregano

Directions:
1. Preheat air fryer to 370°F(185°C).Smear½tsp of butter on only one side of each slice of bread and sprinkle with oregano.On one of the slices,layer 2 slices of ham,2 slices of cheese,and 2 slices of tomato on the unbuttered side.Place the unbuttered side of another piece of bread onto the toppings.Place the sandwiches butter side down into the air fryer.Bake for 8 minutes,flipping once until crispy.Let cool slightly,cut in half and serve.

Buttermilk Biscuits
Servings:4
Cooking Time:9 Minutes
Ingredients:
- 1 cup flour
- 1½teaspoons baking powder
- ¼teaspoon baking soda
- ¼teaspoon salt
- ¼cup butter,cut into tiny cubes
- ¼cup buttermilk,plus 2 tablespoons
- cooking spray

Directions:
1. Preheat air fryer to 330°F(165°C).
2. Combine flour,baking powder,soda,and salt in a medium bowl.Stir together.
3. Add cubed butter and cut into flour using knives or a pastry blender.
4. Add buttermilk and stir into a stiff dough.
5. Divide dough into 4 portions and shape each into a large biscuit.If dough is too sticky to handle,stir in 1 or 2 more tablespoons of flour before shaping.Biscuits should be firm enough to hold their shape.Otherwise they will stick to the air fryer basket.
6. Spray air fryer basket with nonstick cooking spray.
7. Place biscuits in basket and cook at 330°F(165°C)for 9 minutes.

Coconut&Peanut Rice Cereal
Servings:4
Cooking Time:15 Minutes
Ingredients:
- 4 cups rice cereal
- 1 cup coconut shreds
- 2 tbsp peanut butter
- 1 tsp vanilla extract
- ¼cup honey
- 1 tbsp light brown sugar
- 2 tsp ground cinnamon
- ¼cup hazelnut flour
- Salt to taste

Directions:
1. Preheat air fryer at 350ºF.Combine the rice cereal,coconut shreds,peanut butter,vanilla extract,honey,brown sugar,cinnamon,hazelnut flour,and salt in a bowl.Press mixture into a greased cake pan.Place cake pan in the frying basket and Air Fry for 5 minutes,stirring once.Let cool completely for 10 minutes before crumbling.Store it into an airtight container up to 5 days.

Blueberry Muffins

Servings:8
Cooking Time:14 Minutes
Ingredients:

- 1⅓cups flour
- ½cup sugar
- 2 teaspoons baking powder
- ¼teaspoon salt
- ⅓cup canola oil
- 1 egg
- ½cup milk
- ⅔cup blueberries,fresh or frozen and thawed
- 8 foil muffin cups including paper liners

Directions:

1. Preheat air fryer to 330°F(165°C).
2. In a medium bowl,stir together flour,sugar,baking powder,and salt.
3. In a separate bowl,combine oil,egg,and milk and mix well.
4. Add egg mixture to dry ingredients and stir just until moistened.
5. Gently stir in blueberries.
6. Spoon batter evenly into muffin cups.
7. Place 4 muffin cups in air fryer basket and bake at 330°F(165°C)for 14 minutes or until tops spring back when touched lightly.
8. Repeat previous step to cook remaining muffins.

Tri-color Frittata

Servings:4
Cooking Time:30 Minutes
Ingredients:

- 8 eggs,beaten
- 1 red bell pepper,diced
- Salt and pepper to taste
- 1 garlic clove,minced
- ½tsp dried oregano
- ½cup ricotta

Directions:

1. Preheat air fryer to 360°F(180°C).Place the beaten eggs,bell pepper,oregano,salt,black pepper,and garlic and mix well.Fold in¼cup half of ricotta cheese.
2. Pour the egg mixture into a greased cake pan and top with the remaining ricotta.Place into the air fryer and Bake for 18-20 minutes or until the eggs are set in the center.Let the frittata cool for 5 minutes.Serve sliced.

Apricot-cheese Mini Pies

Servings:6
Cooking Time:35 Minutes
Ingredients:

- 2 refrigerated piecrusts
- 1/3 cup apricot preserves
- 1 tsp cornstarch
- ½cup vanilla yogurt
- 1 oz cream cheese
- 1 tsp sugar
- Rainbow sprinkles

Directions:

1. Preheat air fryer to 370°F(185°C).Lay out pie crusts on a flat surface.Cut each sheet of pie crust with a knife into three rectangles for a total of 6 rectangles.Mix apricot preserves and cornstarch in a small bowl.Cover the top half of one rectangle with 1 tbsp of the preserve mixture.Repeat for all rectangles.Fold the bottom of the crust over the preserve-covered top.Crimp and seal all edges with a fork.
2. Lightly coat each tart with cooking oil,then place into the air fryer without stacking.Bake for 10 minutes.Meanwhile,prepare the frosting by mixing yogurt,cream cheese,and sugar.When tarts are done,let cool completely in the air fryer.Frost the tarts and top with sprinkles.Serve.

Thyme Beef&Eggs

Servings:1
Cooking Time:25 Minutes
Ingredients:

- 2 tbsp butter
- 1 rosemary sprig
- 2 garlic cloves,pressed
- 8 oz sirloin steak
- Salt and pepper to taste
- ⅛tsp cayenne pepper
- 2 eggs
- 1 tsp dried thyme

Directions:

1. Preheat air fryer to 400°F(205°C).On a clean cutting board,place butter and half of the rosemary spring in the center.Set aside.Season both sides of the steak with salt,black pepper,thyme,pressed garlic,and cayenne pepper.Transfer the steak to the frying basket and top with the other half of the rosemary sprig.Cook for 4 minutes,then flip the steak.Cook for another 3 minutes.
2. Remove the steak and set it on top of the butter and rosemary sprig on the cutter board.Tent with foil and let it rest.Grease ramekin and crack both eggs into it.Season with salt and pepper.Transfer the ramekin to the frying basket and bake for 4-5 minutes until the egg white is cooked and set.Remove the foil from the steak and slice.Serve with eggs and enjoy.

Bagels With Avocado&Tomatoes

Servings:2
Cooking Time:35 Minutes
Ingredients:

- 2/3 cup all-purpose flour
- ½tsp active dry yeast
- 1/3 cup Greek yogurt
- 8 cherry tomatoes
- 1 ripe avocado
- 1 tbsp lemon juice
- 2 tbsp chopped red onions
- Black pepper to taste

Directions:

1. Preheat air fryer to 400°F(205°C).Beat the flour,dry yeast,and Greek yogurt until you get a smooth dough,adding more flour if necessary.Make 2 equal balls out of the mixture.
2. Using a rolling pin,roll each ball into a 9-inch long strip.Form a ring with each strip and press the ends together to create 2 bagels.In a bowl with hot water,soak the bagels

for 1 minute.Shake excess water and let rise for 15 minutes in the fryer.Bake for 5 minutes,turn the bagels,top with tomatoes,and Bake for another 5 minutes.

3.   Cut avocado in half,discard the pit and remove the flesh into a bowl.Mash with a fork and stir in lemon juice and onions.Once the bagels are ready,let cool slightly and cut them in half.Spread on each half some guacamole,top with 2 slices of Baked tomatoes,and sprinkle with pepper.Serve immediately.

White Wheat Walnut Bread

Servings:8
Cooking Time:25 Minutes
Ingredients:
* 1 cup lukewarm water(105–115°F(40-45°C))
* 1 packet RapidRise yeast
* 1 tablespoon light brown sugar
* 2 cups whole-grain white wheat flour
* 1 egg,room temperature,beaten with a fork
* 2 teaspoons olive oil
* ½teaspoon salt
* ½cup chopped walnuts
* cooking spray

Directions:
1.   In a small bowl,mix the water,yeast,and brown sugar.
2.   Pour yeast mixture over flour and mix until smooth.
3.   Add the egg,olive oil,and salt and beat with a wooden spoon for 2minutes.
4.   Stir in chopped walnuts.You will have very thick batter rather than stiff bread dough.
5.   Spray air fryer baking pan with cooking spray and pour in batter,smoothing the top.
6.   Let batter rise for 15minutes.
7.   Preheat air fryer to 360°F(180°C).
8.   Cook bread for 25 minutes,until toothpick pushed into center comes out with crumbs clinging.Let bread rest for 10minutes before removing from pan.

Fancy Cranberry Muffins

Servings:6
Cooking Time:30 Minutes
Ingredients:
* 1 cup all-purpose flour
* 2 tbsp whole wheat flour
* 1 tsp baking powder
* ⅛tsp baking soda
* Pinch of salt
* 3 tbsp sugar
* ½cup dried cranberries
* 1 egg
* 1/3 cup buttermilk
* 3 tbsp butter,melted

Directions:
1.   Preheat the air fryer to 350°F(175°C).Sift together all-purpose and whole wheat flours,baking powder,baking soda,and salt into a bowl and stir in the sugar.Add in the cranberries and stir;set aside.Whisk the egg,buttermilk,and

melted butter into a bowl until combined.Fold the egg mixture into the flour mixture and stir to combine.
2.   Grease 6 silicone muffin cups with baking spray.Fill each muffin cup about 2/3,leaving room at the top for rising.Put the muffin cups in the frying basket and bake 14-18 minutes or until a skewer inserted into the center comes out clean.Set on a wire rack for cooling,then serve.

Western Omelet

Servings:2
Cooking Time:22 Minutes
Ingredients:
* ¼cup chopped onion
* ¼cup chopped bell pepper,green or red
* ¼cup diced ham
* 1 teaspoon butter
* 4 large eggs
* 2 tablespoons milk
* ⅛teaspoon salt
* ¾cup grated sharp Cheddar cheese

Directions:
1.   Place onion,bell pepper,ham,and butter in air fryer baking pan.Cook at 390°F(200°C)for 1 minute and stir.Continue cooking 5minutes,until vegetables are tender.
2.   Beat together eggs,milk,and salt.Pour over vegetables and ham in baking pan.Cook at 360°F(180°C)for 15minutes or until eggs set and top has browned slightly.
3.   Sprinkle grated cheese on top of omelet.Cook 1 minute or just long enough to melt the cheese.

Brown Sugar Grapefruit

Servings:2
Cooking Time:4 Minutes
Ingredients:
* 1 grapefruit
* 2 to 4 teaspoons brown sugar

Directions:
1.   Preheat the air fryer to 400°F(205°C).
2.   While the air fryer is Preheating,cut the grapefruit in half horizontally(in other words not through the stem or blossom end of the grapefruit).Slice the bottom of the grapefruit to help it sit flat on the counter if necessary.Using a sharp paring knife(serrated is great),cut around the grapefruit between the flesh of the fruit and the peel.Then,cut each segment away from the membrane so that it is sitting freely in the fruit.
3.   Sprinkle 1 to 2 teaspoons of brown sugar on each half of the prepared grapefruit.Set up a rack in the air fryer basket(use an air fryer rack or make your own rack with some crumpled up aluminum foil).You don't have to use a rack,but doing so will get the grapefruit closer to the element so that the brown sugar can caramelize a little better.Transfer the grapefruit half to the rack in the air fryer basket.Depending on how big your grapefruit are and what size air fryer you have,you may need to do each half separately to make sure they sit flat.
4.   Air-fry at 400°F(205°C)for 4 minutes.
5.   Remove and let it cool for just a minute before enjoying.

Vegetable Side Dishes Recipes

Basic Corn On The Cob

Servings:4
Cooking Time:15 Minutes
Ingredients:
- 3 ears of corn,shucked and halved
- 2 tbsp butter,melted
- Salt and pepper to taste
- 1 tsp minced garlic
- 1 tsp paprika

Directions:
1. Preheat air fryer at 400ºF.Toss all ingredients in a bowl.Place corn in the frying basket and Bake for 7 minutes,turning once.Serve immediately.

Fried Eggplant Slices

Servings:3
Cooking Time:12 Minutes
Ingredients:
- 1½sleeves(about 60 saltines)Saltine crackers
- ¾cup Cornstarch
- 2 Large egg(s),well beaten
- 1 medium(about¾pound)Eggplant,stemmed,peeled,and cut into¼-inch-thick rounds
- Olive oil spray

Directions:
1. Preheat the air fryer to 400°F(205°C).Also,position the rack in the center of the oven and heat the oven to 175°F(80°C).
2. Grind the saltines,in batches if necessary,in a food processor,pulsing the machine and rearranging the saltine pieces every few pulses.Or pulverize the saltines in a large,heavy zip-closed plastic bag with the bottom of a heavy saucepan.In either case,you want small bits of saltines,not just crumbs.
3. Set up and fill three shallow soup plates or small pie plates on your counter:one for the cornstarch,one for the beaten egg(s),and one for the pulverized saltines.
4. Set an eggplant slice in the cornstarch and turn it to coat on both sides.Use a brush to lightly remove any excess.Dip it into the beaten egg(s)and turn to coat both sides.Let any excess egg slip back into the rest,then set the slice in the saltines.Turn several times,pressing gently to coat both sides evenly but not heavily.Coat both sides of the slice with olive oil spray and set it aside.Continue dipping and coating the remaining slices.
5. Set one,two,or maybe three slices in the basket.There should be at least½inch between them for proper air flow.Air-fry undisturbed for 12 minutes,or until crisp and browned.
6. Use a nonstick-safe spatula to transfer the slice(s)to a large baking sheet.Slip it into the oven to keep the slices warm as you air-fry more batches,as needed,always transferring the slices to the baking sheet to stay warm.

Cheesy Texas Toast

Servings:2
Cooking Time:4 Minutes
Ingredients:
- 2 1-inch-thick slice(s)Italian bread(each about 4 inches across)
- 4 teaspoons Softened butter
- 2 teaspoons Minced garlic
- ¼cup(about¾ounce)Finely grated Parmesan cheese

Directions:
1. Preheat the air fryer to 400°F(205°C).
2. Spread one side of a slice of bread with 2 teaspoons butter.Sprinkle with 1 teaspoon minced garlic,followed by 2 tablespoons grated cheese.Repeat this process if you're making one or more additional toasts.
3. When the machine is at temperature,put the bread slice(s)cheese side up in the basket(with as much air space between them as possible if you're making more than one).Air-fry undisturbed for 4 minutes,or until browned and crunchy.
4. Use a nonstick-safe spatula to transfer the toasts cheese side up to a wire rack.Cool for 5 minutes before serving.

Fried Cauliflowerwith Parmesan Lemon Dressing

Servings:2
Cooking Time:12 Minutes
Ingredients:
- 4 cups cauliflower florets(about half a large head)
- 1 tablespoon olive oil
- salt and freshly ground black pepper
- 1 teaspoon finely chopped lemon zest
- 1 tablespoon fresh lemon juice(about half a lemon)
- ¼cup grated Parmigiano-Reggiano cheese
- 4 tablespoons extra virgin olive oil
- ¼teaspoon salt
- lots of freshly ground black pepper
- 1 tablespoon chopped fresh parsley

Directions:
1. Preheat the air fryer to 400°F(205°C).
2. Toss the cauliflower florets with the olive oil,salt and freshly ground black pepper.Air-fry for 12 minutes,shaking the basket a couple of times during the cooking process.
3. While the cauliflower is frying,make the dressing.Combine the lemon zest,lemon juice,Parmigiano-Reggiano cheese and olive oil in a small bowl.Season with salt and lots of freshly ground black pepper.Stir in the parsley.
4. Turn the fried cauliflower out onto a serving platter and drizzle the dressing over the top.

Green Peas With Mint

Servings:4
Cooking Time:5 Minutes
Ingredients:
- 1 cup shredded lettuce
- 1 10-ounce package frozen green peas,thawed
- 1 tablespoon fresh mint,shredded
- 1 teaspoon melted butter

Directions:
1. Lay the shredded lettuce in the air fryer basket.
2. Toss together the peas,mint,and melted butter and spoon over the lettuce.
3. Cook at 360°F(180°C)for 5minutes,until peas are warm and lettuce wilts.

Roasted Corn Salad

Servings:3
Cooking Time:15 Minutes
Ingredients:
- 3 4-inch lengths husked and de-silked corn on the cob
- Olive oil spray
- 1 cup Packed baby arugula leaves
- 12 Cherry tomatoes,halved
- Up to 3 Medium scallion(s),trimmed and thinly sliced
- 2 tablespoons Lemon juice
- 1 tablespoon Olive oil
- 1½teaspoons Honey
- ¼teaspoon Mild paprika
- ¼teaspoon Dried oregano
- ¼teaspoon,plus more to taste Table salt
- ¼teaspoon Ground black pepper

Directions:
1. Preheat the air fryer to 400°F(205°C).
2. When the machine is at temperature,lightly coat the pieces of corn on the cob with olive oil spray.Set the pieces of corn in the basket with as much air space between them as possible.Air-fry undisturbed for 15 minutes,or until the corn is charred in a few spots.
3. Use kitchen tongs to transfer the corn to a wire rack.Cool for 15 minutes.
4. Cut the kernels off the ears by cutting the fat end off each piece so it will stand up straight on a cutting board,then running a knife down the corn.(Or you can save your fingers and buy a fancy tool to remove kernels from corn cobs.Check it out at online kitchenware stores.)Scoop the kernels into a serving bowl.
5. Chop the arugula into bite-size bits and add these to the kernels.Add the tomatoes and scallions,too.Whisk the lemon juice,olive oil,honey,paprika,oregano,salt,and pepper in a small bowl until the honey dissolves.Pour over the salad and toss well to coat,tasting for extra salt before serving.

Veggie Fritters

Servings:4
Cooking Time:35 Minutes
Ingredients:
- ¼cup crumbled feta cheese
- 1 grated zucchini
- ¼cup Parmesan cheese
- 2 tbsp minced onion
- 1 tbs powder garlic
- 1 tbsp flour
- 1 tbsp cornmeal
- 1 tbsp butter,melted
- 1 egg
- 2 tsp chopped dill
- 2 tsp chopped parsley
- Salt and pepper to taste
- 1 cup bread crumbs

Directions:
1. Preheat air fryer at 350ºF.Squeeze grated zucchini between paper towels to remove excess moisture.In a bowl,combine all ingredients except breadcrumbs.Form mixture into 12 balls,about 2 tbsp each.In a shallow bowl,add breadcrumbs.Roll each ball in breadcrumbs,covering all sides.Place fritters on an ungreased pizza pan.Place in the frying basket and Air Fry for 11 minutes,flipping once.Serve.

Mashed Potato Tots

Servings:18
Cooking Time:10 Minutes
Ingredients:
- 1 medium potato or 1 cup cooked mashed potatoes
- 1 tablespoon real bacon bits
- 2 tablespoons chopped green onions,tops only
- ¼teaspoon onion powder
- 1 teaspoon dried chopped chives
- salt
- 2 tablespoons flour
- 1 egg white,beaten
- ½cup panko breadcrumbs
- oil for misting or cooking spray

Directions:
1. If using cooked mashed potatoes,jump to step 4.
2. Peel potato and cut into½-inch cubes.(Small pieces cook more quickly.)Place in saucepan,add water to cover,and heat to boil.Lower heat slightly and continue cooking just until tender,about 10minutes.
3. Drain potatoes and place in ice cold water.Allow to cool for a minute or two,then drain well and mash.
4. Preheat air fryer to 390°F(200°C).
5. In a large bowl,mix together the potatoes,bacon bits,onions,onion powder,chives,salt to taste,and flour.Add egg white and stir well.
6. Place panko crumbs on a sheet of wax paper.
7. For each tot,use about 2 teaspoons of potato mixture.To shape,drop the measure of potato mixture onto panko crumbs and push crumbs up and around potatoes to coat edges.Then turn tot over to coat other side with crumbs.
8. Mist tots with oil or cooking spray and place in air fryer basket,crowded but not stacked.
9. Cook at 390°F(200°C)for 10 minutes,until browned and crispy.
10. Repeat steps 8 and 9 to cook remaining tots.

Simple Peppared Carrot Chips

Servings:4
Cooking Time:15 Minutes
Ingredients:
- 3 carrots,cut into coins
- 1 tbsp sesame oil
- Salt and pepper to taste

Directions:
1. Preheat air fryer at 375ºF.Combine all ingredients in a bowl.Place carrots in the frying basket and Roast for 10 minutes,tossing once.Serve right away.

Crispy Brussels Sprouts

Servings:3
Cooking Time:12 Minutes
Ingredients:
- 1¼pounds Medium,2-inch-in-length Brussels sprouts
- 1½tablespoons Olive oil
- ¾teaspoon Table salt

Directions:
1. Preheat the air fryer to 400°F(205°C).

2. Halve each Brussels sprout through the stem end,pulling off and discarding any discolored outer leaves.Put the sprout halves in a large bowl,add the oil and salt,and stir well to coat evenly,until the Brussels sprouts are glistening.

3. When the machine is at temperature,scrape the contents of the bowl into the basket,gently spreading the Brussels sprout halves into as close to one layer as possible.Air-fry for 12 minutes,gently tossing and rearranging the vegetables twice to get all covered or touching parts exposed to the air currents,until crisp and browned at the edges.

4. Gently pour the contents of the basket onto a wire rack.Cool for a minute or two before serving.

Balsamic Beet Chips

Servings:4
Cooking Time:40 Minutes
Ingredients:
- ½tsp balsamic vinegar
- 4 beets,peeled and sliced
- 1 garlic clove,minced
- 2 tbsp chopped mint
- Salt and pepper to taste
- 3 tbsp olive oil

Directions:
1. Preheat air fryer to 380°F(195°C).Coat all ingredients in a bowl,except balsamic vinegar.Pour the beet mixture into the frying basket and Roast for 25-30 minutes,stirring once.Serve,drizzled with vinegar and enjoy!

Cheese-rice Stuffed Bell Peppers

Servings:4
Cooking Time:30 Minutes
Ingredients:
- 2 red bell peppers,halved and seeds and stem removed
- 1 cup cooked brown rice
- 2 tomatoes,diced
- 1 garlic clove,minced
- Salt and pepper to taste
- 4 oz goat cheese
- 3 tbsp basil,chopped
- 3 tbsp oregano,chopped
- 1 tbsp parsley,chopped
- ¼cup grated Parmesan

Directions:
1. Preheat air fryer to 360°F(180°C).Place the brown rice,tomatoes,garlic,salt,and pepper in a bowl and stir.Divide the rice filling evenly among the bell pepper halves.Combine the goat cheese,basil,parsley and oregano in a small bowl.Sprinkle each bell pepper with the herbed cheese.Arrange the bell peppers on the air fryer and Bake for 20 minutes.Serve topped with grated Parmesan and parsley.

Thyme Sweet Potato Wedges

Servings:4
Cooking Time:30 Minutes
Ingredients:
- 2 peeled sweet potatoes,cubed
- ¼cup grated Parmesan
- 1 tbsp olive oil
- Salt and pepper to taste
- ½tsp dried thyme
- ½tsp ground cumin

Directions:
1. Preheat air fryer to 330°F(165°C).Add sweet potato cubes to the frying basket,then drizzle with oil.Toss to gently coat.Season with salt,pepper,thyme,and cumin.Roast the potatoes for about 10 minutes.Shake the basket and continue roasting for another 10 minutes.Shake the basket again,this time adding Parmesan cheese.Shake and return to the air fryer.Roast until the potatoes are tender,4-6 minutes.Serve and enjoy!

Broccoli Tots

Servings:24
Cooking Time:10 Minutes
Ingredients:
- 2 cups broccoli florets(about½pound broccoli crowns)
- 1 egg,beaten
- ⅛teaspoon onion powder
- ¼teaspoon salt
- ⅛teaspoon pepper
- 2 tablespoons grated Parmesan cheese
- ¼cup panko breadcrumbs
- oil for misting

Directions:
1. Steam broccoli for 2minutes.Rinse in cold water,drain well,and chop finely.
2. In a large bowl,mix broccoli with all other ingredients except the oil.
3. Scoop out small portions of mixture and shape into 24 tots.Lay them on a cookie sheet or wax paper as you work.
4. Spray tots with oil and place in air fryer basket in single layer.
5. Cook at 390°F(200°C)for 5minutes.Shake basket and spray with oil again.Cook 5minutes longer or until browned and crispy.

Roasted Fennel Salad

Servings:3
Cooking Time:20 Minutes
Ingredients:
- 3 cups(about¾pound)Trimmed fennel(see the headnote),roughly chopped
- 1½tablespoons Olive oil
- ¼teaspoon Table salt
- ¼teaspoon Ground black pepper
- 1½tablespoons White balsamic vinegar(see here)

Directions:
1. Preheat the air fryer to 400°F(205°C).
2. Toss the fennel,olive oil,salt,and pepper in a large bowl until the fennel is well coated in the oil.
3. When the machine is at temperature,pour the fennel into the basket,spreading it out into as close to one layer as possible.Air-fry for 20 minutes,tossing and rearranging the fennel pieces twice so that any covered or touching parts get exposed to the air currents,until golden at the edges and softened.
4. Pour the fennel into a serving bowl.Add the vinegar while hot.Toss well,then cool a couple of minutes before serving.Or serve at room temperature.

Curried Fruit

Servings:6
Cooking Time:20 Minutes
Ingredients:
- 1 cup cubed fresh pineapple
- 1 cup cubed fresh pear(firm,not overly ripe)
- 8 ounces frozen peaches,thawed
- 1 15-ounce can dark,sweet,pitted cherries with juice
- 2 tablespoons brown sugar
- 1 teaspoon curry powder

Directions:
1. Combine all ingredients in large bowl.Stir gently to mix in the sugar and curry.
2. Pour into air fryer baking pan and cook at 360°F(180°C)for 10minutes.
3. Stir fruit and cook 10 more minutes.
4. Serve hot.

Balsamic Stuffed Mushrooms

Servings:4
Cooking Time:30 Minutes
Ingredients:
- ¼cup chopped roasted red peppers
- 12 portobello mushroom caps
- 2 tsp grated Parmesan cheese
- 10 oz spinach,chopped
- 3 scallions,chopped
- ¼cup chickpea flour
- 1 tsp garlic powder
- 1 tbsp balsamic vinegar
- ½lemon

Directions:
1. Preheat air fryer to 360°F(180°C).In a bowl,squeeze any excess water from the spinach;discard the water.Stir in scallions,red pepper,chickpea flour,Parmesan cheese,garlic,and balsamic vinegar until well combined.Fill each mushroom cap with spinach mixture until covering the tops,pressing down slightly.Bake for 12 minutes until crispy.Drizzle with lemon juice before serving.

Classic Stuffed Shells

Servings:4
Cooking Time:35 Minutes
Ingredients:
- 1 cup chopped spinach,cooked
- 1 cup shredded mozzarella
- 4 cooked jumbo shells
- 1 tsp dry oregano
- 1 cup ricotta cheese
- 1 egg,beaten
- 1 cup marinara sauce
- 1 tbsp basil leaves

Directions:
1. Preheat air fryer to 360°F(180°C).Place the beaten egg,oregano,ricotta,mozzarella,and chopped spinach in a bowl and mix until all the ingredients are combined.Fill the mixture into the cooked pasta shells.Spread half of the marinara sauce on a baking pan,then place the stuffed shells over the sauce.Spoon the remaining marinara sauce over the shells.Bake in the air fryer for 25 minutes or until the stuffed shells are wonderfully cooked,crispy on the outside with the spinach and cheeses inside gooey and delicious.Sprinkle with basil leaves and serve warm.

Greek-inspired Ratatouille

Servings:6
Cooking Time:55 Minutes
Ingredients:
- 1 cup cherry tomatoes
- ½bulb fennel,finely sliced
- 2 russet potatoes,cubed
- ½cup tomatoes,cubed
- 1 eggplant,cubed
- 1 zucchini,cubed
- 1 red onion,chopped
- 1 red bell pepper,chopped
- 2 garlic cloves,minced
- 1 tsp dried mint
- 1 tsp dried parsley
- 1 tsp dried oregano
- Salt and pepper to taste
- ¼tsp red pepper flakes
- 1/3 cup olive oil
- 1 can tomato paste
- ¼cup vegetable broth

Directions:
1. Preheat air fryer to 320°F(160°C).Mix the potatoes,tomatoes,fennel,eggplant,zucchini,onion,bell pepper,garlic,mint,parsley,oregano,salt,black pepper,and red pepper flakes in a bowl.Whisk the olive oil,tomato paste,broth,and¼cup of water in a small bowl.Toss the mixture with the vegetables.
2. Pour the coated vegetables into the air frying basket in a single layer and Roast for 20 minutes.Stir well and spread out again.Roast for an additional 10 minutes,then repeat the process and cook for another 10 minutes.Serve and enjoy!

Roasted Broccoli And Red Bean Salad

Servings:3
Cooking Time:14 Minutes
Ingredients:
- 3 cups(about 1 pound)1-to 1½-inch fresh broccoli florets(not frozen)
- 1½tablespoons Olive oil spray
- 1¼cups Canned red kidney beans,drained and rinsed
- 3 tablespoons Minced yellow or white onion
- 2 tablespoons plus 1 teaspoon Red wine vinegar
- ¾teaspoon Dried oregano
- ¼teaspoon Table salt
- ¼teaspoon Ground black pepper

Directions:
1. Preheat the air fryer to 375°F(190°C).
2. Put the broccoli florets in a big bowl,coat them generously with olive oil spray,then toss to coat all surfaces,even down into the crannies,spraying them a couple of times more.
3. Pour the florets into the basket,spreading them into as close to one layer as you can.Air-fry for 12 minutes,tossing and rearranging the florets twice so that any touching or

covered parts are eventually exposed to the air currents,until light browned but still a bit firm.(If the machine is at 360°F(180°C),you may need to add 2 minutes to the cooking time.)

4.   Dump the contents of the basket onto a large cutting board.Cool for a minute or two,then chop the florets into small bits.Scrape these into a bowl and add the kidney beans,onion,vinegar,oregano,salt,and pepper.Toss well and serve warm or at room temperature.

Salmon Salad With Steamboat Dressing

Servings:4
Cooking Time:18 Minutes
Ingredients:
- ¼teaspoon salt
- 1½teaspoons dried dill weed
- 1 tablespoon fresh lemon juice
- 8 ounces fresh or frozen salmon fillet(skin on)
- 8 cups shredded romaine,Boston,or other leaf lettuce
- 8 spears cooked asparagus,cut in 1-inch pieces
- 8 cherry tomatoes,halved or quartered

Directions:
1.   Mix the salt and dill weed together.Rub the lemon juice over the salmon on both sides and sprinkle the dill and salt all over.Refrigerate for 15 to 20minutes.
2.   Make Steamboat Dressing and refrigerate while cooking salmon and preparing salad.
3.   Cook salmon in air fryer basket at 330°F(165°C)for 18 minutes.Cooking time will vary depending on thickness of fillets.When done,salmon should flake with fork but still be moist and tender.
4.   Remove salmon from air fryer and cool slightly.At this point,the skin should slide off easily.Cut salmon into 4 pieces and discard skin.
5.   Divide the lettuce among 4 plates.Scatter asparagus spears and tomato pieces evenly over the lettuce,allowing roughly 2 whole spears and 2 whole cherry tomatoes per plate.
6.   Top each salad with one portion of the salmon and drizzle with a tablespoon of dressing.Serve with additional dressing to pass at the table.

Cinnamon Roasted Pumpkin

Servings:2
Cooking Time:25 Minutes
Ingredients:
- 1 lb pumpkin,halved crosswise and seeded
- 1 tsp coconut oil
- 1 tsp sugar
- ½tsp ground nutmeg
- 1 tsp ground cinnamon

Directions:
1.   Prepare the pumpkin by rubbing coconut oil on the cut sides.In a small bowl,combine sugar,nutmeg and cinnamon.Sprinkle over the pumpkin.Preheat air fryer to 325°F(160°C).Put the pumpkin in the greased frying basket,cut sides up.Bake until the squash is soft in the center,15 minutes.Test with a knife to ensure softness.Serve.

Chicken Eggrolls

Servings:10
Cooking Time:17 Minutes
Ingredients:
- 1 tablespoon vegetable oil
- ¼cup chopped onion
- 1 clove garlic,minced
- 1 cup shredded carrot
- ½cup thinly sliced celery
- 2 cups cooked chicken
- 2 cups shredded white cabbage
- ½cup teriyaki sauce
- 20 egg roll wrappers
- 1 egg,whisked
- 1 tablespoon water

Directions:
1.   Preheat the air fryer to 390°F(200°C).
2.   In a large skillet,heat the oil over medium-high heat.Add in the onion and sautéfor 1 minute.Add in the garlic and sautéfor 30 seconds.Add in the carrot and celery and cook for 2 minutes.Add in the chicken,cabbage,and teriyaki sauce.Allow the mixture to cook for 1 minute,stirring to combine.Remove from the heat.
3.   In a small bowl,whisk together the egg and water for brushing the edges.
4.   Lay the eggroll wrappers out at an angle.Place¼cup filling in the center.Fold the bottom corner up first and then fold in the corners;roll up to complete eggroll.
5.   Place the eggrolls in the air fryer basket,spray with cooking spray,and cook for 8 minutes,turn over,and cook another 2 to 4 minutes.

Crunchy Green Beans

Servings:4
Cooking Time:15 Minutes
Ingredients:
- 1 tbsp tahini
- 1 tbsp lemon juice
- 1 tsp allspice
- 1 lb green beans,trimmed

Directions:
1.   Preheat air fryer to 400°F(205°C).Whisk tahini,lemon juice,1 tbsp of water,and allspice in a bowl.Put in the green beans and toss to coat.Roast for 5 minutes until golden brown and cooked.Serve immediately.

Roasted Cauliflower With Garlic And Capers

Servings:3
Cooking Time:10 Minutes
Ingredients:
- 3 cups(about 15 ounces)1-inch cauliflower florets
- 2 tablespoons Olive oil
- 1½tablespoons Drained and rinsed capers,chopped
- 2 teaspoons Minced garlic
- ¼teaspoon Table salt
- Up to¼teaspoon Red pepper flakes

Directions:
1.   Preheat the air fryer to 375°F(190°C).

2. Stir the cauliflower florets,olive oil,capers,garlic,salt,and red pepper flakes in a large bowl until the florets are evenly coated.

3. When the machine is at temperature,put the florets in the basket,spreading them out to as close to one layer as you can.Air-fry for 10 minutes,tossing once to get any covered pieces exposed to the air currents,until tender and lightly browned.

4. Dump the contents of the basket into a serving bowl or onto a serving platter.Cool for a minute or two before serving.

Herbed Baby Red Potato Hasselback

Servings:4
Cooking Time:35 Minutes
Ingredients:
- 6 baby red potatoes,scrubbed
- 3 tsp shredded cheddar cheese
- 1 tbsp olive oil
- 2 tbsp butter,melted
- 1 tbsp chopped thyme
- Salt and pepper to taste
- 3 tsp sour cream
- ¼cup chopped parsley

Directions:
1. Preheat air fryer at 350ºF.Make slices in the width of each potato about¼-inch apart without cutting through.Rub potato slices with olive oil,both outside and in between slices.Place potatoes in the frying basket and Air Fry for 20 minutes,tossing once,brush with melted butter,and scatter with thyme.Remove them to a large serving dish.Sprinkle with salt,black pepper and top with a dollop of cheddar cheese,sour cream.Scatter with parsley to serve.

Fried Pearl Onions With Balsamic Vinegar And Basil

Servings:2
Cooking Time:10 Minutes
Ingredients:
- 1 pound fresh pearl onions
- 1 tablespoon olive oil
- salt and freshly ground black pepper
- 1 teaspoon high quality aged balsamic vinegar
- 1 tablespoon chopped fresh basil leaves(or mint)

Directions:
1. Preheat the air fryer to 400°F(205°C).
2. Decide whether you want to peel the onions before or after they cook.Peeling them ahead of time is a little more laborious.Peeling after they cook is easier,but a little messier since the onions are hot and you may discard more of the onion than you'd like to.If you opt to peel them first,trim the tiny root of the onions off and pinch off any loose papery skins.(It's ok if there are some skins left on the onions.)Toss the pearl onions with the olive oil,salt and freshly ground black pepper.
3. Air-fry for 10 minutes,shaking the basket a couple of times during the cooking process.(If your pearl onions are very large,you may need to add a couple of minutes to this cooking time.)
4. Let the onions cool slightly and then slip off any remaining skins.

5. Toss the onions with the balsamic vinegar and basil and serve.

Dijon Roasted Purple Potatoes

Servings:4
Cooking Time:25 Minutes
Ingredients:
- 1 lb purple potatoes,scrubbed and halved
- 1 tbsp olive oil
- 1 tsp Dijon mustard
- 1 tsp lemon juice
- 2 cloves garlic,minced
- Salt and pepper to taste
- 2 tbsp butter,melted
- 1 tbsp chopped cilantro
- 1 tsp fresh rosemary

Directions:
1. Mix the olive oil,mustard,garlic,lemon juice,pepper,salt and rosemary in a bowl.Let chill covered in the fridge until ready to use.
2. Preheat air fryer at 350ºF.Toss the potatoes,salt,pepper,and butter in a bowl,place the potatoes in the frying basket,and Roast for 18-20 minutes,tossing once.Transfer them into a bowl.Drizzle potatoes with the dressing and toss to coat.Garnish with cilantro to serve.

Creole Potato Wedges

Servings:4
Cooking Time:10 Minutes
Ingredients:
- 1 pound medium Yukon gold potatoes
- ½teaspoon cayenne pepper
- ½teaspoon thyme
- ½teaspoon garlic powder
- ½teaspoon salt
- ½teaspoon smoked paprika
- 1 cup dry breadcrumbs
- oil for misting or cooking spray

Directions:
1. Wash potatoes,cut into thick wedges,and drop wedges into a bowl of water to prevent browning.
2. Mix together the cayenne pepper,thyme,garlic powder,salt,paprika,and breadcrumbs and spread on a sheet of wax paper.
3. Remove potatoes from water and,without drying them,roll in the breadcrumb mixture.
4. Spray air fryer basket with oil or cooking spray and pile potato wedges into basket.It's okay if they form more than a single layer.
5. Cook at 390°F(200°C)for 8minutes.Shake basket,then continue cooking for 2 minutes longer,until coating is crisp and potato centers are soft.Total cooking time will vary,depending on thickness of potato wedges.

Cheese Sage Cauliflower

Servings:4
Cooking Time:25 Minutes
Ingredients:
- 1 head cauliflower,cut into florets
- 3 tbsp butter,melted
- 2 tbsp grated asiago cheese

- 2 tsp dried sage
- ½tsp garlic powder
- ¼tsp salt

Directions:
1. Preheat air fryer to 350°F.Mix all ingredients in a bowl.Add cauliflower mixture to the frying basket and Air Fry for 6 minutes,shaking once.Serve immediately.

Citrusy Brussels Sprouts

Servings:4
Cooking Time:15 Minutes
Ingredients:
- 1 lb Brussels sprouts,quartered
- 1 clementine,cut into rings
- 2 garlic cloves,minced
- 1 tbsp olive oil
- 1 tbsp butter,melted
- ½tsp salt

Directions:
1. Preheat air fryer to 360°F(180°C).Add the quartered Brussels sprouts with the garlic,olive oil,butter and salt in a bowl and toss until well coated.Pour the Brussels sprouts into the air fryer,top with the clementine slices,and Roast for 10 minutes.Remove from the air fryer and set the clementines aside.Toss the Brussels sprouts and serve.

Zucchini Fries

Servings:3
Cooking Time:12 Minutes
Ingredients:
- 1 large Zucchini
- ½cup All-purpose flour or tapioca flour
- 2 Large egg(s),well beaten
- 1 cup Seasoned Italian-style dried bread crumbs(gluten-free,if a concern)
- Olive oil spray

Directions:
1. Preheat the air fryer to 400°F(205°C).
2. Trim the zucchini into a long rectangular block,taking off the ends and four"sides"to make this shape.Cut the block lengthwise into½-inch-thick slices.Lay these slices flat and cut in half widthwise.Slice each of these pieces into½-inch-thick batons.
3. Set up and fill three shallow soup plates or small pie plates on your counter:one for the flour,one for the beaten egg(s),and one for the bread crumbs.
4. Set a zucchini baton in the flour and turn it several times to coat all sides.Gently shake off any excess flour,then dip it in the egg(s),turning it to coat.Let any excess egg slip back into the rest,then set the baton in the bread crumbs and turn it several times,pressing gently to coat all sides,even the ends.Set aside on a cutting board and continue coating the remainder of the batons in the same way.
5. Lightly coat the batons on all sides with olive oil spray.Set them in two flat layers in the basket,the top layer at a 90-degree angle to the bottom one,with a little air space between the batons in each layer.In the end,the whole thing will look like a crosshatch pattern.Air-fry undisturbed for 6 minutes.
6. Use kitchen tongs to gently rearrange the batons so that any covered parts are now uncovered.The batons no longer need to be in a crosshatch pattern.Continue air-frying undisturbed for 6 minutes,or until lightly browned and crisp.
7. Gently pour the contents of the basket onto a wire rack.Spread the batons out and cool for only a minute or two before serving.

Sweet Potato Fries

Servings:4
Cooking Time:30 Minutes
Ingredients:
- 2 pounds sweet potatoes
- 1 teaspoon dried marjoram
- 2 teaspoons olive oil
- sea salt

Directions:
1. Peel and cut the potatoes into¼-inch sticks,4 to 5 inches long.
2. In a sealable plastic bag or bowl with lid,toss sweet potatoes with marjoram and olive oil.Rub seasonings in to coat well.
3. Pour sweet potatoes into air fryer basket and cook at 390°F(200°C)for approximately 30 minutes,until cooked through with some brown spots on edges.
4. Season to taste with sea salt.

Roasted Sesame Carrots

Servings:4
Cooking Time:25 Minutes
Ingredients:
- 1 lb baby carrots
- 1 tbsp sesame oil
- Salt and pepper to taste
- 6 cloves garlic,peeled
- 3 tbsp sesame seeds
- 1 tbsp green onions

Directions:
1. Preheat air fryer to 380°F(195°C).In a bowl,add baby carrots,sesame oil,salt,and pepper.Toss to coat.Transfer the carrots to the frying basket.Roast for about 4 minutes.Shake the basket and continue roasting for another 4 minutes or until the garlic and carrots are slightly brown.Pour into a serving bowl and top with sesame seeds and green onions.Enjoy!

Sriracha Green Beans

Servings:4
Cooking Time:30 Minutes
Ingredients:
- ½tbsp toasted sesame seeds
- 1 tbsp tamari
- ½tbsp Sriracha sauce
- 4 tsp canola oil
- 12 oz trimmed green beans
- 1 tbsp cilantro,chopped

Directions:
1. Mix the tamari,sriracha,and 1 tsp of canola oil in a small bowl.In a large bowl,toss green beans with the remaining oil.Preheat air fryer to 375°F(190°C).Place the green beans in the frying basket and Air Fry for 8 minutes,shaking the basket once until the beans are charred and tender.Toss the beans with sauce,cilantro,and sesame seeds.Serve.

Perfect Broccoli

Servings:4
Cooking Time:12 Minutes
Ingredients:
- 5 cups(about 1 pound 10 ounces)1-to 1½-inch fresh broccoli florets(not frozen)
- Olive oil spray
- ¾teaspoon Table salt

Directions:
1. Preheat the air fryer to 375°F(190°C).
2. Put the broccoli florets in a big bowl,coat them generously with olive oil spray,then toss to coat all surfaces,even down into the crannies,spraying them in a couple of times more.Sprinkle the salt on top and toss again.
3. When the machine is at temperature,pour the florets into the basket.Air-fry for 10 minutes,tossing and rearranging the pieces twice so that all the covered or touching bits are eventually exposed to the air currents,until lightly browned but still crunchy.(If the machine is at 360°F(180°C),you may have to add 2 minutes to the cooking time.)
4. Pour the florets into a serving bowl.Cool for a minute or two,then serve hot.

Charred Radicchio Salad

Servings:4
Cooking Time:5 Minutes
Ingredients:
- 2 Small 5-to 6-ounce radicchio head(s)
- 3 tablespoons Olive oil
- ½teaspoon Table salt
- 2 tablespoons Balsamic vinegar
- Up to¼teaspoon Red pepper flakes

Directions:
1. Preheat the air fryer to 375°F(190°C).
2. Cut the radicchio head(s)into quarters through the stem end.Brush the oil over the heads,particularly getting it between the leaves along the cut sides.Sprinkle the radicchio quarters with the salt.
3. When the machine is at temperature,set the quarters cut sides up in the basket with as much air space between them as possible.They should not touch.Air-fry undisturbed for 5 minutes,watching carefully because they burn quickly,until blackened in bits and soft.
4. Use a nonstick-safe spatula to transfer the quarters to a cutting board.Cool for a minute or two,then cut out the thick stems inside the heads.Discard these tough bits and chop the remaining heads into bite-size bits.Scrape them into a bowl.Add the vinegar and red pepper flakes.Toss well and serve warm.

Almond Green Beans

Servings:4
Cooking Time:20 Minutes
Ingredients:
- 2 cups green beans,trimmed
- ¼cup slivered almonds
- 2 tbsp butter,melted
- Salt and pepper to taste
- 2 tsp lemon juice
- Lemon zest and slices

Directions:
1. Preheat air fryer at 375ºF.Add almonds to the frying basket and Air Fry for 2 minutes,tossing once.Set aside in a small bowl.Combine the remaining ingredients,except 1 tbsp of butter,in a bowl.
2. Place green beans in the frying basket and Air Fry for 10 minutes,tossing once.Then,transfer them to a large serving dish.Scatter with the melted butter,lemon juice and roasted almonds and toss.Serve immediately garnished with lemon zest and lemon slices.

Butternut Medallions With Honey Butter And Sage

Servings:2
Cooking Time:15 Minutes
Ingredients:
- 1 butternut squash,peeled
- olive oil,in a spray bottle
- salt and freshly ground black pepper
- 2 tablespoons butter,softened
- 2 tablespoons honey
- pinch ground cinnamon
- pinch ground nutmeg
- chopped fresh sage

Directions:
1. Preheat the air fryer to 370°F(185°C).
2. Cut the neck of the butternut squash into disks about½-inch thick.(Use the base of the butternut squash for another use.)Brush or spray the disks with oil and season with salt and freshly ground black pepper.
3. Transfer the butternut disks to the air fryer in one layer(or just ever so slightly overlapping).Air-fry at 370°F(185°C)for 5 minutes.
4. While the butternut squash is cooking,combine the butter,honey,cinnamon and nutmeg in a small bowl.Brush this mixture on the butternut squash,flip the disks over and brush the other side as well.Continue to air-fry at 370°F(185°C)for another 5 minutes.Flip the disks once more,brush with more of the honey butter and air-fry for another 5 minutes.The butternut should be browning nicely around the edges.
5. Remove the butternut squash from the air-fryer and repeat with additional batches if necessary.Transfer to a serving platter,sprinkle with the fresh sage and serve.

Pork Tenderloin Salad

Servings:4
Cooking Time:25 Minutes
Ingredients:
- Pork Tenderloin
- ½teaspoon smoked paprika
- ¼teaspoon salt
- ¼teaspoon garlic powder
- ½teaspoon onion powder
- ⅛teaspoon ginger
- 1 teaspoon extra-light olive oil

- ¾pound pork tenderloin
- Dressing
- 3 tablespoons extra-light olive oil
- 2 tablespoons red wine vinegar
- 2 tablespoons Dijon mustard
- 1 tablespoon honey
- Salad
- ¼sweet red bell pepper
- 1 large Granny Smith apple
- 8 cups shredded Napa cabbage

Directions:
1. Mix the tenderloin seasonings together with oil and rub all over surface of meat.
2. Place pork tenderloin in the air fryer basket and cook at 390°F(200°C)for 25minutes,until meat registers 130°F(55°C)on a meat thermometer.
3. Allow meat to rest while preparing salad and dressing.
4. In a jar,shake all dressing ingredients together until well mixed.
5. Cut the bell pepper into slivers,then core,quarter,and slice the apple crosswise.
6. In a large bowl,toss together the cabbage,bell pepper,apple,and dressing.
7. Divide salad mixture among 4 plates.
8. Slice pork tenderloin into½-inch slices and divide among the 4 salads.
9. Serve with sweet potato or other vegetable chips.

Sicilian Arancini
Servings:4
Cooking Time:20 Minutes
Ingredients:
- 1/3 minced red bell pepper
- 4 tsp grated Parmesan cheese
- 1¼cup cooked rice
- 1 egg
- 3 tbsp plain flour
- 1/3 cup finely grated carrots
- 2 tbsp minced fresh parsley
- 2 tsp olive oil

Directions:
1. Preheat air fryer to 380°F(195°C).Add the rice,egg,and flour to a bowl and mix well.Add the carrots,bell peppers,parsley,and Parmesan cheese and mix again.Shape into 8 fritters.Brush with olive oil and place the fritters in the frying basket.Air Fry for 8-10 minutes,turning once,until golden.Serve hot and enjoy!

Savory Brussels Sprouts
Servings:4
Cooking Time:15 Minutes
Ingredients:
- 1 lb Brussels sprouts,quartered
- 2 tbsp balsamic vinegar
- 1 tbsp olive oil
- 1 tbsp honey
- Salt and pepper to taste

- 1½tbsp lime juice
- Parsley for sprinkling

Directions:
1. Preheat air fryer at 350ºF.Combine all ingredients in a bowl.Transfer them to the frying basket.Air Fry for 10 minutes,tossing once.Top with lime juice and parsley.

Almond-crusted Zucchini Fries
Servings:2
Cooking Time:30 Minutes
Ingredients:
- ½cup grated Pecorino cheese
- 1 zucchini,cut into fries
- 1 tsp salt
- 1 egg
- 1 tbsp almond milk
- ½cup almond flour

Directions:
1. Preheat air fryer to 370ºF.Distribute zucchini fries evenly over a paper towel,sprinkle with salt,and let sit for 10 minutes to pull out moisture.Pat them dry with paper towels.In a bowl,beat egg and almond milk.In another bowl,combine almond flour and Pecorino cheese.Dip fries in egg mixture and then dredge them in flour mixture.Place zucchini fries in the lightly greased frying basket and Air Fry for 10 minutes,flipping once.Serve.

Brussels Sprouts
Serving:3
Cooking Time:5 Minutes
Ingredients:
- 1 10-ounce package frozen brussels sprouts,thawed and halved
- 2 teaspoons olive oil
- salt and pepper

Directions:
1. Toss the brussels sprouts and olive oil together.
2. Place them in the air fryer basket and season to taste with salt and pepper.
3. Cook at 360°F(180°C)for approximately 5minutes,until the edges begin to brown.

Fried Eggplant Balls
Servings:4
Cooking Time:40 Minutes
Ingredients:
- 1 medium eggplant(about 1 pound)
- olive oil
- salt and freshly ground black pepper
- 1 cup grated Parmesan cheese
- 2 cups fresh breadcrumbs
- 2 tablespoons chopped fresh parsley
- 2 tablespoons chopped fresh basil
- 1 clove garlic,minced
- 1 egg,lightly beaten
- ½cup fine dried breadcrumbs

Directions:
1. Preheat the air fryer to 400°F(205°C).

2. Quarter the eggplant by cutting it in half both lengthwise and horizontally.Make a few slashes in the flesh of the eggplant but not through the skin.Brush the cut surface of the eggplant generously with olive oil and transfer to the air fryer basket,cut side up.Air-fry for 10 minutes.Turn the eggplant quarters cut side down and air-fry for another 15 minutes or until the eggplant is soft all the way through.You may need to rotate the pieces in the air fryer so that they cook evenly.Transfer the eggplant to a cutting board to cool.

3. Place the Parmesan cheese,the fresh breadcrumbs,fresh herbs,garlic and egg in a food processor.Scoop the flesh out of the eggplant,discarding the skin and any pieces that are tough.You should have about 1 to 1½cups of eggplant.Add the eggplant to the food processor and process everything together until smooth.Season with salt and pepper.Refrigerate the mixture for at least 30 minutes.

4. Place the dried breadcrumbs into a shallow dish or onto a plate.Scoop heaping tablespoons of the eggplant mixture into the dried breadcrumbs.Roll the dollops of eggplant in the breadcrumbs and then shape into small balls.You should have 16 to 18 eggplant balls at the end.Refrigerate until you are ready to air-fry.

5. Preheat the air fryer to 350°F(175°C).

6. Spray the eggplant balls and the air fryer basket with olive oil.Air-fry the eggplant balls for 15 minutes,rotating the balls during the cooking process to brown evenly.

Five-spice Roasted Sweet Potatoes

Servings:4
Cooking Time:12 Minutes
Ingredients:
- ½teaspoon ground cinnamon
- ¼teaspoon ground cumin
- ¼teaspoon paprika
- 1 teaspoon chile powder
- ⅛teaspoon turmeric
- ½teaspoon salt(optional)
- freshly ground black pepper
- 2 large sweet potatoes,peeled and cut into¾-inch cubes(about 3 cups)
- 1 tablespoon olive oil

Directions:
1. In a large bowl,mix together cinnamon,cumin,paprika,chile powder,turmeric,salt,and pepper to taste.
2. Add potatoes and stir well.
3. Drizzle the seasoned potatoes with the olive oil and stir until evenly coated.
4. Place seasoned potatoes in the air fryer baking pan or an ovenproof dish that fits inside your air fryer basket.
5. Cook for 6minutes at 390°F(200°C),stop,and stir well.
6. Cook for an additional 6minutes.

Ricotta&Broccoli Cannelloni

Servings:4
Cooking Time:35 Minutes
Ingredients:

- 1 cup shredded mozzarella cheese
- ½cup cooked broccoli,chopped
- ½cup cooked spinach,chopped
- 4 cooked cannelloni shells
- 1 cup ricotta cheese
- ½tsp dried marjoram
- 1 egg
- 1 cup passata
- 1 tbsp basil leaves

Directions:
1. Preheat air fryer to 360°F(180°C).Beat the egg in a bowl until fluffy.Add the ricotta,marjoram,half of the mozzarella,broccoli,and spinach and stir to combine.Cover the base of a baking dish with a layer of passata.Fill the cannelloni with the cheese mixture and place them on top of the sauce.Spoon the remaining passata over the tops and top with the rest of the mozzarella cheese.Put the dish in the frying basket and Bake for 25 minutes until the cheese is melted and golden.Top with basil.

Mashed Potato Pancakes

Servings:6
Cooking Time:10 Minutes
Ingredients:
- 2 cups leftover mashed potatoes
- ½cup grated cheddar cheese
- ¼cup thinly sliced green onions
- ½teaspoon salt
- ¼teaspoon black pepper
- 1 cup breadcrumbs

Directions:
1. Preheat the air fryer to 380°F(195°C).
2. In a large bowl,mix together the potatoes,cheese,and onions.Using a¼cup measuring cup,measure out 6 patties.Form the potatoes into½-inch thick patties.Season the patties with salt and pepper on both sides.
3. In a small bowl,place the breadcrumbs.Gently press the potato pancakes into the breadcrumbs.
4. Place the potato pancakes into the air fryer basket and spray with cooking spray.Cook for 5 minutes,turn the pancakes over,and cook another 3 to 5 minutes or until golden brown on the outside and cooked through on the inside.

Mediterranean Roasted Vegetables

Servings:4
Cooking Time:30 Minutes
Ingredients:
- 1 red bell pepper,cut into chunks
- 1 cup sliced mushrooms
- 1 cup green beans,diced
- 1 zucchini,sliced
- 1/3 cup diced red onion
- 3 garlic cloves,sliced
- 2 tbsp olive oil
- 1 tsp rosemary

- ½tsp flaked sea salt

Directions:

1. Preheat air fryer to 350°F(175°C).Add the bell pepper,mushrooms,green beans,red onion,zucchini,rosemary,and garlic to a bowl and mix,then spritz with olive oil.Stir until well-coated.Put the veggies in the frying basket and Air Fry for 14-18 minutes.The veggies should be soft and crispy.Serve sprinkled with flaked sea salt.

Broccoli Au Gratin

Servings:2

Cooking Time:25 Minutes

Ingredients:

- 2 cups broccoli florets,chopped
- 6 tbsp grated Gruyère cheese
- 1 tbsp grated Pecorino cheese
- ½tbsp olive oil
- 1 tbsp flour
- 1/3 cup milk
- ½tsp ground coriander
- Salt and black pepper
- 2 tbsp panko bread crumbs

Directions:

1. Whisk the olive oil,flour,milk,coriander,salt,and pepper in a bowl.Incorporate broccoli,Gruyere cheese,panko bread crumbs,and Pecorino cheese until well combined.Pour in a greased baking dish.

2. Preheat air fryer to 330°F(165°C).Put the baking dish into the frying basket.Bake until the broccoli is crisp-tender and the top is golden,or about 12-15 minutes.Serve warm.

Beef, pork&Lamb Recipes

Extra Crispy Country-style Pork Riblets

Servings:3
Cooking Time:30 Minutes
Ingredients:
- ⅓cup Tapioca flour
- 2½tablespoons Chile powder
- ¾teaspoon Table salt(optional)
- 1¼pounds Boneless country-style pork ribs,cut into 1½-inch chunks
- Vegetable oil spray

Directions:
1.   Preheat the air fryer to 375°F(190°C).
2.   Mix the tapioca flour,chile powder,and salt(if using)in a large bowl until well combined.Add the country-style rib chunks and toss well to coat thoroughly.
3.   When the machine is at temperature,gently shake off any excess tapioca coating from the chunks.Generously coat them on all sides with vegetable oil spray.Arrange the chunks in the basket in one(admittedly fairly tight)layer.The pieces may touch.Air-fry for 30 minutes,rearranging the pieces at the 10-and 20-minute marks to expose any touching bits,until very crisp and well browned.
4.   Gently pour the contents of the basket onto a wire rack.Cool for 5 minutes before serving.

Coffee-rubbed Pork Tenderloin

Servings:4
Cooking Time:30 Minutes
Ingredients:
- 1 tbsp packed brown sugar
- 2 tsp espresso powder
- 1 tsp bell pepper powder
- ½tsp dried parsley
- 1 tbsp honey
- ½tbsp lemon juice
- 2 tsp olive oil
- 1 pound pork tenderloin

Directions:
1.   Preheat air fryer to 400°F(205°C).Toss the brown sugar,espresso powder,bell pepper powder,and parsley in a bowl and mix together.Add the honey,lemon juice,and olive oil,then stir well.Smear the pork with the mix,then allow to marinate for 10 minutes before putting it in the air fryer.Roast for 9-11 minutes until the pork is cooked through.Slice before serving.

Traditional Italian Beef Meatballs

Servings:4
Cooking Time:35 Minutes
Ingredients:
- 1/3 cup grated Parmesan
- 1 lb ground beef
- 1 egg,beaten
- 2 tbsp tomato paste
- ½tsp Italian seasonings
- ¼cup ricotta cheese
- 3 cloves garlic,minced
- ¼cup grated yellow onion
- Salt and pepper to taste
- ¼cup almond flour
- ¼cup chopped basil
- 2 cups marinara sauce

Directions:
1.   Preheat air fryer to 400ºF.In a large bowl,combine ground beef,egg,tomato paste,Italian seasoning,ricotta cheese,Parmesan cheese,garlic,onion,salt,pepper,flour,and basil.Form mixture into 4 meatballs.Add them to the greased frying basket and Air Fry for 20 minutes.Warm the marinara sauce in a skillet over medium heat for 3 minutes.Add in cooked meatballs and roll them around in sauce for 2 minutes.Serve with sauce over the top.

Natchitoches Meat Pies

Servings:8
Cooking Time:12 Minutes
Ingredients:
- Filling
- ½pound lean ground beef
- ¼cup finely chopped onion
- ¼cup finely chopped green bell pepper
- ⅛teaspoon salt
- ½teaspoon garlic powder
- ½teaspoon red pepper flakes
- 1 tablespoon low sodium Worcestershire sauce
- Crust
- 2 cups self-rising flour
- ¼cup butter,finely diced
- 1 cup milk
- Egg Wash
- 1 egg
- 1 tablespoon water or milk
- oil for misting or cooking spray

Directions:
1.   Mix all filling ingredients well and shape into 4 small patties.
2.   Cook patties in air fryer basket at 390°F(200°C)for 10 to 12minutes or until well done.
3.   Place patties in large bowl and use fork and knife to crumble meat into very small pieces.Set aside.
4.   To make the crust,use a pastry blender or fork to cut the butter into the flour until well mixed.Add milk and stir until dough stiffens.
5.   Divide dough into 8 equal portions.
6.   On a lightly floured surface,roll each portion of dough into a circle.The circle should be thin and about 5 inches in diameter,but don't worry about getting a perfect shape.Uneven circles result in a rustic look that many people prefer.
7.   Spoon 2 tablespoons of meat filling onto each dough circle.
8.   Brush egg wash all the way around the edge of dough circle,about½-inch deep.

9. Fold each circle in half and press dough with tines of a dinner fork to seal the edges all the way around.
10. Brush tops of sealed meat pies with egg wash.
11. Cook filled pies in a single layer in air fryer basket at 360°F(180°C)for 4minutes.Spray tops with oil or cooking spray,turn pies over,and spray bottoms with oil or cooking spray.Cook for an additional 2minutes.
12. Repeat previous step to cook remaining pies.

Rib Eye Cheesesteaks With Fried Onions

Servings:2
Cooking Time:20 Minutes
Ingredients:
- 1(12-ounce)rib eye steak
- 2 tablespoons Worcestershire sauce
- salt and freshly ground black pepper
- ½onion,sliced
- 2 tablespoons butter,melted
- 4 ounces sliced Cheddar or provolone cheese
- 2 long hoagie rolls,lightly toasted

Directions:
1. Place the steak in the freezer for 30 minutes to make it easier to slice.When it is well-chilled,thinly slice the steak against the grain and transfer it to a bowl.Pour the Worcestershire sauce over the steak and season it with salt and pepper.Allow the meat to come to room temperature.
2. Preheat the air fryer to 400°F(205°C).
3. Toss the sliced onion with the butter and transfer it to the air fryer basket.Air-fry at 400°F(205°C)for 12 minutes,shaking the basket a few times during the cooking process.Place the steak on top of the onions and air-fry for another 6 minutes,stirring the meat and onions together halfway through the cooking time.
4. When the air fryer has finished cooking,divide the steak and onions in half in the air fryer basket,pushing each half to one side of the air fryer basket.Place the cheese on top of each half,push the drawer back into the turned off air fryer and let it sit for 2 minutes,until the cheese has melted.
5. Transfer each half of the cheesesteak mixture into a toasted roll with the cheese side up and dig in!

Corned Beef Hash

Servings:6
Cooking Time:15 Minutes
Ingredients:
- 3 cups(about 14 ounces)Frozen unseasoned hash brown cubes(no need to thaw)
- 9 ounces Deli corned beef,cut into¾-inch-thick slices,then cubed
- ¾cup Roughly chopped yellow or white onion
- ¾cup Stemmed,cored,and roughly chopped red bell pepper
- 2½tablespoons Olive oil
- ¼teaspoon Dried thyme
- ¼teaspoon Dried sage leaves
- Up to a⅛teaspoon Cayenne

Directions:
1. Preheat the air fryer to 400°F(205°C).
2. Mix all the ingredients in a large or very large bowl until the potato cubes and corned beef are coated in the spices.

3. Spread the mixture in the basket in as close to an even layer as you can.Air-fry for 15 minutes,tossing and rearranging the pieces at the 5-and 10-minute marks to expose covered bits,until the potatoes are browned,even crisp,and the mixture is very fragrant.
4. Pour the contents of the basket onto a serving platter or divide between serving plates.Cool for a couple of minutes before serving.

Kentucky-style Pork Tenderloin

Servings:2
Cooking Time:30 Minutes
Ingredients:
- 1 lb pork tenderloin,halved crosswise
- 1 tbsp smoked paprika
- 2 tsp ground cumin
- 1 tsp garlic powder
- 1 tsp shallot powder
- ¼tsp chili pepper
- Salt and pepper to taste
- 1 tsp Italian seasoning
- 2 tbsp butter,melted
- 1 tsp Worcestershire sauce

Directions:
1. Preheat air fryer to 350ºF.In a shallow bowl,combine all spices.Set aside.In another bowl,whisk butter and Worcestershire sauce and brush over pork tenderloin.Sprinkle with the seasoning mix.Place pork in the lightly greased frying basket and Air Fry for 16 minutes,flipping once.Let sit onto a cutting board for 5 minutes before slicing.Serve immediately.

Vietnamese Beef Lettuce Wraps

Servings:4
Cooking Time:12 Minutes
Ingredients:
- ⅓cup low-sodium soy sauce*
- 2 teaspoons fish sauce*
- 2 teaspoons brown sugar
- 1 tablespoon chili paste
- juice of 1 lime
- 2 cloves garlic,minced
- 2 teaspoons fresh ginger,minced
- 1 pound beef sirloin
- Sauce
- ⅓cup low-sodium soy sauce*
- juice of 2 limes
- 1 tablespoon mirin wine
- 2 teaspoons chili paste
- Serving
- 1 head butter lettuce
- ½cup julienned carrots
- ½cup julienned cucumber
- ½cup sliced radishes,sliced into half moons
- 2 cups cooked rice noodles
- ⅓cup chopped peanuts

Directions:
1. Combine the soy sauce,fish sauce,brown sugar,chili paste,lime juice,garlic and ginger in a bowl.Slice the beef into thin slices,then cut those slices in half.Add the beef to

the marinade and marinate for 1 to 3 hours in the refrigerator.When you are ready to cook,remove the steak from the refrigerator and let it sit at room temperature for 30 minutes.

2. Preheat the air fryer to 400°F(205°C).

3. Transfer the beef and marinade to the air fryer basket.Air-fry at 400°F(205°C)for 12 minutes,shaking the basket a few times during the cooking process.

4. While the beef is cooking,prepare a wrap-building station.Combine the soy sauce,lime juice,mirin wine and chili paste in a bowl and transfer to a little pouring vessel.Separate the lettuce leaves from the head of lettuce and put them in a serving bowl.Place the carrots,cucumber,radish,rice noodles and chopped peanuts all in separate serving bowls.

5. When the beef has finished cooking,transfer it to another serving bowl and invite your guests to build their wraps.To build the wraps,place some beef in a lettuce leaf and top with carrots,cucumbers,some rice noodles and chopped peanuts.Drizzle a little sauce over top,fold the lettuce around the ingredients and enjoy!

Cowboy Rib Eye Steak

Servings:2
Cooking Time:20 Minutes
Ingredients:
- ¼cup barbecue sauce
- 1 clove garlic,minced
- ⅛tsp chili pepper
- ¼tsp sweet paprika
- ¼tsp cumin
- 1 rib-eye steak

Directions:
1. Preheat air fryer to 400ºF.In a bowl,whisk the barbecue sauce,garlic,chili pepper,paprika,and cumin.Divide in half and brush the steak with half of the sauce.Add steak to the lightly greased frying basket and Air Fry for 10 minutes until you reach your desired doneness,turning once and brushing with the remaining sauce.Let rest for 5 minutes onto a cutting board before slicing.Serve warm.

Italian Sausage Bake

Servings:4
Cooking Time:25 Minutes
Ingredients:
- 1 cup red bell pepper,strips
- ¾lb Italian sausage,sliced
- ½cup minced onions
- 3 tbsp brown sugar
- 1/3 cup ketchup
- 2 tbsp mustard
- 2 tbsp apple cider vinegar
- ½cup chicken broth

Directions:
1. Preheat air fryer to 350°F(175°C).Combine the Italian sausage,bell pepper,and minced onion into a bowl.Stir well.Mix together brown sugar,ketchup,mustard,apple cider vinegar,and chicken broth in a small bowl.Pour over the sausage.Place the bowl in the air fryer,and Bake until the sausage is hot,the vegetables are tender,and the sauce is bubbling and thickened,10-15 minutes.Serve and enjoy!

Barbecue-style London Broil

Servings:5
Cooking Time:17 Minutes
Ingredients:
- ¾teaspoon Mild smoked paprika
- ¾teaspoon Dried oregano
- ¾teaspoon Table salt
- ¾teaspoon Ground black pepper
- ¼teaspoon Garlic powder
- ¼teaspoon Onion powder
- 1½pounds Beef London broil(in one piece)
- Olive oil spray

Directions:
1. Preheat the air fryer to 400°F(205°C).

2. Mix the smoked paprika,oregano,salt,pepper,garlic powder,and onion powder in a small bowl until uniform.

3. Pat and rub this mixture across all surfaces of the beef.Lightly coat the beef on all sides with olive oil spray.

4. When the machine is at temperature,lay the London broil flat in the basket and air-fry undisturbed for 8 minutes for the small batch,10 minutes for the medium batch,or 12 minutes for the large batch for medium-rare,until an instant-read meat thermometer inserted into the center of the meat registers 130°F(55°C)(not USDA-approved).Add 1,2,or 3 minutes,respectively(based on the size of the cut)for medium,until an instant-read meat thermometer registers 135°F(60°C)(not USDA-approved).Or add 3,4,or 5 minutes respectively for medium,until an instant-read meat thermometer registers 145°F(65°C)(USDA-approved).

5. Use kitchen tongs to transfer the London broil to a cutting board.Let the meat rest for 10 minutes.It needs a long time for the juices to be reincorporated into the meat's fibers.Carve it against the grain into very thin(less than¼-inch-thick)slices to serve.

Pork Kabobs With Pineapple

Servings:4
Cooking Time:30 Minutes
Ingredients:
- 2 cans juice-packed pineapple chunks,juice reserved
- 1 green bell pepper,cut into½-inch chunks
- 1 red bell pepper,cut into½-inch chunks
- 1 lb pork tenderloin,cubed
- Salt and pepper to taste
- 1 tbsp honey
- ½tsp ground ginger
- ½tsp ground coriander
- 1 red chili,minced

Directions:
1. Preheat the air fryer to 375°F(190°C).Mix the coriander,chili,salt,and pepper in a bowl.Add the pork and toss to coat.Then,thread the pork pieces,pineapple chunks,and bell peppers onto skewers.Combine the pineapple juice,honey,and ginger and mix well.Use all the mixture as you brush it on the kebabs.Put the kebabs in the greased frying basket and Air Fry for 10-14 minutes or until cooked through.Serve and enjoy!

Spanish-style Meatloaf With Manzanilla Olives

Servings:6
Cooking Time:35 Minutes
Ingredients:
- 2 oz Manchego cheese,grated
- 1 lb lean ground beef
- 2 eggs
- 2 tomatoes,diced
- ½white onion,diced
- ½cup bread crumbs
- 1 tsp garlic powder
- 1 tsp dried oregano
- 1 tsp dried thyme
- Salt and pepper to taste
- 4 Manzanilla olives,minced
- 1 tbsp olive oil
- 2 tbsp chopped parsley

Directions:
1. Preheat the oven to 380°F(195°C).Combine the ground beef,eggs,tomatoes,onion,bread crumbs,garlic powder,oregano,thyme,salt,pepper,olives and cheese in a bowl and mix well.Form into a loaf,flattening to 1-inch thick.Lightly brush the top with olive oil,then place the meatloaf into the frying basket.Bake for 25 minutes.Allow to rest for 5 minutes.Top with parsley and slice.Serve warm.

Crispy Pork Pork Escalopes

Servings:4
Cooking Time:20 Minutes
Ingredients:
- 4 pork loin steaks
- Salt and pepper to taste
- ¼cup flour
- 2 tbsp bread crumbs

Directions:
1. Preheat air fryer to 380°F(195°C).Season pork with salt and pepper.In one shallow bowl,add flour.In another,add bread crumbs.Dip the steaks first in the flour,then in the crumbs.Place them in the fryer and spray with oil.Bake for 12-14 minutes,flipping once until crisp.Serve.

Meatball Subs

Servings:4
Cooking Time:11 Minutes
Ingredients:
- Marinara Sauce
- 1 15-ounce can diced tomatoes
- 1 teaspoon garlic powder
- 1 teaspoon dried basil
- ½teaspoon oregano
- ⅛teaspoon salt
- 1 tablespoon robust olive oil
- Meatballs
- ¼pound ground turkey
- ¾pound very lean ground beef
- 1 tablespoon milk
- ½cup torn bread pieces
- 1 egg
- ¼teaspoon salt
- ½teaspoon dried onion
- 1 teaspoon garlic powder
- ¼teaspoon smoked paprika
- ¼teaspoon crushed red pepper
- 1½teaspoons dried parsley
- ¼teaspoon oregano
- 2 teaspoons Worcestershire sauce
- Sandwiches
- 4 large whole-grain sub or hoagie rolls,split
- toppings,sliced or chopped:
- mushrooms
- jalapeño or banana peppers
- red or green bell pepper
- red onions
- grated cheese

Directions:
1. Place all marinara ingredients in saucepan and bring to a boil.Lower heat and simmer 10minutes,uncovered.
2. Combine all meatball ingredients in large bowl and stir.Mixture should be well blended but don't overwork it.Excessive mixing will toughen the meatballs.
3. Divide meat into 16 equal portions and shape into balls.
4. Cook the balls at 360°F(180°C)until meat is done and juices run clear,about 11 minutes.
5. While meatballs are cooking,taste marinara.If you prefer stronger flavors,add more seasoning and simmer another 5minutes.
6. When meatballs finish cooking,drain them on paper towels.
7. To assemble subs,place 4 meatballs on each sub roll,spoon sauce over meat,and add preferred toppings.Serve with additional marinara for dipping.

Steakhouse Filets Mignons

Servings:3
Cooking Time:12-15 Minutes
Ingredients:
- ¾ounce Dried porcini mushrooms
- ¼teaspoon Granulated white sugar
- ¼teaspoon Ground white pepper
- ¼teaspoon Table salt
- 6¼-pound filets mignons or beef tenderloin steaks
- 6 Thin-cut bacon strips(gluten-free,if a concern)

Directions:
1. Preheat the air fryer to 400°F(205°C).
2. Grind the dried mushrooms in a clean spice grinder until powdery.Add the sugar,white pepper,and salt.Grind to blend.
3. Rub this mushroom mixture into both cut sides of each filet.Wrap the circumference of each filet with a strip of bacon.(It will loop around the beef about 1½times.)
4. Set the filets mignons in the basket on their sides with the bacon seam side down.Do not let the filets touch;keep at least¼inch open between them.Air-fry undisturbed for 12 minutes for rare,or until an instant-read meat thermometer inserted into the center of a filet registers 125°F(50°C)(not USDA-approved);13 minutes for medium-rare,or until an instant-read meat thermometer inserted into the center of a filet registers 132°F(55°C)(not USDA-approved);or 15 minutes for medium,or until an instant-read meat thermometer inserted into the center of a filet registers 145°F(65°C)(USDA-approved).
5. Use kitchen tongs to transfer the filets to a wire rack,setting them cut side down.Cool for 5 minutes before serving.

Flank Steak With Roasted Peppers And Chimichurri

Servings:4
Cooking Time:22 Minutes
Ingredients:

- 2 cups flat-leaf parsley leaves
- ¼cup fresh oregano leaves
- 3 cloves garlic
- ½cup olive oil
- ¼cup red wine vinegar
- ½teaspoon salt
- freshly ground black pepper
- ¼teaspoon crushed red pepper flakes
- ½teaspoon ground cumin
- 1 pound flank steak
- 1 red bell pepper,cut into strips
- 1 yellow bell pepper,cut into strips

Directions:

1. Make the chimichurri sauce by chopping the parsley,oregano and garlic in a food processor.Add the olive oil,vinegar and seasonings and process again.Pour half of the sauce into a shallow dish with the flank steak and set the remaining sauce aside.Pierce the flank steak with a needle-style meat tenderizer or a paring knife and marinate the steak for 2 to 24 hours in the refrigerator.When you are ready to cook,remove the steak from the refrigerator and let it sit at room temperature for 30 minutes.
2. Preheat the air fryer to 400°F(205°C).
3. Cut the flank steak in half so that it fits more easily into the air fryer and transfer both pieces to the air fryer basket.Air-fry for 14 minutes,depending on how you like your steak cooked(10 minutes will give you medium for a 1-inch thick flank steak).Flip the steak over halfway through the cooking time.
4. When the flank steak is cooked to your liking,transfer it to a cutting board,loosely tent with foil and let it rest while you cook the peppers.
5. Toss the peppers in a little olive oil,salt and freshly ground black pepper and transfer them to the air fryer basket.Air-fry at 400°F(205°C)for 8 minutes,shaking the basket once or twice throughout the cooking process.To serve,slice the flank steak against the grain of the meat and top with the roasted peppers.Drizzle the reserved chimichurri sauce on top,thinning the sauce with another tablespoon of olive oil if desired.

Pork Schnitzel

Servings:4
Cooking Time:14 Minutes
Ingredients:

- 4 boneless pork chops,pounded to¼-inch thickness
- 1 teaspoon salt,divided
- 1 teaspoon black pepper,divided
- ½cup all-purpose flour
- 2 eggs
- 1 cup breadcrumbs
- ¼teaspoon paprika
- 1 lemon,cut into wedges

Directions:

1. Season both sides of the pork chops with½teaspoon of the salt and½teaspoon of the pepper.
2. On a plate,place the flour.
3. In a large bowl,whisk the eggs.
4. In another large bowl,place the breadcrumbs.
5. Season the flour with the paprika and season the breadcrumbs with the remaining½teaspoon of salt and½teaspoon of pepper.
6. To bread the pork,place a pork chop in the flour,then into the whisked eggs,and then into the breadcrumbs.Place the breaded pork onto a plate and finish breading the remaining pork chops.
7. Preheat the air fryer to 390°F(200°C).
8. Place the pork chops into the air fryer,not overlapping and working in batches as needed.Spray the pork chops with cooking spray and cook for 8 minutes;flip the pork and cook for another 4 to 6 minutes or until cooked to an internal temperature of 145°F(65°C).
9. Serve with lemon wedges.

Meatloaf With Tangy Tomato Glaze

Servings:6
Cooking Time:50 Minutes
Ingredients:

- 1 pound ground beef
- ½pound ground pork
- ½pound ground veal(or turkey)
- 1 medium onion,diced
- 1 small clove of garlic,minced
- 2 egg yolks,lightly beaten
- ½cup tomato ketchup
- 1 tablespoon Worcestershire sauce
- ½cup plain breadcrumbs*
- 2 teaspoons salt
- freshly ground black pepper
- ½cup chopped fresh parsley,plus more for garnish
- 6 tablespoons ketchup
- 1 tablespoon balsamic vinegar
- 2 tablespoons brown sugar

Directions:

1. Combine the meats,onion,garlic,egg yolks,ketchup,Worcestershire sauce,breadcrumbs,salt,pepper and fresh parsley in a large bowl and mix well.
2. Preheat the air fryer to 350°F(175°C)and pour a little water into the bottom of the air fryer drawer.(This will help prevent the grease that drips into the bottom drawer from burning and smoking.)
3. Transfer the meatloaf mixture to the air fryer basket,packing it down gently.Run a spatula around the meatloaf to create a space about½-inch wide between the meat and the side of the air fryer basket.
4. Air-fry at 350°F(175°C)for 20 minutes.Carefully invert the meatloaf onto a plate(remember to remove the basket from the air fryer drawer so you don't pour all the grease out)and slide it back into the air fryer basket to turn it over.Re-shape the meatloaf with a spatula if necessary.Air-fry for another 20 minutes at 350°F(175°C).
5. Combine the ketchup,balsamic vinegar and brown sugar in a bowl and spread the mixture over the meatloaf.Air-fry

for another 10 minutes,until an instant read thermometer inserted into the center of the meatloaf registers 160°F(70°C).

6. Allow the meatloaf to rest for a few more minutes and then transfer it to a serving platter using a spatula.Slice the meatloaf,sprinkle a little chopped parsley on top if desired,and serve.

Italian Meatballs

Servings:4
Cooking Time:12 Minutes
Ingredients:
- 12 ounces lean ground beef
- 4 ounces Italian sausage,casing removed
- ½cup breadcrumbs
- 1 cup grated Parmesan cheese
- 1 egg
- 2 tablespoons milk
- 2 teaspoons Italian seasoning
- ½teaspoon onion powder
- ½teaspoon garlic powder
- Pinch of red pepper flakes

Directions:
1. In a large bowl,place all the ingredients and mix well.Roll out 24 meatballs.
2. Preheat the air fryer to 360°F(180°C).
3. Place the meatballs in the air fryer basket and cook for 12 minutes,tossing every 4 minutes.Using a food thermometer,check to ensure the internal temperature of the meatballs is 165°F(75°C).

Cheesy Mushroom-stuffed Pork Loins

Servings:3
Cooking Time:30 Minutes
Ingredients:
- ¾cup diced mushrooms
- 2 tsp olive oil
- 1 shallot,diced
- Salt and pepper to taste
- 3 center-cut pork loins
- 6 Gruyère cheese slices

Directions:
1. Warm the olive oil in a skillet over medium heat.Add in shallot and mushrooms and stir-fry for 3 minutes.Sprinkle with salt and pepper and cook for 1 minute.
2. Preheat air fryer to 350°F.Cut a pocket into each pork loin and set aside.Stuff an even amount of mushroom mixture into each chop pocket and top with 2 Gruyere cheese slices into each pocket.Place the pork in the lightly greased frying basket and Air Fry for 11 minutes cooked through and the cheese has melted.Let sit onto a cutting board for 5 minutes before serving.

Pepper Steak

Servings:4
Cooking Time:30 Minutes
Ingredients:
- 2 tablespoons cornstarch
- 1 tablespoon sugar
- ¾cup beef broth
- ¼cup hoisin sauce
- 3 tablespoons soy sauce
- 1 teaspoon sesame oil
- ½teaspoon freshly ground black pepper
- 1½pounds boneless New York strip steaks,sliced into½-inch strips
- 1 onion,sliced
- 3 small bell peppers,red,yellow and green,sliced

Directions:
1. Whisk the cornstarch and sugar together in a large bowl to break up any lumps in the cornstarch.Add the beef broth and whisk until combined and smooth.Stir in the hoisin sauce,soy sauce,sesame oil and freshly ground black pepper.Add the beef,onion and peppers,and toss to coat.Marinate the beef and vegetables at room temperature for 30 minutes,stirring a few times to keep meat and vegetables coated.
2. Preheat the air fryer to 350°F(175°C).
3. Transfer the beef,onion,and peppers to the air fryer basket with tongs,reserving the marinade.Air-fry the beef and vegetables for 30 minutes,stirring well two or three times during the cooking process.
4. While the beef is air-frying,bring the reserved marinade to a simmer in a small saucepan over medium heat on the stovetop.Simmer for 5 minutes until the sauce thickens.
5. When the steak and vegetables have finished cooking,transfer them to a serving platter.Pour the hot sauce over the pepper steak and serve with white rice.

Tonkatsu

Servings:3
Cooking Time:10 Minutes
Ingredients:
- ½cup All-purpose flour or tapioca flour
- 1 Large egg white(s),well beaten
- ¾cup Plain panko bread crumbs(gluten-free,if a concern)
- 3 4-ounce center-cut boneless pork loin chops(about½inch thick)
- Vegetable oil spray

Directions:
1. Preheat the air fryer to 375°F(190°C).
2. Set up and fill three shallow soup plates or small pie plates on your counter:one for the flour,one for the beaten egg white(s),and one for the bread crumbs.
3. Set a chop in the flour and roll it to coat all sides,even the ends.Gently shake off any excess flour and set it in the egg white(s).Gently roll and turn it to coat all sides.Let any excess egg white slip back into the rest,then set the chop in the bread crumbs.Turn it several times,pressing gently to get an even coating on all sides and the ends.Generously coat the breaded chop with vegetable oil spray,then set it aside so you can dredge,coat,and spray the remaining chop(s).
4. Set the chops in the basket with as much air space between them as possible.Air-fry undisturbed for 10 minutes,or until golden brown and crisp.
5. Use kitchen tongs to transfer the chops to a wire rack and cool for a couple of minutes before serving.

Beef Meatballs With Herbs

Servings:6
Cooking Time:30 Minutes
Ingredients:
- 1 medium onion,minced
- 2 garlic cloves,minced
- 1 tsp olive oil
- 1 bread slice,crumbled
- 3 tbsp milk
- 1 tsp dried sage
- 1 tsp dried thyme
- 1 lb ground beef

Directions:
1. Preheat air fryer to 380°F(195°C).Toss the onion,garlic,and olive oil in a baking pan,place it in the air fryer,and Air Fry for 2-4 minutes.The veggies should be crispy but tender.Transfer the veggies to a bowl and add in the breadcrumbs,milk,thyme,and sage,then toss gently to combine.Add in the ground beef and mix with your hands.Shape the mixture into 24 meatballs.Put them in the frying basket and Air Fry for 12-16 minutes or until the meatballs are browned on all sides.Serve and enjoy!

Mustard-crusted Rib-eye

Servings:2
Cooking Time:9 Minutes
Ingredients:
- Two 6-ounce rib-eye steaks,about 1-inch thick
- 1 teaspoon coarse salt
- ½teaspoon coarse black pepper
- 2 tablespoons Dijon mustard

Directions:
1. Rub the steaks with the salt and pepper.Then spread the mustard on both sides of the steaks.Cover with foil and let the steaks sit at room temperature for 30 minutes.
2. Preheat the air fryer to 390°F(200°C).
3. Cook the steaks for 9 minutes.Check for an internal temperature of 140°F(60°C)and immediately remove the steaks and let them rest for 5 minutes before slicing.

Kochukaru Pork Lettuce Cups

Servings:4
Cooking Time:25 Minutes
Ingredients:
- 1 tsp kochukaru(chili pepper flakes)
- 12 baby romaine lettuce leaves
- 1 lb pork tenderloin,sliced
- Salt and pepper to taste
- 3 scallions,chopped
- 3 garlic cloves,crushed
- ¼cup soy sauce
- 2 tbsp gochujang
- ½tbsp light brown sugar
- ½tbsp honey
- 1 tbsp grated fresh ginger
- 2 tbsp rice vinegar
- 1 tsp toasted sesame oil
- 2¼cups cooked brown rice
- ½tbsp sesame seeds
- 2 spring onions,sliced

Directions:
1. Mix the scallions,garlic,soy sauce,kochukaru,honey,brown sugar,and ginger in a small bowl.Mix well.Place the pork in a large bowl.Season with salt and pepper.Pour the marinade over the pork,tossing the meat in the marinade until coated.Cover the bowl with plastic wrap and allow to marinate overnight.When ready to cook,
2. Preheat air fryer to 400°F(205°C).Remove the pork from the bowl and discard the marinade.Place the pork in the greased frying basket and Air Fry for 10 minutes,flipping once until browned and cooked through.Meanwhile,prepare the gochujang sauce.Mix the gochujang,rice vinegar,and sesame oil until smooth.To make the cup,add 3 tbsp of brown rice on the lettuce leaf.Place a slice of pork on top,drizzle a tsp of gochujang sauce and sprinkle with some sesame seeds and spring onions.Wrap the lettuce over the mixture similar to a burrito.Serve warm.

Bacon Wrapped Filets Mignons

Servings:4
Cooking Time:18 Minutes
Ingredients:
- 4 slices bacon(not thick cut)
- 4(8-ounce)filets mignons
- 1 tablespoon fresh thyme leaves
- salt and freshly ground black pepper

Directions:
1. Preheat the air fryer to 400°F(205°C).
2. Lay the bacon slices down on a cutting board and sprinkle the thyme leaves on the bacon slices.Remove any string tying the filets and place the steaks down on their sides on top of the bacon slices.Roll the bacon around the side of the filets and secure the bacon to the fillets with a toothpick or two.
3. Season the steaks generously with salt and freshly ground black pepper and transfer the steaks to the air fryer.
4. Air-fry for 18 minutes,turning the steaks over halfway through the cooking process.This should cook your steaks to about medium,depending on how thick they are.If you'd prefer your steaks medium-rare or medium-well,simply add or subtract two minutes from the cooking time.Remove the steaks from the air fryer and let them rest for 5 minutes before removing the toothpicks and serving.(Just enough time to quickly air-fry some vegetables to go with them!)

Zesty London Broil

Servings:4
Cooking Time:28 Minutes
Ingredients:
- ⅔cup ketchup
- ¼cup honey
- ¼cup olive oil
- 2 tablespoons apple cider vinegar
- 2 tablespoons Worcestershire sauce
- 2 tablespoons minced onion
- ½teaspoon paprika
- 1 teaspoon salt
- 1 teaspoon freshly ground black pepper
- 2 pounds London broil,top round or flank steak(about 1-inch thick)

Directions:

1. Combine the ketchup,honey,olive oil,apple cider vinegar,Worcestershire sauce,minced onion,paprika,salt and pepper in a small bowl and whisk together.
2. Generously pierce both sides of the meat with a fork or meat tenderizer and place it in a shallow dish.Pour the marinade mixture over the steak,making sure all sides of the meat get coated with the marinade.Cover and refrigerate overnight.
3. Preheat the air fryer to 400°F(205°C).
4. Transfer the London broil to the air fryer basket and air-fry for 28 minutes,depending on how rare or well done you like your steak.Flip the steak over halfway through the cooking time.
5. Remove the London broil from the air fryer and let it rest for five minutes on a cutting board.To serve,thinly slice the meat against the grain and transfer to a serving platter.

French-style Steak Salad
Servings:4
Cooking Time:25 Minutes
Ingredients:
- 1 cup sliced strawberries
- 4 tbsp crumbled blue cheese
- ¼cup olive oil
- Salt and pepper to taste
- 1 flank steak
- ¼cup balsamic vinaigrette
- 1 tbsp Dijon mustard
- 2 tbsp lemon juice
- 8 cups baby arugula
- ½red onion,sliced
- 4 tbsp pecan pieces
- 4 tbsp sunflower seeds
- 1 sliced kiwi
- 1 sliced orange

Directions:
1. In a bowl,whisk olive oil,salt,lemon juice and pepper.Toss in flank steak and let marinate covered in the fridge for 30 minutes up to overnight.Preheat air fryer at 325ºF.Place flank steak in the greased frying basket and Bake for 18-20 minutes until rare,flipping once.Let rest for 5 minutes before slicing thinly against the grain.
2. In a salad bowl,whisk balsamic vinaigrette and mustard.Stir in arugula,salt,and pepper.Divide between 4 serving bowls.Top each salad with blue cheese,onion,pecan,sunflower seeds,strawberries,kiwi,orange and sliced steak.Serve immediately.

Venison Backstrap
Servings:4
Cooking Time:10 Minutes
Ingredients:
- 2 eggs
- ¼cup milk
- 1 cup whole wheat flour
- ½teaspoon salt
- ¼teaspoon pepper
- 1 pound venison backstrap,sliced
- salt and pepper
- oil for misting or cooking spray

Directions:
1. Beat together eggs and milk in a shallow dish.
2. In another shallow dish,combine the flour,salt,and pepper.Stir to mix well.
3. Sprinkle venison steaks with additional salt and pepper to taste.Dip in flour,egg wash,then in flour again,pressing in coating.
4. Spray steaks with oil or cooking spray on both sides.
5. Cooking in 2 batches,place steaks in the air fryer basket in a single layer.Cook at 360°F(180°C)for 8minutes.Spray with oil,turn over,and spray other side.Cook for 2 minutes longer,until coating is crispy brown and meat is done to your liking.
6. Repeat to cook remaining venison.

Beef Brazilian Empanadas
Servings:6
Cooking Time:40 Minutes
Ingredients:
- 1 cup shredded Pepper Jack cheese
- 1/3 minced green bell pepper
- 1 cup shredded mozzarella
- 2 garlic cloves,chopped
- 1/3 onion,chopped
- 8 oz ground beef
- 1 tsp allspice
- ½tsp paprika
- ½teaspoon chili powder
- Salt and pepper to taste
- 15 empanada wrappers
- 1 tbsp butter

Directions:
1. Spray a skillet with cooking oil.Over medium heat,stir-fry garlic,green pepper,and onion for 2 minutes or until aromatic.Add beef,allspice,chili,paprika,salt and pepper.Use a spoon to break up the beef.Cook until brown.Drain the excess fat.On a clean work surface,glaze each empanada wrapper edge with water using a basting brush to soften the crust.Mound 2-3 tbsp of meat onto each wrapper.Top with mozzarella and pepper Jack cheese.Fold one side of the wrapper to the opposite side.Press the edges with the back of a fork to seal.
2. Preheat air fryer to 400°F(205°C).Place the empanadas in the air fryer and spray with cooking oil.Bake for 8 minutes,then flip the empanadas.Cook for another 4 minutes.Melt butter in a microwave-safe bowl for 20 seconds.Brush melted butter over the top of each empanada.Serve warm.

Traditional Moo Shu Pork Lettuce Wraps
Servings:4
Cooking Time:40 Minutes
Ingredients:
- ½cup sliced shiitake mushrooms
- 1 lb boneless pork loin,cubed
- 3 tbsp cornstarch
- 2 tbsp rice vinegar
- 3 tbsp hoisin sauce
- 1 tsp oyster sauce

- 3 tsp sesame oil
- 1 tsp sesame seeds
- ¼tsp ground ginger
- 1 egg
- 2 tbsp flour
- 1 bag coleslaw mix
- 1 cup chopped baby spinach
- 3 green onions,sliced
- 8 iceberg lettuce leaves

Directions:

1.   Preheat air fryer at 350ºF.Make a slurry by whisking 1 tbsp of cornstarch and 1 tbsp of water in a bowl.Set aside.Warm a saucepan over heat,add in rice vinegar,hoisin sauce,oyster sauce,1 tsp of sesame oil,and ginger,and cook for 3 minutes,stirring often.Add in cornstarch slurry and cook for 1 minute.Set aside and let the mixture thicken.Beat the egg,flour,and the remaining cornstarch in a bowl.Set aside.

2.   Dredge pork cubes in the egg mixture.Shake off any excess.Place them in the greased frying basket and Air Fry for 8 minutes,shaking once.Warm the remaining sesame oil in a skillet over medium heat.Add in coleslaw mix,baby spinach,green onions,and mushrooms and cook for 5 minutes until the coleslaw wilts.Turn the heat off.Add in cooked pork,pour in oyster sauce mixture,and toss until coated.Divide mixture between lettuce leaves,sprinkle with sesame seed,roll them up,and serve.

Grilled Pork&Bell Pepper Salad

Servings:4
Cooking Time:25 Minutes
Ingredients:

- 1 cup sautéed button mushrooms,sliced
- 2 lb pork tenderloin,sliced
- 1 tsp olive oil
- 1 tsp dried marjoram
- 6 tomato wedges
- 6 green olives
- 6 cups mixed salad greens
- 1 red bell pepper,sliced
- 1/3 cup vinaigrette dressing

Directions:

1.   Preheat air fryer to 400°F(205°C).Combine the pork and olive oil,making sure the pork is well-coated.Season with marjoram.Lay the pork in the air fryer.Grill for 4-6 minutes,turning once until the pork is cooked through.

2.   While the pork is cooking,toss the salad greens,red bell pepper,tomatoes,olives,and mushrooms into a bowl.Lay the pork slices on top of the salad,season with vinaigrette,and toss.Serve while the pork is still warm.

Crispy Ham And Eggs

Servings:3
Cooking Time:9 Minutes
Ingredients:

- 2 cups Rice-puff cereal,such as Rice Krispies
- ¼cup Maple syrup
- ½pound¼-to½-inch-thick ham steak(gluten-free,if a concern)
- 1 tablespoon Unsalted butter
- 3 Large eggs

- ⅛teaspoon Table salt
- ⅛teaspoon Ground black pepper

Directions:

1.   Preheat the air fryer to 400°F(205°C).

2.   Pour the cereal into a food processor,cover,and process until finely ground.Pour the ground cereal into a shallow soup plate or a small pie plate.

3.   Smear the maple syrup on both sides of the ham,then set the ham into the ground cereal.Turn a few times,pressing gently,until evenly coated.

4.   Set the ham steak in the basket and air-fry undisturbed for 5 minutes,or until browned.

5.   Meanwhile,melt the butter in a medium or large nonstick skillet set over medium heat.Crack the eggs into the skillet and cook until the whites are set and the yolks are hot,about 3 minutes(or 4 minutes for a more set yolk.)Season with the salt and pepper.

6.   When the ham is ready,transfer it to a serving platter,then slip the eggs from the skillet on top of it.Divide into portions to serve.

Beef&Spinach Sautée

Servings:4
Cooking Time:30 Minutes
Ingredients:

- 2 tomatoes,chopped
- 2 tbsp crumbled Goat cheese
- ½lb ground beef
- 1 shallot,chopped
- 2 garlic cloves,minced
- 2 cups baby spinach
- 2 tbsp lemon juice
- 1/3 cup beef broth

Directions:

1.   Preheat air fryer to 370°F(185°C).Crumble the beef in a baking pan and place it in the air fryer.Air Fry for 3-7 minutes,stirring once.Drain the meat and make sure it's browned.Toss in the tomatoes,shallot,and garlic and Air Fry for an additional 4-8 minutes until soft.Toss in the spinach,lemon juice,and beef broth and cook for 2-4 minutes until the spinach wilts.Top with goat cheese and serve.

Pizza Tortilla Rolls

Servings:4
Cooking Time:8 Minutes
Ingredients:

- 1 teaspoon butter
- ½medium onion,slivered
- ½red or green bell pepper,julienned
- 4 ounces fresh white mushrooms,chopped
- 8 flour tortillas(6-or 7-inch size)
- ½cup pizza sauce
- 8 thin slices deli ham
- 24 pepperoni slices(about 1½ounces)
- 1 cup shredded mozzarella cheese(about 4 ounces)
- oil for misting or cooking spray

Directions:

1.   Place butter,onions,bell pepper,and mushrooms in air fryer baking pan.Cook at 390°F(200°C)for 3minutes.Stir and

cook 4 minutes longer until just crisp and tender.Remove pan and set aside.

2.   To assemble rolls,spread about 2 teaspoons of pizza sauce on one half of each tortilla.Top with a slice of ham and 3 slices of pepperoni.Divide sautéed vegetables among tortillas and top with cheese.

3.   Roll up tortillas,secure with toothpicks if needed,and spray with oil.

4.   Place 4 rolls in air fryer basket and cook for 4minutes.Turn and cook 4 minutes,until heated through and lightly browned.

5.   Repeat step 4 to cook remaining pizza rolls.

Fusion Tender Flank Steak

Servings:4
Cooking Time:25 Minutes
Ingredients:
- 2 tbsp cilantro,chopped
- 2 tbsp chives,chopped
- ¼tsp red pepper flakes
- 1 jalapeño pepper,minced
- 1 lime,juiced
- 3 tbsp olive oil
- Salt and pepper to taste
- 2 tbsp sesame oil
- 5 tbsp tamari sauce
- 3 tsp honey
- 1 tbsp grated fresh ginger
- 2 green onions,minced
- 2 garlic cloves,minced
- 1¼pounds flank steak

Directions:
1.   Combine the jalapeño pepper,cilantro,chives,lime juice,olive oil,salt,and pepper in a bowl.Set aside.Mix the sesame oil,tamari sauce,honey,ginger,green onions,garlic,and pepper flakes in another bowl.Stir until the honey is dissolved.Put the steak into the bowl and massage the marinade onto the meat.Marinate for 2 hours in the fridge.Preheat air fryer to 390 F.

2.   Remove the steak from the marinade and place it in the greased frying basket.Air Fry for about 6 minutes,flip,and continue cooking for 6-8 more minutes.Allow to rest for a few minutes,slice thinly against the grain and top with the prepared dressing.Serve and enjoy!

Spiced Beef Empanadas

Servings:4
Cooking Time:35 Minutes
Ingredients:
- 2 tbsp olive oil
- 6 oz ground beef
- 1 shallot,diced
- ½tsp ground cumin
- ½tsp nutmeg
- ½tsp ground cloves
- 1 pinch of brown sugar
- 2 tsp red chili powder
- 4 empanada dough shells

Directions:

1.   Preheat air fryer to 350°F(175°C).Warm the olive oil in a saucepan over medium heat.Crumble and cook the ground beef for 4-5 minutes.Add in the shallot,cumin,nutmeg,chili powder,and clove and stir-fry for 3 minutes.Kill the heat and let the mixture cool slightly.Divide the beef mixture between the empanada shells.Fold the empanada shells over and use a fork to seal the edges.Sprinkle brown sugar over.Place the empanadas in the foil-lined frying basket and Bake for 15 minutes.Halfway through,flip the empanadas.Cook them until golden.Serve and enjoy!

Steak Fajitas

Servings:4
Cooking Time:20 Minutes
Ingredients:
- 1 lb beef flank steak,cut into strips
- 1 red bell pepper,cut into strips
- 1 green bell pepper,cut into strips
- ½cup sweet corn
- 1 shallot,cut into strips
- 2 tbsp fajita seasoning
- Salt and pepper to taste
- 2 tbsp olive oil
- 8 flour tortillas

Directions:
1.   Preheat air fryer to 380°F(195°C).Combine beef,bell peppers,corn,shallot,fajita seasoning,salt,pepper,and olive oil in a large bowl until well mixed.

2.   Pour the beef and vegetable mixture into the air fryer.Air Fry for 9-11 minutes,shaking the basket once halfway through.Spoon a portion of the beef and vegetables in each of the tortillas and top with favorite toppings.Serve.

Albóndigas

Servings:4
Cooking Time:15 Minutes
Ingredients:
- 1 pound Lean ground pork
- 3 tablespoons Very finely chopped trimmed scallions
- 3 tablespoons Finely chopped fresh cilantro leaves
- 3 tablespoons Plain panko bread crumbs(gluten-free,if a concern)
- 3 tablespoons Dry white wine,dry sherry,or unsweetened apple juice
- 1½teaspoons Minced garlic
- 1¼teaspoons Mild smoked paprika
- ¾teaspoon Dried oregano
- ¾teaspoon Table salt
- ¼teaspoon Ground black pepper
- Olive oil spray

Directions:
1.   Preheat the air fryer to 400°F(205°C).

2.   Mix the ground pork,scallions,cilantro,bread crumbs,wine or its substitute,garlic,smoked paprika,oregano,salt,and pepper in a bowl until the herbs and spices are evenly distributed in the mixture.

3.   Lightly coat your clean hands with olive oil spray,then form the ground pork mixture into balls,using 2 tablespoons for each one.Spray your hands frequently so that the meat mixture doesn't stick.

4. Set the balls in the basket so that they're not touching,even if they're close together.Air-fry undisturbed for 15 minutes,or until well browned and an instant-read meat thermometer inserted into one or two balls registers 165°F(75°C).

5. Use a nonstick-safe spatula and kitchen tongs for balance to gently transfer the fragile balls to a wire rack to cool for 5 minutes before serving.

Lemon Pork Escalopes

Servings:4
Cooking Time:45 Minutes
Ingredients:
- 4 pork loin chops
- 1 cup breadcrumbs
- 2 eggs,beaten
- Salt and pepper to taste
- ½tbsp thyme,chopped
- ½tsp smoked paprika
- ½tsp ground cumin
- 1 lemon,zested

Directions:
1. Preheat air fryer to 350°F(175°C).Mix the breadcrumbs,thyme,smoked paprika,cumin,lemon zest,salt,and pepper in a bowl.Add the pork chops and toss to coat.Dip in the beaten eggs,then dip again into the dry ingredients.Place the coated chops in the greased frying basket and Air Fry for 16-18 minutes,turning once.Serve and enjoy!

Skirt Steak With Horseradish Cream

Servings:2
Cooking Time:20 Minutes
Ingredients:
- 1 cup heavy cream
- 3 tbsp horseradish sauce
- 1 lemon,zested
- 1 skirt steak,halved
- 2 tbsp olive oil
- Salt and pepper to taste

Directions:
1. Mix together the heavy cream,horseradish sauce,and lemon zest in a small bowl.Let chill in the fridge.
2. Preheat air fryer to 400ºF.Brush steak halves with olive oil and sprinkle with salt and pepper.Place steaks in the frying basket and Air Fry for 10 minutes or until you reach your desired doneness,flipping once.Let sit onto a cutting board for 5 minutes.Thinly slice against the grain and divide between 2 plates.Drizzle with the horseradish sauce over.Serve and enjoy!

Cinnamon-stick Kofta Skewers

Servings:8
Cooking Time:15 Minutes
Ingredients:
- 1 pound Lean ground beef
- ½teaspoon Ground cumin
- ½teaspoon Onion powder
- ½teaspoon Ground dried turmeric
- ½teaspoon Ground cinnamon
- ½teaspoon Table salt
- Up to a⅛teaspoon Cayenne
- 8 3½-to 4-inch-long cinnamon sticks(see the headnote)
- Vegetable oil spray

Directions:
1. Preheat the air fryer to 375°F(195°C).
2. Gently mix the ground beef,cumin,onion powder,turmeric,cinnamon,salt,and cayenne in a bowl until the meat is evenly mixed with the spices.(Clean,dry hands work best!)Divide this mixture into 2-ounce portions,each about the size of a golf ball.
3. Wrap one portion of the meat mixture around a cinnamon stick,using about three-quarters of the length of the stick,covering one end but leaving a little"handle"of cinnamon stick protruding from the other end.Set aside and continue making more kofta skewers.
4. Generously coat the formed kofta skewers on all sides with vegetable oil spray.Set them in the basket with as much air space between them as possible.Air-fry undisturbed for 13 minutes,or until browned and cooked through.If the machine is at 360°F(180°C),you may need to add 2 minutes to the cooking time.
5. Use a nonstick-safe spatula,and perhaps kitchen tongs for balance,to gently transfer the kofta skewers to a wire rack.Cool for at least 5 minutes or up to 20 minutes before serving.

Crispy Steak Subs

Servings:2
Cooking Time:30 Minutes
Ingredients:
- 1 hoagie bun baguette,halved
- 6 oz flank steak,sliced
- ½white onion,sliced
- ½red pepper,sliced
- 2 mozzarella cheese slices

Directions:
1. Preheat air fryer to 320°F(160°C).Place the flank steak slices,onion,and red pepper on one side of the frying basket.Add the hoagie bun halves,crusty side up,to the other half of the air fryer.Bake for 10 minutes.Flip the hoagie buns.Cover both sides with one slice of mozzarella cheese.Gently stir the steak,onions,and peppers.Cook for 6 more minutes until the cheese is melted and the steak is juicy on the inside and crispy on the outside.
2. Remove the cheesy hoagie halves to a serving plate.Cover one side with the steak,and top with the onions and peppers.Close with the other cheesy hoagie half,slice into two pieces,and enjoy!

Sloppy Joes

Servings:4
Cooking Time:17 Minutes
Ingredients:
- oil for misting or cooking spray
- 1 pound very lean ground beef
- 1 teaspoon onion powder
- ⅓cup ketchup
- ¼cup water
- ½teaspoon celery seed
- 1 tablespoon lemon juice

- 1½teaspoons brown sugar
- 1¼teaspoons low-sodium Worcestershire sauce
- ½teaspoon salt(optional)
- ½teaspoon vinegar
- ⅛teaspoon dry mustard
- hamburger or slider buns

Directions:
1. Spray air fryer basket with nonstick cooking spray or olive oil.
2. Break raw ground beef into small chunks and pile into basket.
3. Cook at 390°F(200°C)for 5minutes.Stir to break apart and cook 3minutes.Stir and cook 4 minutes longer or until meat is well done.
4. Remove meat from air fryer,drain,and use a knife and fork to crumble into small pieces.
5. Give your air fryer basket a quick rinse to remove any bits of meat.
6. Place all the remaining ingredients except the buns in a 6 x 6-inch baking pan and mix together.
7. Add meat and stir well.
8. Cook at 330°F(165°C)for 5minutes.Stir and cook for 2minutes.
9. Scoop onto buns.

Basil Cheese&Ham Stromboli

Servings:6
Cooking Time:30 Minutes
Ingredients:
- 1 can refrigerated pizza dough
- ½cup shredded mozzarella
- ½red bell pepper,sliced
- 2 tsp all-purpose flour
- 6 Havarti cheese slices
- 12 deli ham slices
- ½tsp dried basil
- 1 tsp garlic powder
- ½tsp oregano
- Black pepper to taste

Directions:
1. Preheat air fryer to 400°F(205°C).Flour a flat work surface and roll out the pizza dough.Use a knife to cut into 6 equal-sized rectangles.On each rectangle,add 1 slice of Havarti,1 tbsp of mozzarella,2 slices of ham,and some red pepper slices.Season with basil,garlic,oregano,and black pepper.Fold one side of the dough over the filling to the opposite side.Press the edges with the back of a fork to seal them.Place one batch of stromboli in the fryer and lightly spray with cooking oil.Air Fry for 10 minutes.Serve and enjoy!

Indian Fry Bread Tacos

Servings:4
Cooking Time:20 Minutes
Ingredients:
- 1 cup all-purpose flour
- 1½teaspoons salt,divided
- 1½teaspoons baking powder
- ¼cup milk

- ¼cup warm water
- ½pound lean ground beef
- One 14.5-ounce can pinto beans,drained and rinsed
- 1 tablespoon taco seasoning
- ½cup shredded cheddar cheese
- 2 cups shredded lettuce
- ¼cup black olives,chopped
- 1 Roma tomato,diced
- 1 avocado,diced
- 1 lime

Directions:
1. In a large bowl,whisk together the flour,1 teaspoon of the salt,and baking powder.Make a well in the center and add in the milk and water.Form a ball and gently knead the dough four times.Cover the bowl with a damp towel,and set aside.
2. Preheat the air fryer to 380°F(195°C).
3. In a medium bowl,mix together the ground beef,beans,and taco seasoning.Crumble the meat mixture into the air fryer basket and cook for 5 minutes;toss the meat and cook an additional 2 to 3 minutes,or until cooked fully.Place the cooked meat in a bowl for taco assembly;season with the remaining½teaspoon salt as desired.
4. On a floured surface,place the dough.Cut the dough into 4 equal parts.Using a rolling pin,roll out each piece of dough to 5 inches in diameter.Spray the dough with cooking spray and place in the air fryer basket,working in batches as needed.Cook for 3 minutes,flip over,spray with cooking spray,and cook for an additional 1 to 3 minutes,until golden and puffy.
5. To assemble,place the fry breads on a serving platter.Equally divide the meat and bean mixture on top of the fry bread.Divide the cheese,lettuce,olives,tomatoes,and avocado among the four tacos.Squeeze lime over the top prior to serving.

Wasabi Pork Medallions

Servings:4
Cooking Time:20 Minutes+Marinate Time
Ingredients:
- 1 lb pork medallions
- 1 cup soy sauce
- 1 tbsp mirin
- ½cup olive oil
- 3 cloves garlic,crushed
- 1 tsp fresh grated ginger
- 1 tsp wasabi paste
- 1 tbsp brown sugar

Directions:
1. Place all ingredients,except for the pork,in a resealable bag and shake to combine.Add the pork medallions to the bag,shake again,and place in the fridge to marinate for 2 hours.Preheat air fryer to 360°F(180°C).Remove pork medallions from the marinade and place them in the frying basket in rows.Air Fry for 14-16 minutes or until the medallions are cooked through and juicy.Serve.

Lamb Meatballs With Quick Tomato Sauce

Servings:4
Cooking Time:8 Minutes
Ingredients:

- ½small onion,finely diced
- 1 clove garlic,minced
- 1 pound ground lamb
- 2 tablespoons fresh parsley,finely chopped(plus more for garnish)
- 2 teaspoons fresh oregano,finely chopped
- 2 tablespoons milk
- 1 egg yolk
- salt and freshly ground black pepper
- ½cup crumbled feta cheese,for garnish
- Tomato Sauce:
- 2 tablespoons butter
- 1 clove garlic,smashed
- pinch crushed red pepper flakes
- ¼teaspoon ground cinnamon
- 1(28-ounce)can crushed tomatoes
- salt,to taste

Directions:
1. Combine all ingredients for the meatballs in a large bowl and mix just until everything is combined.Shape the mixture into 1½-inch balls or shape the meat between two spoons to make quenelles(little three-sided footballs).
2. Preheat the air fryer to 400°F(205°C).
3. While the air fryer is Preheating,start the quick tomato sauce.Place the butter,garlic and red pepper flakes in a sautépan and heat over medium heat on the stovetop.Let the garlic sizzle a little,but before the butter starts to brown,add the cinnamon and tomatoes.Bring to a simmer and simmer for 15 minutes.Season to taste with salt(but not too much as the feta that you will be sprinkling on at the end will be salty).
4. Brush the bottom of the air fryer basket with a little oil and transfer the meatballs to the air fryer basket in one layer,air-frying in batches if necessary.
5. Air-fry at 400°F(205°C)for 8 minutes,giving the basket a shake once during the cooking process to turn the meatballs over.
6. To serve,spoon a pool of the tomato sauce onto plates and add the meatballs in a decorative manner.Sprinkle the feta cheese on top and garnish with more fresh parsley.Serve immediately.

Perfect Pork Chops

Servings:3
Cooking Time:10 Minutes
Ingredients:

- ¾teaspoon Mild paprika
- ¾teaspoon Dried thyme
- ¾teaspoon Onion powder
- ¼teaspoon Garlic powder
- ¼teaspoon Table salt
- ¼teaspoon Ground black pepper
- 3 6-ounce boneless center-cut pork loin chops
- Vegetable oil spray

Directions:
1. Preheat the air fryer to 400°F(205°C).

2. Mix the paprika,thyme,onion powder,garlic powder,salt,and pepper in a small bowl until well combined.Massage this mixture into both sides of the chops.Generously coat both sides of the chops with vegetable oil spray.
3. When the machine is at temperature,set the chops in the basket with as much air space between them as possible.Air-fry undisturbed for 10 minutes,or until an instant-read meat thermometer inserted into the thickest part of a chop registers 145°F(65°C).
4. Use kitchen tongs to transfer the chops to a cutting board or serving plates.Cool for 5 minutes before serving.

Tender Steak With Salsa Verde

Servings:4
Cooking Time:20 Minutes
Ingredients:

- 1 flank steak,halved
- 1½cups salsa verde
- ½tsp black pepper

Directions:
1. Toss steak and 1 cup of salsa verde in a bowl and refrigerate covered for 2 hours.Preheat air fryer to 400ºF.Add steaks to the lightly greased frying basket and Air Fry for 10-12 minutes or until you reach your desired doneness,flipping once.Let sit onto a cutting board for 5 minutes.Thinly slice against the grain and divide between 4 plates.Spoon over the remaining salsa verde and serve sprinkled with black pepper to serve.

Marinated Rib-eye Steak With Herb Roasted Mushrooms

Servings:2
Cooking Time:10-15 Minutes
Ingredients:

- 2 tablespoons Worcestershire sauce
- ¼cup red wine
- 2(8-ounce)boneless rib-eye steaks
- coarsely ground black pepper
- 8 ounces baby bella(cremini)mushrooms,stems trimmed and caps halved
- 2 tablespoons olive oil
- 1 teaspoon dried parsley
- 1 teaspoon fresh thyme leaves
- salt and freshly ground black pepper
- chopped fresh chives or parsley

Directions:
1. Combine the Worcestershire sauce and red wine in a shallow baking dish.Add the steaks to the marinade,pierce them several times with the tines of a fork or a meat tenderizer and season them generously with the coarsely ground black pepper.Flip the steaks over and pierce the other side in a similar fashion,seasoning again with the coarsely ground black pepper.Marinate the steaks for 2 hours.
2. Preheat the air fryer to 400°F(205°C).
3. Toss the mushrooms in a bowl with the olive oil,dried parsley,thyme,salt and freshly ground black pepper.Transfer the steaks from the marinade to the air fryer basket,season with salt and scatter the mushrooms on top.

4. Air-fry the steaks for 10 minutes for medium-rare,12 minutes for medium,or 15 minutes for well-done,flipping the steaks once halfway through the cooking time.

5. Serve the steaks and mushrooms together with the chives or parsley sprinkled on top.A good steak sauce or some horseradish would be a nice accompaniment.

T-bone Steak With Roasted Tomato,Corn And Asparagus Salsa

Servings:2
Cooking Time:15-20 Minutes
Ingredients:
- 1(20-ounce)T-bone steak
- salt and freshly ground black pepper
- Salsa
- 1½cups cherry tomatoes
- ¾cup corn kernels(fresh,or frozen and thawed)
- 1½cups sliced asparagus(1-inch slices)(about½bunch)
- 1 tablespoon+1 teaspoon olive oil,divided
- salt and freshly ground black pepper
- 1½teaspoons red wine vinegar
- 3 tablespoons chopped fresh basil
- 1 tablespoon chopped fresh chives

Directions:
1. Preheat the air fryer to 400°F(205°C).
2. Season the steak with salt and pepper and air-fry at 400°F(205°C)for 10 minutes(medium-rare),12 minutes(medium),or 15 minutes(well-done),flipping the steak once halfway through the cooking time.
3. In the meantime,toss the tomatoes,corn and asparagus in a bowl with a teaspoon or so of olive oil,salt and freshly ground black pepper.
4. When the steak has finished cooking,remove it to a cutting board,tent loosely with foil and let it rest.Transfer the vegetables to the air fryer and air-fry at 400°F(205°C)for 5 minutes,shaking the basket once or twice during the cooking process.Transfer the cooked vegetables back into the bowl and toss with the red wine vinegar,remaining olive oil and fresh herbs.
5. To serve,slice the steak on the bias and serve with some of the salsa on top.

Spicy Hoisin Bbq Pork Chops

Servings:2
Cooking Time:12 Minutes
Ingredients:
- 3 tablespoons hoisin sauce
- ¼cup honey
- 1 tablespoon soy sauce
- 3 tablespoons rice vinegar
- 2 tablespoons brown sugar

- 1½teaspoons grated fresh ginger
- 1 to 2 teaspoons Sriracha sauce,to taste
- 2 to 3 bone-in center cut pork chops,1-inch thick(about 1¼pounds)
- chopped scallions,for garnish

Directions:
1. Combine the hoisin sauce,honey,soy sauce,rice vinegar,brown sugar,ginger,and Sriracha sauce in a small saucepan.Whisk the ingredients together and bring the mixture to a boil over medium-high heat on the stovetop.Reduce the heat and simmer the sauce until it has reduced in volume and thickened slightly–about 10 minutes.
2. Preheat the air fryer to 400°F(205°C).
3. Place the pork chops into the air fryer basket and pour half the hoisin BBQ sauce over the top.Air-fry for 6 minutes.Then,flip the chops over,pour the remaining hoisin BBQ sauce on top and air-fry for 6 more minutes,depending on the thickness of the pork chops.The internal temperature of the pork chops should be 155°F(70°C)when tested with an instant read thermometer.
4. Let the pork chops rest for 5 minutes before serving.You can spoon a little of the sauce from the bottom drawer of the air fryer over the top if desired.Sprinkle with chopped scallions and serve.

Tacos Norteños

Servings:4
Cooking Time:25 Minutes
Ingredients:
- ½cup minced purple onions
- 5 radishes,julienned
- 2 tbsp white wine vinegar
- ½tsp granulated sugar
- Salt and pepper to taste
- ¼cup olive oil
- ½tsp ground cumin
- 1 flank steak
- 10 mini flour tortillas
- 1 cup shredded red cabbage
- ½cup cucumber slices
- ½cup fresh radish slices

Directions:
1. Combine the radishes,vinegar,sugar,and salt in a bowl.Let sit covered in the fridge until ready to use.Whisk the olive oil,salt,black pepper and cumin in a bowl.Toss in flank steak and let marinate in the fridge for 30 minutes.
2. Preheat air fryer at 325ºF.Place flank steak in the frying basket and Bake for 18-20 minutes,tossing once.Let rest onto a cutting board for 5 minutes before slicing thinly against the grain.Add steak slices to flour tortillas along with red cabbage,chopped purple onions,cucumber slices,radish slices and fresh radish slices.Serve warm.

Fish And Seafood Recipes

Catalan Sardines With Romesco Sauce

Servings:2
Cooking Time:15 Minutes
Ingredients:
- 2 cans skinless,boneless sardines in oil,drained
- ½cup warmed romesco sauce
- ½cup bread crumbs

Directions:
1. Preheat air fryer to 350ºF.In a shallow dish,add bread crumbs.Roll in sardines to coat.Place sardines in the greased frying basket and Air Fry for 6 minutes,turning once.Serve with romesco sauce.

Classic Shrimp Po' boy Sandwiches

Servings:4
Cooking Time:20 Minutes
Ingredients:
- 1 lb peeled shrimp,deveined
- 1 egg
- ½cup flour
- ¾cup cornmeal
- Salt and pepper to taste
- ½cup mayonnaise
- 1 tsp Creole mustard
- 1 tsp Worcestershire sauce
- 1 tsp minced garlic
- 2 tbsp sweet pickle relish
- 1 tsp Louisiana hot sauce
- ½tsp Creole seasoning
- 4 rolls
- 2 cups shredded lettuce
- 8 tomato slices

Directions:
1. Preheat air fryer to 400°F(205°C).Set up three small bowls.In the first,add flour.In the second,beat the egg.In the third,mix cornmeal with salt and pepper.First dip the shrimp in the flour,then dredge in the egg,then dip in the cornmeal.Place in the greased frying basket.Air Fry for 8 minutes,flipping once until crisp.Let cool slightly.
2. While the shrimp is cooking,mix mayonnaise,mustard,Worcestershire,garlic,pickle relish juice,hot sauce,and Creole seasoning in a small bowl.Set aside.To assemble the po'boys,split rolls along the crease and spread the inside with remoulade.Layer¼of the shrimp,½cup shredded lettuce,and 2 slices of tomato.Serve and enjoy!

Fried Shrimp

Servings:3
Cooking Time:7 Minutes
Ingredients:
- 1 Large egg white
- 2 tablespoons Water
- 1 cup Plain dried bread crumbs(gluten-free,if a concern)
- ¼cup All-purpose flour or almond flour
- ¼cup Yellow cornmeal

- 1 teaspoon Celery salt
- 1 teaspoon Mild paprika
- Up to½teaspoon Cayenne(optional)
- ¾pound Large shrimp(20–25 per pound),peeled and deveined
- Vegetable oil spray

Directions:
1. Preheat the air fryer to 400°F(205°C).
2. Set two medium or large bowls on your counter.In the first,whisk the egg white and water until foamy.In the second,stir the bread crumbs,flour,cornmeal,celery salt,paprika,and cayenne(if using)until well combined.
3. Pour all the shrimp into the egg white mixture and stir gently until all the shrimp are coated.Use kitchen tongs to pick them up one by one and transfer them to the bread-crumb mixture.Turn each in the bread-crumb mixture to coat it evenly and thoroughly on all sides before setting it on a cutting board.When you're done coating the shrimp,coat them all on both sides with the vegetable oil spray.
4. Set the shrimp in as close to one layer in the basket as you can.Some may overlap.Air-fry for 7 minutes,gently rearranging the shrimp at the 4-minute mark to get covered surfaces exposed,until golden brown and firm but not hard.
5. Use kitchen tongs to gently transfer the shrimp to a wire rack.Cool for only a minute or two before serving.

Lightened-up Breaded Fish Filets

Servings:4
Cooking Time:10 Minutes
Ingredients:
- ½cup all-purpose flour
- ½teaspoon cayenne pepper
- 1 teaspoon garlic powder
- ½teaspoon black pepper
- ¼teaspoon salt
- 2 eggs,whisked
- 1½cups panko breadcrumbs
- 1 pound boneless white fish filets
- 1 cup tartar sauce
- 1 lemon,sliced into wedges

Directions:
1. In a medium bowl,mix the flour,cayenne pepper,garlic powder,pepper,and salt.
2. In a shallow dish,place the eggs.
3. In a third dish,place the breadcrumbs.
4. Cover the fish in the flour,dip them in the egg,and coat them with panko.Repeat until all fish are covered in the breading.
5. Liberally spray the metal trivet that fits inside the air fryer basket with olive oil mist.Place the fish onto the trivet,leaving space between the filets to flip.Cook for 5 minutes,flip the fish,and cook another 5 minutes.Repeat until all the fish is cooked.
6. Serve warm with tartar sauce and lemon wedges.

Lobster Tails With Lemon Garlic Butter

Servings:2
Cooking Time:5 Minutes
Ingredients:
- 4 ounces unsalted butter
- 1 tablespoon finely chopped lemon zest
- 1 clove garlic,thinly sliced
- 2(6-ounce)lobster tails
- salt and freshly ground black pepper
- ½cup white wine
- ½lemon,sliced
- vegetable oil

Directions:
1. Start by making the lemon garlic butter.Combine the butter,lemon zest and garlic in a small saucepan.Melt and simmer the butter on the stovetop over the lowest possible heat while you prepare the lobster tails.
2. Prepare the lobster tails by cutting down the middle of the top of the shell.Crack the bottom shell by squeezing the sides of the lobster together so that you can access the lobster meat inside.Pull the lobster tail up out of the shell,but leave it attached at the base of the tail.Lay the lobster meat on top of the shell and season with salt and freshly ground black pepper.Pour a little of the lemon garlic butter on top of the lobster meat and transfer the lobster to the refrigerator so that the butter solidifies a little.
3. Pour the white wine into the air fryer drawer and add the lemon slices.Preheat the air fryer to 400°F(205°C)for 5 minutes.
4. Transfer the lobster tails to the air fryer basket.Air-fry at 370°for 5 minutes,brushing more butter on halfway through cooking.(Add a minute or two if your lobster tail is more than 6-ounces.)Remove and serve with more butter for dipping or drizzling.

Fish Piccata With Crispy Potatoes

Servings:4
Cooking Time:30 Minutes
Ingredients:
- 4 cod fillets
- 1 tbsp butter
- 2 tsp capers
- 1 garlic clove,minced
- 2 tbsp lemon juice
- ½lb asparagus,trimmed
- 2 large potatoes,cubed
- 1 tbsp olive oil
- Salt and pepper to taste
- ¼tsp garlic powder
- 1 tsp dried rosemary
- 1 tsp dried parsley
- 1 tsp chopped dill

Directions:
1. Preheat air fryer to 380°F(195°C).Place each fillet on a large piece of foil.Top each fillet with butter,capers,dill,garlic,and lemon juice.Fold the foil over the fish and seal the edges to make a pouch.Mix asparagus,parsley,potatoes,olive oil,salt,rosemary,garlic powder,and pepper in a large bowl.Place asparagus in the frying basket.Roast for 4 minutes,then shake the basket.Top vegetable with foil packets and Roast for another 8

minutes.Turn off air fryer and let it stand for 5 minutes.Serve warm and enjoy.

Piña Colada Shrimp

Servings:4
Cooking Time:25 Minutes
Ingredients:
- 1 lb large shrimp,deveined and shelled
- 1 can crushed pineapple
- ½cup sour cream
- ¼cup pineapple preserves
- 2 egg whites
- 1 tbsp dark rum
- 2/3 cup cornstarch
- 2/3 cup sweetened coconut
- 1 cup panko bread crumbs

Directions:
1. Preheat air fryer to 400°F(205°C).Drain the crushed pineapple and reserve the juice.Next,transfer the pineapple to a small bowl and mix with sour cream and preserves.Set aside.In a shallow bowl,beat egg whites with 1 tbsp of the reserved pineapple juice and rum.On a separate plate,add the cornstarch.On another plate,stir together coconut and bread crumbs.Coat the shrimp with the cornstarch.Then,dip the shrimp into the egg white mixture.Shake off drips and then coat with the coconut mixture.Place the shrimp in the greased frying basket.Air Fry until crispy and golden,7 minutes.Serve warm.

Quick Shrimp Scampi

Servings:2
Cooking Time:5 Minutes
Ingredients:
- 16 to 20 raw large shrimp,peeled,deveined and tails removed
- ½cup white wine
- freshly ground black pepper
- ¼cup+1 tablespoon butter,divided
- 1 clove garlic,sliced
- 1 teaspoon olive oil
- salt,to taste
- juice of½lemon,to taste
- ¼cup chopped fresh parsley

Directions:
1. Start by marinating the shrimp in the white wine and freshly ground black pepper for at least 30 minutes,or as long as 2 hours in the refrigerator.
2. Preheat the air fryer to 400°F(205°C).
3. Melt¼cup of butter in a small saucepan on the stovetop.Add the garlic and let the butter simmer,but be sure to not let it burn.
4. Pour the shrimp and marinade into the air fryer,letting the marinade drain through to the bottom drawer.Drizzle the olive oil on the shrimp and season well with salt.Air-fry at 400°F(205°C)for 3 minutes.Turn the shrimp over(don't shake the basket because the marinade will splash around)and pour the garlic butter over the shrimp.Air-fry for another 2 minutes.
5. Remove the shrimp from the air fryer basket and transfer them to a bowl.Squeeze lemon juice over all the shrimp and toss with the chopped parsley and remaining tablespoon of butter.Season to taste with salt and serve immediately.

Spiced Salmon Croquettes

Servings:6
Cooking Time:20 Minutes
Ingredients:
- 1 can Alaskan pink salmon,bones removed
- 1 lime,zested
- 1 red chili,minced
- 2 tbsp cilantro,chopped
- 1 egg,beaten
- ½cup bread crumbs
- 2 scallions,diced
- 1 tsp garlic powder
- Salt and pepper to taste

Directions:
1. Preheat air fryer to 400°F(205°C).Mix salmon,beaten egg,bread crumbs and scallions in a large bowl.Add garlic,lime,red chili,cilantro,salt and pepper.Divide into 6 even portions and shape into patties.Place them in the greased frying basket and Air Fry for 7 minutes.Flip them and cook for 4 minutes or until golden.Serve.

Fish Sticks With Tartar Sauce

Servings:2
Cooking Time:6 Minutes
Ingredients:
- 12 ounces cod or flounder
- ½cup flour
- ½teaspoon paprika
- 1 teaspoon salt
- lots of freshly ground black pepper
- 2 eggs,lightly beaten
- 1½cups panko breadcrumbs
- 1 teaspoon salt
- vegetable oil
- Tartar Sauce:
- ¼cup mayonnaise
- 2 teaspoons lemon juice
- 2 tablespoons finely chopped sweet pickles
- salt and freshly ground black pepper

Directions:
1. Cut the fish into¾-inch wide sticks or strips.Set up a dredging station.Combine the flour,paprika,salt and pepper in a shallow dish.Beat the eggs lightly in a second shallow dish.Finally,mix the breadcrumbs and salt in a third shallow dish.Coat the fish sticks by dipping the fish into the flour,then the egg and finally the breadcrumbs,coating on all sides in each step and pressing the crumbs firmly onto the fish.Place the finished sticks on a plate or baking sheet while you finish all the sticks.
2. Preheat the air fryer to 400°F(205°C).
3. Spray the fish sticks with the oil and spray or brush the bottom of the air fryer basket.Place the fish into the basket and air-fry at 400°F(205°C)for 4 minutes,turn the fish sticks over,and air-fry for another 2 minutes.
4. While the fish is cooking,mix the tartar sauce ingredients together.
5. Serve the fish sticks warm with the tartar sauce and some French fries on the side.

Salmon Patties With Lemon-dill Sauce

Servings:4
Cooking Time:40 Minutes
Ingredients:
- 2 tbsp diced red bell peppers
- ¼cup sour cream
- 6 tbsp mayonnaise
- 2 cloves garlic,minced
- 2 tbsp cup onion
- 2 tbsp chopped dill
- 2 tsp lime juice
- 1 tsp honey
- 1 can salmon
- 1 egg
- ½cup bread crumbs
- Salt and pepper to taste

Directions:
1. Mix the sour cream,2 tbsp of mayonnaise,honey,onion,garlic,dill,lime juice,salt and pepper in a bowl.Let chill the resulting dill sauce in the fridge until ready to use.
2. Preheat air fryer at 400ºF.Combine the salmon,remaining mayonnaise,egg,bell peppers,breadcrumbs,and salt in a bowl.Form mixture into patties.Place salmon cakes in the greased frying basket and Air Fry for 10 minutes,flipping once.Let rest for 5 minutes before serving with dill sauce on the side.

Sesame-crusted Tuna Steaks

Servings:3
Cooking Time:10-13 Minutes
Ingredients:
- ½cup Sesame seeds,preferably a blend of white and black
- 1½tablespoons Toasted sesame oil
- 3 6-ounce skinless tuna steaks

Directions:
1. Preheat the air fryer to 400°F(205°C).
2. Pour the sesame seeds on a dinner plate.Use½tablespoon of the sesame oil as a rub on both sides and the edges of a tuna steak.Set it in the sesame seeds,then turn it several times,pressing gently,to create an even coating of the seeds,including around the steak's edge.Set aside and continue coating the remaining steak(s).
3. When the machine is at temperature,set the steaks in the basket with as much air space between them as possible.Air-fry undisturbed for 10 minutes for medium-rare(not USDA-approved),or 12 to 13 minutes for cooked through(USDA-approved).
4. Use a nonstick-safe spatula to transfer the steaks to serving plates.Serve hot.

Lime Bay Scallops

Servings:4
Cooking Time:10 Minutes
Ingredients:
- 2 tbsp butter,melted
- 1 lime,juiced
- ¼tsp salt
- 1 lb bay scallops
- 2 tbsp chopped cilantro

Directions:
1.   Preheat air fryer to 350ºF.Combine all ingredients in a bowl,except for the cilantro.Place scallops in the frying basket and Air Fry for 5 minutes,tossing once.Serve immediately topped with cilantro.

Chinese Fish Noodle Bowls

Servings:4
Cooking Time:40 Minutes
Ingredients:
- 1 can crushed pineapple,drained
- 1 shallot,minced
- 2 tbsp chopped cilantro
- 2½tsp lime juice
- 1 tbsp honey
- Salt and pepper to taste
- 1½cups grated red cabbage
- ¼chopped green beans
- 2 grated baby carrots
- ½tsp granulated sugar
- 2 tbsp mayonnaise
- 1 clove garlic,minced
- 8 oz cooked rice noodles
- 2 tsp sesame oil
- 1 tsp sesame seeds
- 4 cod fillets
- 1 tsp Chinese five-spice

Directions:
1.   Preheat air fryer at 350ºF.Combine the pineapple,shallot,1 tbsp of cilantro,honey,2 tsp of lime juice,salt,and black pepper in a bowl.Let chill the salsa covered in the fridge until ready to use.Mix the cabbage,green beans,carrots,sugar,remaining lime juice,mayonnaise,garlic,salt,and pepper in a bowl.Let chill covered in the fridge until ready to use.In a bowl,toss cooked noodles and sesame oil,stirring occasionally to avoid sticking.
2.   Sprinkle cod fillets with salt and five-spice.Place them in the greased frying basket and Air Fry for 10 minutes until the fish is opaque and flakes easily with a fork.Divide noodles into 4 bowls,top each with salsa,slaw,and fish.Serve right away sprinkled with another tbsp of cilantro and sesame seeds.

Basil Crab Cakes With Fresh Salad

Servings:2
Cooking Time:25 Minutes
Ingredients:
- 8 oz lump crabmeat
- 2 tbsp mayonnaise
- ½tsp Dijon mustard
- ½tsp lemon juice
- ½tsp lemon zest
- 2 tsp minced yellow onion
- ¼tsp prepared horseradish
- ¼cup flour
- 1 egg white,beaten
- 1 tbsp basil,minced
- 1 tbsp olive oil
- 2 tsp white wine vinegar
- Salt and pepper to taste
- 4 oz arugula
- ½cup blackberries
- ¼cup pine nuts
- 2 lemon wedges

Directions:
1.   Preheat air fryer to 400ºF.Combine the crabmeat,mayonnaise,mustard,lemon juice and zest,onion,horseradish,flour,egg white,and basil in a bowl.Form mixture into 4 patties.Place the patties in the lightly greased frying basket and Air Fry for 10 minutes,flipping once.Combine olive oil,vinegar,salt,and pepper in a bowl.Toss in the arugula and share into 2 medium bowls.Add 2 crab cakes to each bowl and scatter with blackberries,pine nuts,and lemon wedges.Serve warm.

Stuffed Shrimp Wrapped In Bacon

Servings:4
Cooking Time:30 Minutes
Ingredients:
- 1 lb shrimp,deveined and shelled
- 3 tbsp crumbled goat cheese
- 2 tbsp panko bread crumbs
- ¼tsp soy sauce
- ½tsp prepared horseradish
- ¼tsp garlic powder
- ½tsp chili powder
- 2 tsp mayonnaise
- Black pepper to taste
- 5 slices bacon,quartered
- ¼cup chopped parsley

Directions:
1.   Preheat air fryer to 400ºF.Butterfly shrimp by cutting down the spine of each shrimp without going all the way through.Combine the goat cheese,bread crumbs,soy sauce,horseradish,garlic powder,chili powder,mayonnaise,and black pepper in a bowl.Evenly press goat cheese mixture into shrimp.Wrap a piece of bacon around each piece of shrimp to hold in the cheese mixture.Place them in the frying basket and Air Fry for 8-10 minutes,flipping once.Top with parsley to serve.

Mojito Fish Tacos

Servings:4
Cooking Time:30 Minutes
Ingredients:
- 1½cups chopped red cabbage
- 1 lb cod fillets
- 2 tsp olive oil
- 3 tbsp lemon juice

- 1 large carrot,grated
- 1 tbsp white rum
- ½cup salsa
- 1/3 cup Greek yogurt
- 4 soft tortillas

Directions:
1. Preheat air fryer to 390°F(200°C).Rub the fish with olive oil,then a splash with a tablespoon of lemon juice.Place in the fryer and Air Fry for 9-12 minutes.The fish should flake when done.Mix the remaining lemon juice,red cabbage,carrots,salsa,rum,and yogurt in a bowl.Take the fish out of the fryer and tear into large pieces.Serve with tortillas and cabbage mixture.Enjoy!

Speedy Shrimp Paella

Servings:4
Cooking Time:20 Minutes
Ingredients:
- 2 cups cooked rice
- 1 red bell pepper,chopped
- ¼cup vegetable broth
- ½tsp turmeric
- ½tsp dried thyme
- 1 cup cooked small shrimp
- ½cup baby peas
- 1 tomato,diced

Directions:
1. Preheat air fryer to 340°F(170°C).Gently combine rice,red bell pepper,broth,turmeric,and thyme in a baking pan.Bake in the air fryer until the rice is hot,about 9 minutes.Remove the pan from the air fryer and gently stir in shrimp,peas,and tomato.Return to the air fryer and cook until bubbling and all ingredients are hot,5-8 minutes.Serve and enjoy!

Salmon Croquettes

Servings:4
Cooking Time:8 Minutes
Ingredients:
- 1 tablespoon oil
- ½cup breadcrumbs
- 1 14.75-ounce can salmon,drained and all skin and fat removed
- 1 egg,beaten
- ⅓cup coarsely crushed saltine crackers(about 8 crackers)
- ½teaspoon Old Bay Seasoning
- ½teaspoon onion powder
- ½teaspoon Worcestershire sauce

Directions:
1. Preheat air fryer to 390°F(200°C).
2. In a shallow dish,mix oil and breadcrumbs until crumbly.
3. In a large bowl,combine the salmon,egg,cracker crumbs,Old Bay,onion powder,and Worcestershire.Mix well and shape into 8 small patties about½-inch thick.
4. Gently dip each patty into breadcrumb mixture and turn to coat well on all sides.
5. Cook at 390°F(200°C)for 8minutes or until outside is crispy and browned.

Crunchy Clam Strips

Servings:3
Cooking Time:8 Minutes

Ingredients:
- ½pound Clam strips,drained
- 1 Large egg,well beaten
- ½cup All-purpose flour
- ½cup Yellow cornmeal
- 1½teaspoons Table salt
- 1½teaspoons Ground black pepper
- Up to¾teaspoon Cayenne
- Vegetable oil spray

Directions:
1. Preheat the air fryer to 400°F(205°C).
2. Toss the clam strips and beaten egg in a bowl until the clams are well coated.
3. Mix the flour,cornmeal,salt,pepper,and cayenne in a large zip-closed plastic bag until well combined.Using a flatware fork or small kitchen tongs,lift the clam strips one by one out of the egg,letting any excess egg slip back into the rest.Put the strips in the bag with the flour mixture.Once all the strips are in the bag,seal it and shake gently until the strips are well coated.
4. Use kitchen tongs to pick out the clam strips and lay them on a cutting board(leaving any extra flour mixture in the bag to be discarded).Coat the strips on both sides with vegetable oil spray.
5. When the machine is at temperature,spread the clam strips in the basket in one layer.They may touch in places,but try to leave as much air space as possible around them.Air-fry undisturbed for 8 minutes,or until brown and crunchy.
6. Gently dump the contents of the basket onto a serving platter.Cool for just a minute or two before serving hot.

Horseradish-crusted Salmon Fillets

Servings:3
Cooking Time:8 Minutes
Ingredients:
- ½cup Fresh bread crumbs(see the headnote)
- 4 tablespoons(¼cup/½stick)Butter,melted and cooled
- ¼cup Jarred prepared white horseradish
- Vegetable oil spray
- 4 6-ounce skin-on salmon fillets(for more information,see here)

Directions:
1. Preheat the air fryer to 400°F(205°C).
2. Mix the bread crumbs,butter,and horseradish in a bowl until well combined.
3. Take the basket out of the machine.Generously spray the skin side of each fillet.Pick them up one by one with a nonstick-safe spatula and set them in the basket skin side down with as much air space between them as possible.Divide the bread-crumb mixture between the fillets,coating the top of each fillet with an even layer.Generously coat the bread-crumb mixture with vegetable oil spray.
4. Return the basket to the machine and air-fry undisturbed for 8 minutes,or until the topping has lightly browned and the fish is firm but not hard.
5. Use a nonstick-safe spatula to transfer the salmon fillets to serving plates.Cool for 5 minutes before serving.Because of the butter in the topping,it will stay very hot for quite a while.Take care,especially if you're serving these fillets to children.

Garlic-lemon Steamer Clams

Servings:2
Cooking Time:30 Minutes
Ingredients:
- 25 Manila clams,scrubbed
- 2 tbsp butter,melted
- 1 garlic clove,minced
- 2 lemon wedges

Directions:
1. Add the clams to a large bowl filled with water and let sit for 10 minutes.Drain.Pour more water and let sit for 10 more minutes.Drain.Preheat air fryer to 350ºF.Place clams in the basket and Air Fry for 7 minutes.Discard any clams that don´t open.Remove clams from shells and place them into a large serving dish.Drizzle with melted butter and garlic and squeeze lemon on top.Serve.

Black Cod With Grapes,Fennel,Pecans And Kale

Servings:2
Cooking Time:15 Minutes
Ingredients:
- 2(6-to 8-ounce)fillets of black cod(or sablefish)
- salt and freshly ground black pepper
- olive oil
- 1 cup grapes,halved
- 1 small bulb fennel,sliced¼-inch thick
- ½cup pecans
- 3 cups shredded kale
- 2 teaspoons white balsamic vinegar or white wine vinegar
- 2 tablespoons extra virgin olive oil

Directions:
1. Preheat the air fryer to 400°F(205°C).
2. Season the cod fillets with salt and pepper and drizzle,brush or spray a little olive oil on top.Place the fish,presentation side up(skin side down),into the air fryer basket.Air-fry for 10 minutes.
3. When the fish has finished cooking,remove the fillets to a side plate and loosely tent with foil to rest.
4. Toss the grapes,fennel and pecans in a bowl with a drizzle of olive oil and season with salt and pepper.Add the grapes,fennel and pecans to the air fryer basket and air-fry for 5 minutes at 400°F(205°C),shaking the basket once during the cooking time.
5. Transfer the grapes,fennel and pecans to a bowl with the kale.Dress the kale with the balsamic vinegar and olive oil,season to taste with salt and pepper and serve along side the cooked fish.

Salmon

Servings:4
Cooking Time:8 Minutes
Ingredients:
- Marinade
- 3 tablespoons low-sodium soy sauce
- 3 tablespoons rice vinegar
- 3 tablespoons ketchup
- 3 tablespoons olive oil
- 3 tablespoons brown sugar

- 1 teaspoon garlic powder
- ½teaspoon ground ginger
- 4 salmon fillets(½-inch thick,3 to 4 ounces each)
- cooking spray

Directions:
1. Mix all marinade ingredients until well blended.
2. Place salmon in sealable plastic bag or shallow container with lid.Pour marinade over fish and turn to coat well.Refrigerate for 30minutes.
3. Drain marinade,and spray air fryer basket with cooking spray.
4. Place salmon in basket,skin-side down.
5. Cook at 360°F(180°C)for 10 minutes,watching closely to avoid overcooking.Salmon is done when just beginning to flake and still very moist.

Catfish Nuggets

Servings:4
Cooking Time:7 Minutes Per Batch
Ingredients:
- 2 medium catfish fillets,cut in chunks(approximately 1 x 2 inch)
- salt and pepper
- 2 eggs
- 2 tablespoons skim milk
- ½cup cornstarch
- 1 cup panko breadcrumbs,crushed
- oil for misting or cooking spray

Directions:
1. Season catfish chunks with salt and pepper to your liking.
2. Beat together eggs and milk in a small bowl.
3. Place cornstarch in a second small bowl.
4. Place breadcrumbs in a third small bowl.
5. Dip catfish chunks in cornstarch,dip in egg wash,shake off excess,then roll in breadcrumbs.
6. Spray all sides of catfish chunks with oil or cooking spray.
7. Place chunks in air fryer basket in a single layer,leaving space between for air circulation.
8. Cook at 390°F(200°C)for 4minutes,turn,and cook an additional 3 minutes,until fish flakes easily and outside is crispy brown.
9. Repeat steps 7 and 8 to cook remaining catfish nuggets.

Teriyaki Salmon

Servings:4
Cooking Time:20 Minutes
Ingredients:
- ¼cup raw honey
- 4 garlic cloves,minced
- 1 tbsp olive oil
- ½tsp salt
- ½tsp soy sauce
- ¼tsp blackening seasoning
- 4 salmon fillets

Directions:
1. Preheat air fryer to 380°F(195°C).Combine together the honey,garlic,olive oil,soy sauce,blackening seasoning and salt in a bowl.Put the salmon in a single layer on the greased frying basket.Brush the top of each fillet with the honey-garlic mixture.Roast for 10-12 minutes.Serve and enjoy!

Italian Tuna Roast

Servings:8
Cooking Time:21 Minutes
Ingredients:
- cooking spray
- 1 tablespoon Italian seasoning
- ⅛teaspoon ground black pepper
- 1 tablespoon extra-light olive oil
- 1 teaspoon lemon juice
- 1 tuna loin(approximately 2 pounds,3 to 4 inches thick,large enough to fill a 6 x 6-inch baking dish)

Directions:
1. Spray baking dish with cooking spray and place in air fryer basket.Preheat air fryer to 390°F(200°C).
2. Mix together the Italian seasoning,pepper,oil,and lemon juice.
3. Using a dull table knife or butter knife,pierce top of tuna about every half inch:Insert knife into top of tuna roast and pierce almost all the way to the bottom.
4. Spoon oil mixture into each of the holes and use the knife to push seasonings into the tuna as deeply as possible.
5. Spread any remaining oil mixture on all outer surfaces of tuna.
6. Place tuna roast in baking dish and cook at 390°F(200°C)for 20 minutes.Check temperature with a meat thermometer.Cook for an additional 1 minutes or until temperature reaches 145°F(60°C).
7. Remove basket from fryer and let tuna sit in basket for 10minutes.

Sardinas Fritas

Servings:2
Cooking Time:15 Minutes
Ingredients:
- 2 cans boneless,skinless sardines in mustard sauce
- Salt and pepper to taste
- ½cup bread crumbs
- 2 lemon wedges
- 1 tsp chopped parsley

Directions:
1. Preheat air fryer at 350ºF.Add breadcrumbs,salt and black pepper to a bowl.Roll sardines in the breadcrumbs to coat.Place them in the greased frying basket and Air Fry for 6 minutes,flipping once.Transfer them to a serving dish.Serve topped with parsley and lemon wedges.

Pecan-crusted Tilapia

Servings:4
Cooking Time:8 Minutes
Ingredients:
- 1 pound skinless,boneless tilapia filets
- ¼cup butter,melted
- 1 teaspoon minced fresh or dried rosemary
- 1 cup finely chopped pecans
- 1 teaspoon sea salt
- ¼teaspoon paprika
- 2 tablespoons chopped parsley
- 1 lemon,cut into wedges

Directions:
1. Pat the tilapia filets dry with paper towels.

2. Pour the melted butter over the filets and flip the filets to coat them completely.
3. In a medium bowl,mix together the rosemary,pecans,salt,and paprika.
4. Preheat the air fryer to 350°F(175°C).
5. Place the tilapia filets into the air fryer basket and top with the pecan coating.Cook for 6 to 8 minutes.The fish should be firm to the touch and flake easily when fully cooked.
6. Remove the fish from the air fryer.Top the fish with chopped parsley and serve with lemon wedges.

Super Crunchy Flounder Fillets

Servings:2
Cooking Time:6 Minutes
Ingredients:
- ½cup All-purpose flour or tapioca flour
- 1 Large egg white(s)
- 1 tablespoon Water
- ¾teaspoon Table salt
- 1 cup Plain panko bread crumbs(gluten-free,if a concern)
- 2 4-ounce skinless flounder fillet(s)
- Vegetable oil spray

Directions:
1. Preheat the air fryer to 400°F(205°C).
2. Set up and fill three shallow soup plates or small pie plates on your counter:one for the flour;one for the egg white(s),beaten with the water and salt until foamy;and one for the bread crumbs.
3. Dip one fillet in the flour,turning it to coat both sides.Gently shake off any excess flour,then dip the fillet in the egg white mixture,turning it to coat.Let any excess egg white mixture slip back into the rest,then set the fish in the bread crumbs.Turn it several times,gently pressing it into the crumbs to create an even crust.Generously coat both sides of the fillet with vegetable oil spray.If necessary,set it aside and continue coating the remaining fillet(s)in the same way.
4. Set the fillet(s)in the basket.If working with more than one fillet,they should not touch,although they may be quite close together,depending on the basket's size.Air-fry undisturbed for 6 minutes,or until lightly browned and crunchy.
5. Use a nonstick-safe spatula to transfer the fillet(s)to a wire rack.Cool for only a minute or two before serving.

Shrimp&Grits

Servings:4
Cooking Time:5 Minutes
Ingredients:
- 1 pound raw shelled shrimp,deveined(26–30 count or smaller)
- Marinade
- 2 tablespoons lemon juice
- 2 tablespoons Worcestershire sauce
- 1 tablespoon olive oil
- 1 teaspoon Old Bay Seasoning
- ½teaspoon hot sauce
- Grits
- ¾cup quick cooking grits(not instant)
- 3 cups water
- ½teaspoon salt

- 1 tablespoon butter
- ½cup chopped green bell pepper
- ½cup chopped celery
- ½cup chopped onion
- ½teaspoon oregano
- ¼teaspoon Old Bay Seasoning
- 2 ounces sharp Cheddar cheese,grated

Directions:

1. Stir together all marinade ingredients.Pour marinade over shrimp and set aside.
2. For grits,heat water and salt to boil in saucepan on stovetop.Stir in grits,lower heat to medium-low,and cook about 5minutes or until thick and done.
3. Place butter,bell pepper,celery,and onion in air fryer baking pan.Cook at 390°F(200°C)for 2minutes and stir.Cook 6 or 7minutes longer,until crisp tender.
4. Add oregano and 1 teaspoon Old Bay to cooked vegetables.Stir in grits and cheese and cook at 390°F(200°C)for 1 minute.Stir and cook 1 to 2minutes longer to melt cheese.
5. Remove baking pan from air fryer.Cover with plate to keep warm while shrimp cooks.
6. Drain marinade from shrimp.Place shrimp in air fryer basket and cook at 360°F(180°C)for 3minutes.Stir or shake basket.Cook 2 more minutes,until done.
7. To serve,spoon grits onto plates and top with shrimp.

Timeless Garlic-lemon Scallops

Servings:2
Cooking Time:15 Minutes
Ingredients:

- 2 tbsp butter,melted
- 1 garlic clove,minced
- 1 tbsp lemon juice
- 1 lb jumbo sea scallops

Directions:

1. Preheat air fryer to 400ºF.Whisk butter,garlic,and lemon juice in a bowl.Roll scallops in the mixture to coat all sides.Place scallops in the frying basket and Air Fry for 4 minutes,flipping once.Brush the tops of each scallop with butter mixture and cook for 4 more minutes,flipping once.Serve and enjoy!

Buttery Lobster Tails

Servings:4
Cooking Time:6 Minutes
Ingredients:

- 4 6-to 8-ounce shell-on raw lobster tails
- 2 tablespoons Butter,melted and cooled
- 1 teaspoon Lemon juice
- ½teaspoon Finely grated lemon zest
- ½teaspoon Garlic powder
- ½teaspoon Table salt
- ½teaspoon Ground black pepper

Directions:

1. Preheat the air fryer to 375°F(190°C).
2. To give the tails that restaurant look,you need to butterfly the meat.To do so,place a tail on a cutting board so that the shell is convex.Use kitchen shears to cut a line down the middle of the shell from the larger end to the smaller,cutting only the shell and not the meat below,and stopping before the back fins.Pry open the shell,leaving it intact.Use your clean fingers to separate the meat from the shell's sides and bottom,keeping it attached to the shell at the back near the fins.Pull the meat up and out of the shell through the cut line,laying the meat on top of the shell and closing the shell(as well as you can)under the meat.Make two equidistant cuts down the meat from the larger end to near the smaller end,each about¼inch deep,for the classic restaurant look on the plate.Repeat this procedure with the remaining tail(s).
3. Stir the butter,lemon juice,zest,garlic powder,salt,and pepper in a small bowl until well combined.Brush this mixture over the lobster meat set atop the shells.
4. When the machine is at temperature,place the tails shell side down in the basket with as much air space between them as possible.Air-fry undisturbed for 6 minutes,or until the lobster meat has pink streaks over it and is firm.
5. Use kitchen tongs to transfer the tails to a wire rack.Cool for only a minute or two before serving.

Shrimp,Chorizo And Fingerling Potatoes

Servings:4
Cooking Time:16 Minutes
Ingredients:

- ½red onion,chopped into 1-inch chunks
- 8 fingerling potatoes,sliced into 1-inch slices or halved lengthwise
- 1 teaspoon olive oil
- salt and freshly ground black pepper
- 8 ounces raw chorizo sausage,sliced into 1-inch chunks
- 16 raw large shrimp,peeled,deveined and tails removed
- 1 lime
- ¼cup chopped fresh cilantro
- chopped orange zest(optional)

Directions:

1. Preheat the air fryer to 380°F(195°C).
2. Combine the red onion and potato chunks in a bowl and toss with the olive oil,salt and freshly ground black pepper.
3. Transfer the vegetables to the air fryer basket and air-fry for 6 minutes,shaking the basket a few times during the cooking process.
4. Add the chorizo chunks and continue to air-fry for another 5 minutes.
5. Add the shrimp,season with salt and continue to air-fry,shaking the basket every once in a while,for another 5 minutes.
6. Transfer the tossed shrimp,chorizo and potato to a bowl and squeeze some lime juice over the top to taste.Toss in the fresh cilantro,orange zest and a drizzle of olive oil,and season again to taste.
7. Serve with a fresh green salad.

Crab Cakes

Servings:2
Cooking Time:10 Minutes
Ingredients:

- 1 teaspoon butter
- ⅓cup finely diced onion
- ⅓cup finely diced celery
- ¼cup mayonnaise

- 1 teaspoon Dijon mustard
- 1 egg
- pinch ground cayenne pepper
- 1 teaspoon salt
- freshly ground black pepper
- 16 ounces lump crabmeat
- ½cup+2 tablespoons panko breadcrumbs,divided

Directions:

1. Melt the butter in a skillet over medium heat.Sautéthe onion and celery until it starts to soften,but not brown–about 4 minutes.Transfer the cooked vegetables to a large bowl.Add the mayonnaise,Dijon mustard,egg,cayenne pepper,salt and freshly ground black pepper to the bowl.Gently fold in the lump crabmeat and 2 tablespoons of panko breadcrumbs.Stir carefully so you don't break up all the crab pieces.
2. Preheat the air fryer to 400°F(205°C).
3. Place the remaining panko breadcrumbs in a shallow dish.Divide the crab mixture into 4 portions and shape each portion into a round patty.Dredge the crab patties in the breadcrumbs,coating both sides as well as the edges with the crumbs.
4. Air-fry the crab cakes for 5 minutes.Using a flat spatula,gently turn the cakes over and air-fry for another 5 minutes.Serve the crab cakes with tartar sauce or cocktail sauce,or dress it up with the suggestion below.

Tuscan Salmon

Servings:4
Cooking Time:15 Minutes
Ingredients:

- 2 tbsp olive oil
- 4 salmon fillets
- ½tsp salt
- ¼tsp red pepper flakes
- 1 tsp chopped dill
- 2 tomatoes,diced
- ¼cup sliced black olives
- 4 lemon slices

Directions:

1. Preheat air fryer to 380°F(195°C).Lightly brush the olive oil on both sides of the salmon fillets and season them with salt,red flakes,and dill.Put the fillets in a single layer in the frying basket,then layer the tomatoes and black olives over the top.Top each fillet with a lemon slice.Bake for 8 minutes.Serve and enjoy!

Southeast Asian-style Tuna Steaks

Servings:4
Cooking Time:20 Minutes
Ingredients:

- 1 stalk lemongrass,bent in half
- 4 tuna steaks
- 2 tbsp soy sauce
- 2 tsp sesame oil
- 2 tsp rice wine vinegar
- 1 tsp grated fresh ginger
- ⅛tsp pepper
- 3 tbsp lemon juice

- 2 tbsp chopped cilantro
- 1 sliced red chili

Directions:

1. Preheat air fryer to 390°F(200°C).Place the tuna steak on a shallow plate.Mix together soy sauce,sesame oil,rice wine vinegar,and ginger in a small bowl.Pour over the tuna,rubbing the marinade gently into both sides of the fish.Marinate for about 10 minutes.Then sprinkle with pepper.Place the lemongrass in the frying basket and top with tuna steaks.Add the remaining lemon juice and 1 tablespoon of water in the pan below the basket.Bake until the tuna is cooked through,8-10 minutes.Discard the lemongrass before topping with cilantro and red chili.Serve and enjoy!

Seared Scallops In Beurre Blanc

Servings:4
Cooking Time:15 Minutes
Ingredients:

- 1 lb sea scallops
- Salt and pepper to taste
- 2 tbsp butter,melted
- 1 lemon,zested and juiced
- 2 tbsp dry white wine

Directions:

1. Preheat the air fryer to 400°F(205°C).Sprinkle the scallops with salt and pepper,then set in a bowl.Combine the butter,lemon zest,lemon juice,and white wine in another bowl;mix well.Put the scallops in a baking pan and drizzle over them the mixture.Air Fry for 8-11 minutes,flipping over at about 5 minutes until opaque.Serve and enjoy!

Chili Blackened Shrimp

Servings:4
Cooking Time:15 Minutes
Ingredients:

- 1 lb peeled shrimp,deveined
- 1 tsp paprika
- ½tsp dried dill
- ½tsp red chili flakes
- ½lemon,juiced
- Salt and pepper to taste

Directions:

1. Preheat air fryer to 400°F(205°C).In a resealable bag,add shrimp,paprika,dill,red chili flakes,lemon juice,salt and pepper.Seal and shake well.Place the shrimp in the greased frying basket and Air Fry for 7-8 minutes,shaking the basket once until blackened.Let cool slightly and serve.

Coconut Shrimp With Plum Sauce

Servings:2
Cooking Time:30 Minutes
Ingredients:

- ½lb raw shrimp,peeled
- 2 eggs
- ½cup breadcrumbs
- 1 tsp red chili powder
- 2 tbsp dried coconut flakes
- Salt and pepper to taste
- ½cup plum sauce

Directions:

1. Preheat air fryer to 350°F(175°C).Whisk the eggs with salt and pepper in a bowl.Dip in the shrimp,fully submerging.Combine the bread crumbs,coconut flakes,chili powder,salt,and pepper in another bowl until evenly blended.Coat the shrimp in the crumb mixture and place them in the foil-lined frying basket.Air Fry for 14-16 minutes.Halfway through the cooking time,shake the basket.Serve with plum sauce for dipping and enjoy!

King Prawns Al Ajillo

Servings:4
Cooking Time:15 Minutes
Ingredients:
- 1¼lb peeled king prawns,deveined
- ½cup grated Parmesan
- 1 tbsp olive oil
- 1 tbsp lemon juice
- ½tsp garlic powder
- 2 garlic cloves,minced

Directions:
1. Preheat the air fryer to 350°F(175°C).In a large bowl,add the prawns and sprinkle with olive oil,lemon juice,and garlic powder.Toss in the minced garlic and Parmesan,then toss to coat.Put the prawns in the frying basket and Air Fry for 10-15 minutes or until the prawns cook through.Shake the basket once while cooking.Serve immediately.

Home-style Fish Sticks

Servings:4
Cooking Time:30 Minutes
Ingredients:
- 1 lb cod fillets,cut into sticks
- 1 cup flour
- 1 egg
- ¼cup cornmeal
- Salt and pepper to taste
- ¼tsp smoked paprika
- 1 lemon

Directions:
1. Preheat air fryer at 350ºF.In a bowl,add½cup of flour.In another bowl,beat the egg and in a third bowl,combine the remaining flour,cornmeal,salt,black pepper and paprika.Roll the sticks in the flour,shake off excess flour.Then,dip them in the egg,shake off excess egg.Finally,dredge them in the cornmeal mixture.Place fish fingers in the greased frying basket and Air Fry for 10 minutes,flipping once.Serve with squeezed lemon.

Rich Salmon Burgers With Broccoli Slaw

Servings:4
Cooking Time:25 Minutes
Ingredients:
- 1 lb salmon fillets
- 1 egg
- ¼cup dill,chopped
- 1 cup bread crumbs
- Salt to taste
- ½tsp cayenne pepper
- 1 lime,zested
- 1 tsp fish sauce
- 4 buns

- 3 cups chopped broccoli
- ½cup shredded carrots
- ¼cup sunflower seeds
- 2 garlic cloves,minced
- 1 cup Greek yogurt

Directions:
1. Preheat air fryer to 360°F(180°C).Blitz the salmon fillets in your food processor until they are finely chopped.Remove to a large bowl and add egg,dill,bread crumbs,salt,and cayenne.Stir to combine.Form the mixture into 4 patties.Put them into the frying basket and Bake for 10 minutes,flipping once.Combine broccoli,carrots,sunflower seeds,garlic,salt,lime,fish sauce,and Greek yogurt in a bowl.Serve the salmon burgers onto buns with broccoli slaw.Enjoy!

Baltimore Crab Cakes

Servings:4
Cooking Time:35 Minutes
Ingredients:
- ½lb lump crabmeat,shells discarded
- 2 tbsp mayonnaise
- ½tsp yellow mustard
- ½tsp lemon juice
- ½tbsp minced shallot
- ¼cup bread crumbs
- 1 egg
- Salt and pepper to taste
- 4 poached eggs
- ½cup bechamel sauce
- 2 tsp chopped chives
- 1 lemon,cut into wedges

Directions:
1. Preheat air fryer at 400ºF.Combine all ingredients,except eggs,sauce,and chives,in a bowl.Form mixture into 4 patties.Place crab cakes in the greased frying basket and Air Fry for 10 minutes,flipping once.Transfer them to a serving dish.Top each crab cake with 1 poached egg,drizzle with Bechamel sauce and scatter with chives and lemon wedges.Serve and enjoy!

Parmesan Fish Bites

Servings:2
Cooking Time:30 Minutes
Ingredients:
- 1 haddock fillet,cut into bite-sized pieces
- 1 tbsp shredded cheddar
- 2 tbsp shredded Parmesan
- 2 eggs,beaten
- ½cup breadcrumbs
- Salt and pepper to taste
- ½cup mayoracha sauce

Directions:
1. Preheat air fryer to 350°F(175°C).Dip the strips in the beaten eggs.Place the bread crumbs,Parmesan,cheddar,salt and pepper in a bowl and mix well.Coat the fish strips in the dry mixture and place them on the foil-lined frying basket.Air Fry for 14-16 minutes.Halfway through the cooking time,shake the basket.When the cooking time is over,the fish will be cooked through and crust golden brown.Serve with mayoracha sauce(mixed mayo with sriracha)for dipping and enjoy!

Herb-rubbed Salmon With Avocado

Servings:4
Cooking Time:30 Minutes
Ingredients:
- 1 tbsp sweet paprika
- ½tsp cayenne pepper
- 1 tsp garlic powder
- 1 tsp dried oregano
- ½tsp dried coriander
- 1 tsp dried thyme
- ½tsp dried dill
- Salt and pepper to taste
- 4 wild salmon fillets
- 2 tbsp chopped red onion
- 1½tbsp fresh lemon juice
- 1 tsp olive oil
- 2 tbsp cilantro,chopped
- 1 avocado,diced

Directions:
1. Mix paprika,cayenne,garlic powder,oregano,thyme,dill,coriander,salt,and pepper in a small bowl.Spray and rub cooking oil on both sides of the fish,then cover with the spices.Add red onion,lemon juice,olive oil,cilantro,salt,and pepper in a bowl.Set aside for 5 minutes,then carefully add avocado.
2. Preheat air fryer to 400°F(205°C).Place the salmon skin-side down in the greased frying basket and Bake for 5-7 minutes or until the fish flakes easily with a fork.Transfer to a plate and top with the avocado salsa.

Fish Tortillas With Coleslaw

Servings:4
Cooking Time:30 Minutes
Ingredients:
- 1 tbsp olive oil
- 1 lb cod fillets
- 3 tbsp lemon juice
- 2 cups chopped red cabbage
- ½cup salsa
- 1/3 cup sour cream
- 6 taco shells,warm
- 1 avocado,chopped

Directions:
1. Preheat air fryer to 400°F(205°C).Brush oil on the cod and sprinkle with some lemon juice.Place in the frying basket and Air Fry until the fish flakes with a fork,9-12 minutes.
2. Meanwhile,mix together the remaining lemon juice,red cabbage,salsa,and sour cream in a medium bowl.Put the cooked fish in a bowl,breaking it into large pieces.Then add the cabbage mixture,avocados,and warmed tortilla shells ready for assembly.Enjoy!

Mojo Sea Bass

Servings:2
Cooking Time:15 Minutes
Ingredients:
- 1 tbsp butter,melted
- ¼tsp chili powder
- 2 cloves garlic,minced
- 1 tbsp lemon juice
- ¼tsp salt
- 2 sea bass fillets

- 2 tsp chopped cilantro
Directions:
1. Preheat air fryer to 370ºF.Whisk the butter,chili powder,garlic,lemon juice,and salt in a bowl.Rub mixture over the tops of each fillet.Place the fillets in the frying basket and Air Fry for 7 minutes.Let rest for 5 minutes.Divide between 2 plates and garnish with cilantro to serve.

Tuna Nuggets In Hoisin Sauce

Servings:4
Cooking Time:7 Minutes
Ingredients:
- ½cup hoisin sauce
- 2 tablespoons rice wine vinegar
- 2 teaspoons sesame oil
- 1 teaspoon garlic powder
- 2 teaspoons dried lemongrass
- ¼teaspoon red pepper flakes
- ½small onion,quartered and thinly sliced
- 8 ounces fresh tuna,cut into 1-inch cubes
- cooking spray
- 3 cups cooked jasmine rice

Directions:
1. Mix the hoisin sauce,vinegar,sesame oil,and seasonings together.
2. Stir in the onions and tuna nuggets.
3. Spray air fryer baking pan with nonstick spray and pour in tuna mixture.
4. Cook at 390°F(200°C)for 3minutes.Stir gently.
5. Cook 2minutes and stir again,checking for doneness.Tuna should be barely cooked through,just beginning to flake and still very moist.If necessary,continue cooking and stirring in 1-minute intervals until done.
6. Serve warm over hot jasmine rice.

Crab Stuffed Salmon Roast

Servings:4
Cooking Time:20 Minutes
Ingredients:
- 1(1½-pound)salmon fillet
- salt and freshly ground black pepper
- 6 ounces crabmeat
- 1 teaspoon finely chopped lemon zest
- 1 teaspoon Dijon mustard
- 1 tablespoon chopped fresh parsley,plus more for garnish
- 1 scallion,chopped
- ¼teaspoon salt
- olive oil

Directions:
1. Prepare the salmon fillet by butterflying it.Slice into the thickest side of the salmon,parallel to the countertop and along the length of the fillet.Don't slice all the way through to the other side–stop about an inch from the edge.Open the salmon up like a book.Season the salmon with salt and freshly ground black pepper.
2. Make the crab filling by combining the crabmeat,lemon zest,mustard,parsley,scallion,salt and freshly ground black pepper in a bowl.Spread this filling in the center of the salmon.Fold one side of the salmon over the filling.Then fold the other side over on top.
3. Transfer the rolled salmon to the center of a piece of parchment paper that is roughly 6-to 7-inches wide and about 12-inches long.The parchment paper will act as a

sling,making it easier to put the salmon into the air fryer.Preheat the air fryer to 370°F(185°C).Use the parchment paper to transfer the salmon roast to the air fryer basket and tuck the ends of the paper down beside the salmon.Drizzle a little olive oil on top and season with salt and pepper.

4. Air-fry the salmon at 370°F(185°C)for 20 minutes.

5. Remove the roast from the air fryer and let it rest for a few minutes.Then,slice it,sprinkle some more lemon zest and parsley(or fresh chives)on top and serve.

Shrimp-jalapeño Poppers In Prosciutto

Servings:4
Cooking Time:30 Minutes
Ingredients:
- 1 lb shelled tail on shrimp,deveined,sliced down the spine
- 2 jalapeños,diced
- 2 tbsp grated cheddar
- 3 tbsp mascarpone cheese
- ¼tsp garlic powder
- 1 tbsp mayonnaise
- ¼tsp ground black pepper
- 20 prosciutto slices
- ¼cup chopped parsley
- 1 lemon

Directions:
1. Preheat air fryer at 400°F.Combine the mascarpone and cheddar cheeses,jalapeños,garlic,mayonnaise,and black pepper in a bowl.Press cheese mixture into shrimp.Wrap 1 piece of prosciutto around each shrimp to hold in the cheese mixture.Place wrapped shrimp in the frying basket and Air Fry for 8-10 minutes,flipping once.To serve,scatter with parsley and squeeze lemon.

Tilapia Al Pesto

Servings:4
Cooking Time:25 Minutes
Ingredients:
- 4 tilapia fillets
- 1 egg
- 2 tbsp buttermilk
- 1 cup crushed cornflakes
- Salt and pepper to taste
- 4 tsp pesto
- 2 tbsp butter,melted
- 4 lemon wedges

Directions:
1. Preheat air fryer to 350°F.Whisk egg and buttermilk in a bowl.In another bowl,combine cornflakes,salt,and pepper.Spread 1 tsp of pesto on each tilapia fillet,then tightly roll the fillet from one short end to the other.Secure with a toothpick.Dip each fillet in the egg mixture and dredge in the cornflake mixture.Place fillets in the greased frying basket,drizzle with melted butter,and Air Fry for 6 minutes.Let rest onto a serving dish for 5 minutes before removing the toothpicks.Serve with lemon wedges.

Herby Prawn&Zucchini Bake

Servings:4

Cooking Time:30 Minutes
Ingredients:
- 1¼lb prawns,peeled and deveined
- 2 zucchini,sliced
- 2 tbsp butter,melted
- ½tsp garlic salt
- 1½tsp dried oregano
- ⅛tsp red pepper flakes
- ½lemon,juiced
- 1 tbsp chopped mint
- 1 tbsp chopped dill

Directions:
1. Preheat air fryer to 350°F(175°C).Combine prawns,zucchini,butter,garlic salt,oregano,and pepper flakes in a large bowl.Toss to coat.Put the prawns and zucchini in the greased frying basket and Air Fry for about 6-8 minutes,shaking the basket once until the zucchini is golden and the shrimp are cooked.Remove the shrimp to a serving plate and cover with foil.Serve hot topped with lemon juice,mint,and dill.Enjoy!

Bacon-wrapped Scallops

Servings:4
Cooking Time:8 Minutes
Ingredients:
- 16 large scallops
- 8 bacon strips
- ½teaspoon black pepper
- ¼teaspoon smoked paprika

Directions:
1. Pat the scallops dry with a paper towel.Slice each of the bacon strips in half.Wrap 1 bacon strip around 1 scallop and secure with a toothpick.Repeat with the remaining scallops.Season the scallops with pepper and paprika.
2. Preheat the air fryer to 350°F(175°C).
3. Place the bacon-wrapped scallops in the air fryer basket and cook for 4 minutes, shake the basket,cook another 3 minutes,shake the basket,and cook another 1 to 3 to minutes.When the bacon is crispy,the scallops should be cooked through and slightly firm,but not rubbery.Serve immediately.

Cilantro Sea Bass

Servings:2
Cooking Time:15 Minutes
Ingredients:
- Salt and pepper to taste
- 1 tsp olive oil
- 2 sea bass fillets
- ½tsp berbere seasoning
- 2 tsp chopped cilantro
- 1 tsp dried thyme
- ½tsp garlic powder
- 4 lemon quarters

Directions:
1. Preheat air fryer at 375°F.Rub sea bass fillets with olive oil,thyme,garlic powder,salt and black pepper.Season with berbere seasoning.Place fillets in the greased frying basket and Air Fry for 6-8 minutes.Let rest for 5 minutes on a serving plate.Scatter with cilantro and serve with lemon quarters on the side.

Poultry Recipes

Italian Herb Stuffed Chicken

Servings:4
Cooking Time:30 Minutes
Ingredients:
- 2 tbsp olive oil
- 3 tbsp balsamic vinegar
- 3 garlic cloves,minced
- 1 tomato,diced
- 2 tbsp Italian seasoning
- 1 tbsp chopped fresh basil
- 1 tsp thyme,chopped
- 4 chicken breasts

Directions:
1. Preheat air fryer to 370°F(185°C).Combine the olive oil,balsamic vinegar,garlic,thyme,tomato,half of the Italian seasoning,and basil in a medium bowl.Set aside.
2. Cut 4-5 slits into the chicken breasts¾of the way through.Season with the rest of the Italian seasoning and place the chicken with the slits facing up,in the greased frying basket.Bake for 7 minutes.Spoon the bruschetta mixture into the slits of the chicken.Cook for another 3 minutes.Allow chicken to sit and cool for a few minutes.Serve and enjoy!

Super-simple Herby Turkey

Servings:4
Cooking Time:35 Minutes
Ingredients:
- 2 turkey tenderloins
- 2 tbsp olive oil
- Salt and pepper to taste
- 2 tbsp minced rosemary
- 1 tbsp minced thyme
- 1 tbsp minced sage

Directions:
1. Preheat the air fryer to 350°F(175°C).Brush the tenderloins with olive oil and sprinkle with salt and pepper.Mix rosemary,thyme,and sage,then rub the seasoning onto the meat.Put the tenderloins in the frying basket and Bake for 22-27 minutes,flipping once until cooked through.Lay the turkey on a serving plate,cover with foil,and let stand for 5 minutes.Slice before serving.

Yummy Maple-mustard Chicken Kabobs

Servings:4
Cooking Time:35 Minutes+Chilling Time
Ingredients:
- 1 lb boneless,skinless chicken thighs,cubed
- 1 green bell pepper,chopped
- ½cup honey mustard
- ½yellow onion,chopped
- 8 cherry tomatoes
- 2 tbsp chopped scallions

Directions:

1. Toss chicken cubes and honey mustard in a bowl and let chill covered in the fridge for 30 minutes.Preheat air fryer to 350ºF.Thread chicken cubes,onion,cherry tomatoes,and bell peppers,alternating,onto 8 skewers.Place them on a kebab rack.Place rack in the frying basket and Air Fry for 12 minutes.Top with scallions to serve.

Bacon&Chicken Flatbread

Servings:2
Cooking Time:35 Minutes
Ingredients:
- 1 flatbread dough
- 1 chicken breast,cubed
- 1 cup breadcrumbs
- 2 eggs,beaten
- Salt and pepper to taste
- 2 tsp dry rosemary
- 1 tsp fajita seasoning
- 1 tsp onion powder
- 3 bacon strips
- ½tbsp ranch sauce

Directions:
1. Preheat air fryer to 360°F(180°C).Place the breadcrumbs,onion powder,rosemary,salt,and pepper in a mixing bowl.Coat the chicken with the mixture,dip into the beaten eggs,then roll again into the dry ingredients.Arrange the coated chicken pieces on one side of the greased frying basket.On the other side of the basket,lay the bacon strips.Air Fry for 6 minutes.Turn the bacon pieces over and flip the chicken and cook for another 6 minutes.
2. Roll the flatbread out and spread the ranch sauce all over the surface.Top with the bacon and chicken and sprinkle with fajita seasoning.Close the bread to contain the filling and place it in the air fryer.Cook for 10 minutes,flipping the flatbread once until golden brown.Let it cool for a few minutes.Then slice and serve.

Quick Chicken For Filling

Servings:2
Cooking Time:8 Minutes
Ingredients:
- 1 pound chicken tenders,skinless and boneless
- ½teaspoon ground cumin
- ½teaspoon garlic powder
- cooking spray

Directions:
1. Sprinkle raw chicken tenders with seasonings.
2. Spray air fryer basket lightly with cooking spray to prevent sticking.
3. Place chicken in air fryer basket in single layer.
4. Cook at 390°F(200°C)for 4minutes,turn chicken strips over,and cook for an additional 4minutes.
5. Test for doneness.Thick tenders may require an additional minute or two.

Irresistible Cheesy Chicken Sticks

Servings:2
Cooking Time:30 Minutes
Ingredients:
- 6 mozzarella sticks
- 1 cup flour
- 2 eggs,beaten
- 1 lb ground chicken
- 1½cups breadcrumbs
- ¼tsp crushed chilis
- ¼tsp cayenne pepper
- ½tsp garlic powder
- ¼tsp shallot powder
- ½tsp oregano

Directions:
1. Preheat air fryer to 390°F(200°C).Combine crushed chilis,cayenne pepper,garlic powder,shallot powder,and oregano in a bowl.Add the ground chicken and mix well with your hands until evenly combined.In another mixing bowl,beat the eggs until fluffy and until the yolks and whites are fully combined,and set aside.
2. Pour the beaten eggs,flour,and bread crumbs into 3 separate bowls.Roll the mozzarella sticks in the flour,then dip them in the beaten eggs.With hands,wrap the stick in a thin layer of the chicken mixture.Finally,coat the sticks in the crumbs.Place the sticks in the greased frying basket fryer and Air Fry for 18-20 minutes,turning once until crispy.Serve hot.

Peanut Butter-barbeque Chicken

Servings:4
Cooking Time:20 Minutes
Ingredients:
- 1 pound boneless,skinless chicken thighs
- salt and pepper
- 1 large orange
- ½cup barbeque sauce
- 2 tablespoons smooth peanut butter
- 2 tablespoons chopped peanuts for garnish(optional)
- cooking spray

Directions:
1. Season chicken with salt and pepper to taste.Place in a shallow dish or plastic bag.
2. Grate orange peel,squeeze orange and reserve 1 tablespoon of juice for the sauce.
3. Pour remaining juice over chicken and marinate for 30minutes.
4. Mix together the reserved 1 tablespoon of orange juice,barbeque sauce,peanut butter,and 1 teaspoon grated orange peel.
5. Place¼cup of sauce mixture in a small bowl for basting.Set remaining sauce aside to serve with cooked chicken.
6. Preheat air fryer to 360°F(180°C).Spray basket with nonstick cooking spray.
7. Remove chicken from marinade,letting excess drip off.Place in air fryer basket and cook for 5minutes.Turn chicken over and cook 5minutes longer.
8. Brush both sides of chicken lightly with sauce.
9. Cook chicken 5minutes,then turn thighs one more time,again brushing both sides lightly with sauce.Cook for 5 moreminutes or until chicken is done and juices run clear.

10. Serve chicken with remaining sauce on the side and garnish with chopped peanuts if you like.

Pulled Turkey Quesadillas

Servings:4
Cooking Time:15 Minutes
Ingredients:
- ¾cup pulled cooked turkey breast
- 6 tortilla wraps
- 1/3 cup grated Swiss cheese
- 1 small red onion,sliced
- 2 tbsp Mexican chili sauce

Directions:
1. Preheat air fryer to 400°F(205°C).Lay 3 tortilla wraps on a clean workspace,then spoon equal amounts of Swiss cheese,turkey,Mexican chili sauce,and red onion on the tortillas.Spritz the exterior of the tortillas with cooking spray.Air Fry the quesadillas,one at a time,for 5-8 minutes.The cheese should be melted and the outsides crispy.Serve.

Chicken Flatbread Pizza With Spinach

Servings:1
Cooking Time:15 Minutes
Ingredients:
- ½cup cooked chicken breast,cubed
- ¼cup grated mozzarella
- 1 whole-wheat pita
- 1 tbsp olive oil
- 1 garlic clove,minced
- ¼tsp red pepper flakes
- ½cup kale
- ⅛sliced red onion

Directions:
1. Preheat air fryer to 380°F(195°C).Lightly brush the top of the pita with olive oil and top with the garlic,red pepper flakes,kale,onion,chicken,and mozzarella.Put the pizza into the frying basket and Bake for 7 minutes.Serve.

Cheesy Chicken Tenders

Servings:4
Cooking Time:25 Minutes
Ingredients:
- 1 cup grated Parmesan cheese
- ¼cup grated cheddar
- 1¼lb chicken tenders
- 1 egg,beaten
- 2 tbsp milk
- Salt and pepper to taste
- ½tsp garlic powder
- 1 tsp dried thyme
- ¼tsp shallot powder

Directions:
1. Preheat the air fryer to 400°F(205°C).Stir the egg and milk until combined.Mix the salt,pepper,garlic,thyme,shallot,cheddar cheese,and Parmesan cheese on a plate.Dip the chicken in the egg mix,then in the cheese mix,and press to coat.Lay the tenders in the frying basket in a single layer.Add a raised rack to cook more at one time.Spray all with oil and Bake for 12-16 minutes,flipping once halfway through cooking.Serve hot.

Basic Chicken Breasts[2]

Servings:4
Cooking Time:15 Minutes
Ingredients:
- 2 tsp olive oil
- 2 chicken breasts
- Salt and pepper to taste
- ½tsp garlic powder
- ½tsp rosemary

Directions:
1. Preheat air fryer to 350ºF.Rub the chicken breasts with olive oil over tops and bottom and sprinkle with garlic powder,rosemary,salt,and pepper.Place the chicken in the frying basket and Air Fry for 9 minutes,flipping once.Let rest onto a serving plate for 5 minutes before cutting into cubes.Serve and enjoy!

Coconut Chicken With Apricot-ginger Sauce

Servings:4
Cooking Time:8 Minutes Per Batch
Ingredients:
- 1½pounds boneless,skinless chicken tenders,cut in large chunks(about 1¼inches)
- salt and pepper
- ½cup cornstarch
- 2 eggs
- 1 tablespoon milk
- 3 cups shredded coconut(see below)
- oil for misting or cooking spray
- Apricot-Ginger Sauce
- ½cup apricot preserves
- 2 tablespoons white vinegar
- ¼teaspoon ground ginger
- ¼teaspoon low-sodium soy sauce
- 2 teaspoons white or yellow onion,grated or finely minced

Directions:
1. Mix all ingredients for the Apricot-Ginger Sauce well and let sit for flavors to blend while you cook the chicken.
2. Season chicken chunks with salt and pepper to taste.
3. Place cornstarch in a shallow dish.
4. In another shallow dish,beat together eggs and milk.
5. Place coconut in a third shallow dish.(If also using panko breadcrumbs,as suggested below,stir them to mix well.)
6. Spray air fryer basket with oil or cooking spray.
7. Dip each chicken chunk into cornstarch,shake off excess,and dip in egg mixture.
8. Shake off excess egg mixture and roll lightly in coconut or coconut mixture.Spray with oil.
9. Place coated chicken chunks in air fryer basket in a single layer,close together but without sides touching.
10. Cook at 360°F(180°C)for 4minutes,stop,and turn chunks over.
11. Cook an additional 4 minutes or until chicken is done inside and coating is crispy brown.
12. Repeat steps 9 through 11 to cook remaining chicken chunks.

Nacho Chicken Fries

Servings:4
Cooking Time:7 Minutes
Ingredients:
- 1 pound chicken tenders
- salt
- ¼cup flour
- 2 eggs
- ¾cup panko breadcrumbs
- ¾cup crushed organic nacho cheese tortilla chips
- oil for misting or cooking spray
- Seasoning Mix
- 1 tablespoon chili powder
- 1 teaspoon ground cumin
- ½teaspoon garlic powder
- ½teaspoon onion powder

Directions:
1. Stir together all seasonings in a small cup and set aside.
2. Cut chicken tenders in half crosswise,then cut into strips no wider than about½inch.
3. Preheat air fryer to 390°F(200°C).
4. Salt chicken to taste.Place strips in large bowl and sprinkle with 1 tablespoon of the seasoning mix.Stir well to distribute seasonings.
5. Add flour to chicken and stir well to coat all sides.
6. Beat eggs together in a shallow dish.
7. In a second shallow dish,combine the panko,crushed chips,and the remaining 2 teaspoons of seasoning mix.
8. Dip chicken strips in eggs,then roll in crumbs.Mist with oil or cooking spray.
9. Chicken strips will cook best if done in two batches.They can be crowded and overlapping a little but not stacked in double or triple layers.
10. Cook for 4minutes.Shake basket,mist with oil,and cook 3 moreminutes,until chicken juices run clear and outside is crispy.
11. Repeat step 10 to cook remaining chicken fries.

Chicken Adobo

Servings:6
Cooking Time:12 Minutes
Ingredients:
- 6 boneless chicken thighs
- ¼cup soy sauce or tamari
- ½cup rice wine vinegar
- 4 cloves garlic,minced
- ⅛teaspoon crushed red pepper flakes
- ½teaspoon black pepper

Directions:
1. Place the chicken thighs into a resealable plastic bag with the soy sauce or tamari,the rice wine vinegar,the garlic,and the crushed red pepper flakes.Seal the bag and let the chicken marinate at least 1 hour in the refrigerator.
2. Preheat the air fryer to 400°F(205°C).
3. Drain the chicken and pat dry with a paper towel.Season the chicken with black pepper and liberally spray with cooking spray.
4. Place the chicken in the air fryer basket and cook for 9 minutes,turn over at 9 minutes and check for an internal temperature of 165°F(75°C),and cook another 3 minutes.

Cajun Chicken Livers

Servings:2
Cooking Time:45 Minutes
Ingredients:

- 1 lb chicken livers,rinsed,connective tissue discarded
- 1 cup whole milk
- ½cup cornmeal
- 3/4 cup flour
- 1 tsp salt and black pepper
- 1 tsp Cajun seasoning
- 2 eggs
- 1½cups bread crumbs
- 1 tbsp olive oil
- 2 tbsp chopped parsley

Directions:
1. Pat chicken livers dry with paper towels,then transfer them to a small bowl and pour in the milk and black pepper.Let sit covered in the fridge for 2 hours.
2. Preheat air fryer at 375ºF.In a bowl,combine cornmeal,flour,salt,and Cajun seasoning.In another bowl,beat the eggs,and in a third bowl,add bread crumbs.Dip chicken livers first in the cornmeal mixture,then in the egg,and finally in the bread crumbs.Place chicken livers in the greased frying basket,brush the tops lightly with olive oil,and Air Fry for 16 minutes,turning once.Serve right away sprinkled with parsley.

Harissa Chicken Wings

Servings:4
Cooking Time:25 Minutes
Ingredients:

- 8 whole chicken wings
- 1 tsp garlic powder
- ¼tsp dried oregano
- 1 tbsp harissa seasoning

Directions:
1. Preheat air fryer to 400°F(205°C).Season the wings with garlic,harissa seasoning,and oregano.Place them in the greased frying basket and spray with cooking oil spray.Air Fry for 10 minutes,shake the basket,and cook for another 5-7 minutes until golden and crispy.Serve warm.

Chicken Nuggets

Servings:20
Cooking Time:14 Minutes Per Batch
Ingredients:

- 1 pound boneless,skinless chicken thighs,cut into 1-inch chunks
- ¾teaspoon salt
- ½teaspoon black pepper
- ½teaspoon garlic powder
- ½teaspoon onion powder
- ½cup flour
- 2 eggs,beaten
- ½cup panko breadcrumbs
- 3 tablespoons plain breadcrumbs
- oil for misting or cooking spray

Directions:
1. In the bowl of a food processor,combine chicken,½teaspoon salt,pepper,garlic powder,and onion

powder.Process in short pulses until chicken is very finely chopped and well blended.
2. Place flour in one shallow dish and beaten eggs in another.In a third dish or plastic bag,mix together the panko crumbs,plain breadcrumbs,and¼teaspoon salt.
3. Shape chicken mixture into small nuggets.Dip nuggets in flour,then eggs,then panko crumb mixture.
4. Spray nuggets on both sides with oil or cooking spray and place in air fryer basket in a single layer,close but not overlapping.
5. Cook at 360°F(180°C)for 10minutes.Spray with oil and cook 4 minutes,until chicken is done and coating is golden brown.
6. Repeat step 5 to cook remaining nuggets.

Chicken Pigs In Blankets

Servings:4
Cooking Time:40 Minutes
Ingredients:

- 8 chicken drumsticks,boneless,skinless
- 2 tbsp light brown sugar
- 2 tbsp ketchup
- 1 tbsp grainy mustard
- 8 smoked bacon slices
- 1 tsp chopped fresh sage

Directions:
1. Preheat the air fryer to 350°F(175°C).Mix brown sugar,sage,ketchup,and mustard in a bowl and brush the chicken with it.Wrap slices of bacon around the drumsticks and brush with the remaining mix.Line the frying basket with round parchment paper with holes.Set 4 drumsticks on the paper,add a raised rack and set the other drumsticks on it.Bake for 25-35 minutes,moving the bottom drumsticks to the top,top to the bottom,and flipping at about 14-16 minutes.Sprinkle with sage and serve.

Taquitos

Servings:12
Cooking Time:6 Minutes Per Batch
Ingredients:

- 1 teaspoon butter
- 2 tablespoons chopped green onions
- 1 cup cooked chicken,shredded
- 2 tablespoons chopped green chiles
- 2 ounces Pepper Jack cheese,shredded
- 4 tablespoons salsa
- ½teaspoon lime juice
- ¼teaspoon cumin
- ½teaspoon chile powder
- ⅛teaspoon garlic powder
- 12 corn tortillas
- oil for misting or cooking spray

Directions:
1. Melt butter in a saucepan over medium heat.Add green onions and sautéa minute or two,until tender.
2. Remove from heat and stir in the chicken,green chiles,cheese,salsa,lime juice,and seasonings.
3. Preheat air fryer to 390°F(200°C).
4. To soften refrigerated tortillas,wrap in damp paper towels and microwave for 30 to 60 seconds,until slightly warmed.

5. Remove one tortilla at a time,keeping others covered with the damp paper towels.Place a heaping tablespoon of filling into tortilla,roll up and secure with toothpick.Spray all sides with oil or cooking spray.

6. Place taquitos in air fryer basket,either in a single layer or stacked.To stack,leave plenty of space between taquitos and alternate the direction of the layers,4 on the bottom lengthwise,then 4 more on top crosswise.

7. Cook for 6minutes or until brown and crispy.

8. Repeat steps 6 and 7 to cook remaining taquitos.

9. Serve hot with guacamole,sour cream,salsa or all three!

Asian Meatball Tacos

Servings:4
Cooking Time:10 Minutes
Ingredients:
- 1 pound lean ground turkey
- 3 tablespoons soy sauce
- 1 tablespoon brown sugar
- ½teaspoon onion powder
- ½teaspoon garlic powder
- 1 tablespoon sesame seeds
- 1 English cucumber
- 4 radishes
- 2 tablespoons white wine vinegar
- 1 lime,juiced and divided
- 1 tablespoon avocado oil
- Salt,to taste
- ½cup Greek yogurt
- 1 to 3 teaspoons Sriracha,based on desired spiciness
- 1 cup shredded cabbage
- ¼cup chopped cilantro
- Eight 6-inch flour tortillas

Directions:
1. Preheat the air fryer to 360°F(180°C).
2. In a large bowl,mix the ground turkey,soy sauce,brown sugar,onion powder,garlic powder,and sesame seeds.Form the meat into 1-inch meatballs and place in the air fryer basket.Cook for 5 minutes,shake the basket,and cook another 5 minutes.Using a food thermometer,make sure the internal temperature of the meatballs is 165°F(75°C).
3. Meanwhile,dice the cucumber and radishes and place in a medium bowl.Add the white wine vinegar,1 teaspoon of the lime juice,and the avocado oil,and stir to coat.Season with salt to desired taste.
4. In a large bowl,mix the Greek yogurt,Sriracha,and the remaining lime juice,and stir.Add in the cabbage and cilantro;toss well to create a slaw.
5. In a heavy skillet,heat the tortillas over medium heat for 1 to 2 minutes on each side,or until warmed.
6. To serve,place a tortilla on a plate,top with 5 meatballs,then with cucumber and radish salad,and finish with 2 tablespoons of cabbage slaw.

Garlic Chicken

Servings:4
Cooking Time:30 Minutes
Ingredients:
- 4 bone-in skinless chicken thighs
- 1 tbsp olive oil
- 1 tbsp lemon juice
- 3 tbsp cornstarch
- 1 tsp dried sage
- Black pepper to taste
- 20 garlic cloves,unpeeled

Directions:
1. Preheat air fryer to 370°F(185°C).Brush the chicken with olive oil and lemon juice,then drizzle cornstarch,sage,and pepper.Put the chicken in the frying basket and scatter the garlic cloves on top.Roast for 25 minutes or until the garlic is soft,and the chicken is cooked through.Serve.

Mexican Chicken Roll-ups

Servings:4
Cooking Time:35 Minutes
Ingredients:
- ½red bell pepper,cut into strips
- ½green bell pepper,cut into strips
- 2 chicken breasts
- ½lime,juiced
- 2 tbsp taco seasoning
- 1 spring onion,thinly sliced

Directions:
1. Preheat air fryer to 400°F(205°C).Cut the chicken into cutlets by slicing the chicken breast in half horizontally in order to have 4 thin cutlets.Drizzle with lime juice and season with taco seasoning.Divide the red pepper,green pepper,and spring onion equally between the 4 cutlets.Roll up the cutlets.Secure with toothpicks.Place the chicken roll-ups in the air fryer and lightly spray with cooking oil.Bake for 12 minutes,turning once.Serve warm.

Goat Cheese Stuffed Turkey Roulade

Servings:4
Cooking Time:55 Minutes
Ingredients:
- 1 boneless turkey breast,skinless
- Salt and pepper to taste
- 4 oz goat cheese
- 1 tbsp marjoram
- 1 tbsp sage
- 2 garlic cloves,minced
- 2 tbsp olive oil
- 2 tbsp chopped cilantro

Directions:
1. Preheat air fryer to 380°F(195°C).Butterfly the turkey breast with a sharp knife and season with salt and pepper.Mix together the goat cheese,marjoram,sage,and garlic in a bowl.Spread the cheese mixture over the turkey breast,then roll it up tightly,tucking the ends underneath.
2. Put the turkey breast roulade onto a piece of aluminum foil,wrap it up,and place it into the air fryer.Bake for 30 minutes.Turn the turkey breast,brush the top with oil,and then continue to cook for another 10-15 minutes.Slice and serve sprinkled with cilantro.

Spiced Chicken Breasts

Servings:4
Cooking Time:20 Minutes
Ingredients:
- ½tsp dried oregano
- ½tsp granulated garlic
- ½tsp granulated onion
- ½tsp chili powder
- ¼tsp sweet paprika
- Salt and pepper to taste
- 1 lb chicken breasts,sliced
- 2 tbsp yellow mustard

Directions:
1. Preheat air fryer to 375°F(190°C).Mix together oregano,salt,garlic,onion,chili powder,paprika,and black pepper in a small bowl.Coat the chicken with mustard in a bowl.Sprinkle the seasoning mix over the chicken.Place the chicken in the greased frying basket and Air Fry for 7-8,flipping once until cooked through.Serve immediately.

Sticky Drumsticks

Servings:4
Cooking Time:45 Minutes
Ingredients:
- 1 lb chicken drumsticks
- 1 tbsp chicken seasoning
- 1 tsp dried chili flakes
- Salt and pepper to taste
- ¼cup honey
- 1 cup barbecue sauce

Directions:
1. Preheat air fryer to 390°F(200°C).Season drumsticks with chicken seasoning,chili flakes,salt,and pepper.Place one batch of drumsticks in the greased frying basket and Air Fry for 18-20 minutes,flipping once until golden.
2. While the chicken is cooking,combine honey and barbecue sauce in a small bowl.Remove the drumsticks to a serving dish.Drizzle honey-barbecue sauce over and serve.

Asian Sweet Chili Chicken

Servings:4
Cooking Time:30 Minutes
Ingredients:
- 2 chicken breasts,cut into 1-inch pieces
- 1 cup cornstarch
- 1 tsp chicken seasoning
- Salt and pepper to taste
- 2 eggs
- 1½cups sweet chili sauce

Directions:
1. Preheat air fryer to 360°F(180°C).Mix cornstarch,chicken seasoning,salt and pepper in a large bowl.In another bowl,beat the eggs.Dip the chicken in the cornstarch mixture to coat.Next,dip the chicken into the egg,then return to the cornstarch.Transfer chicken to the air fryer.
2. Lightly spray all of the chicken with cooking oil.Air Fry for 15-16 minutes,shaking the basket once or until golden.Transfer chicken to a serving dish and drizzle with sweet-and-sour sauce.Serve immediately.

Philly Chicken Cheesesteak Stromboli

Servings:2
Cooking Time:28 Minutes
Ingredients:
- ½onion,sliced
- 1 teaspoon vegetable oil
- 2 boneless,skinless chicken breasts,partially frozen and sliced very thin on the bias(about 1 pound)
- 1 tablespoon Worcestershire sauce
- salt and freshly ground black pepper
- ½recipe of Blue Jean Chef pizza dough(see page 229),or 14 ounces of store-bought pizza dough
- 1½cups grated Cheddar cheese
- ½cup Cheese Whiz®(or other jarred cheese sauce),warmed gently in the microwave
- tomato ketchup for serving

Directions:
1. Preheat the air fryer to 400°F(205°C).
2. Toss the sliced onion with oil and air-fry for 8 minutes,stirring halfway through the cooking time.Add the sliced chicken and Worcestershire sauce to the air fryer basket,and toss to evenly distribute the ingredients.Season the mixture with salt and freshly ground black pepper and air-fry for 8 minutes,stirring a couple of times during the cooking process.Remove the chicken and onion from the air fryer and let the mixture cool a little.
3. On a lightly floured surface,roll or press the pizza dough out into a 13-inch by 11-inch rectangle,with the long side closest to you.Sprinkle half of the Cheddar cheese over the dough leaving an empty 1-inch border from the edge farthest away from you.Top the cheese with the chicken and onion mixture,spreading it out evenly.Drizzle the cheese sauce over the meat and sprinkle the remaining Cheddar cheese on top.
4. Start rolling the stromboli away from you and toward the empty border.Make sure the filling stays tightly tucked inside the roll.Finally,tuck the ends of the dough in and pinch the seam shut.Place the seam side down and shape the Stromboli into a U-shape to fit in the air-fry basket.Cut 4 small slits with the tip of a sharp knife evenly in the top of the dough and lightly brush the stromboli with a little oil.
5. Preheat the air fryer to 370°F(185°C).
6. Spray or brush the air fryer basket with oil and transfer the U-shaped stromboli to the air fryer basket.Air-fry for 12 minutes,turning the stromboli over halfway through the cooking time.(Use a plate to invert the stromboli out of the air fryer basket and then slide it back into the basket off the plate.)
7. To remove,carefully flip stromboli over onto a cutting board.Let it rest for a couple of minutes before serving.Slice the stromboli into 3-inch pieces and serve with ketchup for dipping,if desired.

Spiced Mexican Stir-fried Chicken

Servings:4
Cooking Time:30 Minutes
Ingredients:
- 1 lb chicken breasts,cubed
- 2 green onions,chopped
- 1 red bell pepper,chopped
- 1 jalapeño pepper,minced
- 2 tsp olive oil
- 2/3 cup canned black beans
- ½cup salsa
- 2 tsp Mexican chili powder

Directions:
1. Preheat air fryer to 400°F(205°C).Combine the chicken,green onions,bell pepper,jalapeño,and olive oil in a bowl.Transfer to a bowl to the frying basket and Air Fry for 10 minutes,stirring once during cooking.When done,stir in the black beans,salsa,and chili powder.Air Fry for 7-10 minutes or until cooked through.Serve.

Basic Chicken Breasts(1)

Servings:4
Cooking Time:15 Minutes
Ingredients:
- 2 tsp olive oil
- 4 chicken breasts
- Salt and pepper to taste
- 1 tbsp Italian seasoning

Directions:
1. Preheat air fryer at 350ºF.Rub olive oil over chicken breasts and sprinkle with salt,Italian seasoning and black pepper.Place them in the frying basket and Air Fry for 8-10 minutes.Let rest for 5 minutes before cutting.Store it covered in the fridge for up to 1 week.

Vip's Club Sandwiches

Servings:4
Cooking Time:50 Minutes
Ingredients:
- 1 cup buttermilk
- 1 egg
- 1 cup bread crumbs
- 1 tsp garlic powder
- Salt and pepper to taste
- 4 chicken cutlets
- 3 tbsp butter,melted
- 4 hamburger buns
- 4 tbsp mayonnaise
- 4 tsp yellow mustard
- 8 dill pickle chips
- 4 pieccs iceberg lettuce
- ½sliced avocado
- 4 slices cooked bacon
- 8 vine-ripe tomato slices
- 1 tsp chia seeds

Directions:
1. Preheat air fryer at 400ºF.Beat the buttermilk and egg in a bowl.In another bowl,combine breadcrumbs,garlic powder,salt,and black pepper.Dip chicken cutlets in the egg mixture,then dredge them in the breadcrumbs mixture.Brush chicken cutlets lightly with melted butter on both sides,place them in the greased frying basket,and Air Fry for 18-20 minutes.Spread the mayonnaise on the top buns and mustard on the bottom buns.Add chicken onto bottom buns and top with pickles,lettuce,chia seeds,avocado,bacon,and tomato.Cover with the top buns.Serve and enjoy!

Pickle Brined Fried Chicken

Servings:4
Cooking Time:47 Minutes
Ingredients:
- 4 bone-in,skin-on chicken legs,cut into drumsticks and thighs(about 3½pounds)
- pickle juice from a 24-ounce jar of kosher dill pickles
- ½cup flour
- salt and freshly ground black pepper
- 2 eggs
- 1 cup fine breadcrumbs
- 1 teaspoon salt
- 1 teaspoon freshly ground black pepper
- ½teaspoon ground paprika
- ⅛teaspoon ground cayenne pepper
- vegetable or canola oil in a spray bottle

Directions:
1. Place the chicken in a shallow dish and pour the pickle juice over the top.Cover and transfer the chicken to the refrigerator to brine in the pickle juice for 3 to 8 hours.
2. When you are ready to cook,remove the chicken from the refrigerator to let it come to room temperature while you set up a dredging station.Place the flour in a shallow dish and season well with salt and freshly ground black pepper.Whisk the eggs in a second shallow dish.In a third shallow dish,combine the breadcrumbs,salt,pepper,paprika and cayenne pepper.
3. Preheat the air fryer to 370°F(185°C).
4. Remove the chicken from the pickle brine and gently dry it with a clean kitchen towel.Dredge each piece of chicken in the flour,then dip it into the egg mixture,and finally press it into the breadcrumb mixture to coat all sides of the chicken.Place the breaded chicken on a plate or baking sheet and spray each piece all over with vegetable oil.
5. Air-fry the chicken in two batches.Place two chicken thighs and two drumsticks into the air fryer basket.Air-fry for 10 minutes.Then,gently turn the chicken pieces over and air-fry for another 10 minutes.Remove the chicken pieces and let them rest on plate–do not cover.Repeat with the second batch of chicken,air-frying for 20 minutes,turning the chicken over halfway through.
6. Lower the temperature of the air fryer to 340°F(170°C).Place the first batch of chicken on top of the second batch already in the basket and air-fry for an additional 7 minutes.Serve warm and enjoy.

The Ultimate Chicken Bulgogi

Servings:4
Cooking Time:30 Minutes
Ingredients:
- 1½lb boneless,skinless chicken thighs,cubed
- 1 cucumber,thinly sliced
- ¼cup apple cider vinegar

- 4 garlic cloves,minced
- ¼tsp ground ginger
- ⅛tsp red pepper flakes
- 2 tsp honey
- ⅛tsp salt
- 2 tbsp tamari
- 2 tsp sesame oil
- 2 tsp granular honey
- 2 tbsp lemon juice
- ½tsp lemon zest
- 3 scallions,chopped
- 2 cups cooked white rice
- 2 tsp roasted sesame seeds

Directions:
1.   In a bowl,toss the cucumber,vinegar,half of the garlic,half of the ginger,pepper flakes,honey,and salt and store in the fridge covered.Combine the tamari,sesame oil,granular honey,lemon juice,remaining garlic,remaining ginger,and chicken in a large bowl.Toss to coat and marinate in the fridge for 10 minutes.
2.   Preheat air fryer to 350ºF.Place chicken in the frying basket,do not discard excess marinade.Air Fry for 11 minutes,shaking once and pouring excess marinade over.Place the chicken bulgogi over the cooked rice and scatter with scallion greens,pickled cucumbers,and sesame seeds.Serve and enjoy!

Crunchy Chicken Strips

Servings:4
Cooking Time:40 Minutes
Ingredients:
- 1 chicken breast,sliced into strips
- 1 tbsp grated Parmesan cheese
- 1 cup breadcrumbs
- 1 tbsp chicken seasoning
- 2 eggs,beaten
- Salt and pepper to taste

Directions:
1.   Preheat air fryer to 350°F(175°C).Mix the breadcrumbs,Parmesan cheese,chicken seasoning,salt,and pepper in a mixing bowl.Coat the chicken with the crumb mixture,then dip in the beaten eggs.Finally,coat again with the dry ingredients.Arrange the coated chicken pieces on the greased frying basket and Air Fry for 15 minutes.Turn over halfway through cooking and cook for another 15 minutes.Serve immediately.

Za' atar Chicken Drumsticks

Servings:4
Cooking Time:45 Minutes
Ingredients:
- 2 tbsp butter,melted
- 8 chicken drumsticks
- 1½tbsp Za'atar seasoning
- Salt and pepper to taste
- 1 lemon,zested
- 2 tbsp parsley,chopped

Directions:
1.   Preheat air fryer to 390°F(200°C).Mix the Za'atar seasoning,lemon zest,parsley,salt,and pepper in a bowl.Add the chicken drumsticks and toss to coat.Place them in the air fryer and brush them with butter.Air Fry for 18-20 minutes,flipping once until crispy.Serve and enjoy!

Chicken Cutlets With Broccoli Rabe And Roasted Peppers

Servings:2
Cooking Time:10 Minutes
Ingredients:
- ½bunch broccoli rabe
- olive oil,in a spray bottle
- salt and freshly ground black pepper
- ⅔cup roasted red pepper strips
- 2(4-ounce)boneless,skinless chicken breasts
- 2 tablespoons all-purpose flour*
- 1 egg,beaten
- ⅓cup seasoned breadcrumbs*
- 2 slices aged provolone cheese

Directions:
1.   Bring a medium saucepot of salted water to a boil on the stovetop.Blanch the broccoli rabe for 3 minutes in the boiling water and then drain.When it has cooled a little,squeeze out as much water as possible,drizzle a little olive oil on top,season with salt and black pepper and set aside.Dry the roasted red peppers with a clean kitchen towel and set them aside as well.
2.   Place each chicken breast between 2 pieces of plastic wrap.Use a meat pounder to flatten the chicken breasts to about½-inch thick.Season the chicken on both sides with salt and pepper.
3.   Preheat the air fryer to 400°F(205°C).
4.   Set up a dredging station with three shallow dishes.Place the flour in one dish,the egg in a second dish and the breadcrumbs in a third dish.Coat the chicken on all sides with the flour.Shake off any excess flour and dip the chicken into the egg.Let the excess egg drip off and coat both sides of the chicken in the breadcrumbs.Spray the chicken with olive oil on both sides and transfer to the air fryer basket.
5.   Air-fry the chicken at 400°F(205°C)for 5 minutes.Turn the chicken over and air-fry for another minute.Then,top the chicken breast with the broccoli rabe and roasted peppers.Place a slice of the provolone cheese on top and secure it with a toothpick or two.
6.   Air-fry at 360°for 3 to 4 minutes to melt the cheese and warm everything together.

Cajun Fried Chicken

Servings:3
Cooking Time:35 Minutes
Ingredients:
- 1 cup Cajun seasoning
- ½tsp mango powder
- 6 chicken legs,bone-in

Directions:
1.   Preheat air fryer to 360°F(180°C).Place half of the Cajun seasoning and 3/4 cup of water in a bowl and mix well to dissolve any lumps.Add the remaining Cajun seasoning and mango powder to a shallow bowl and stir to combine.Dip the chicken in the batter,then coat it in the mango seasoning.Lightly spritz the chicken with cooking spray.Place the chicken in the air fryer and Air Fry for 14-16 minutes,turning once until the chicken is cooked and the coating is brown.Serve and enjoy!

Turkey Burgers

Servings:4
Cooking Time:13 Minutes
Ingredients:
- 1 pound ground turkey
- ¼cup diced red onion
- 1 tablespoon grilled chicken seasoning
- ½teaspoon dried parsley
- ½teaspoon salt
- 4 slices provolone cheese
- 4 whole-grain sandwich buns
- Suggested toppings:lettuce,sliced tomatoes,dill pickles,and mustard

Directions:
1. Combine the turkey,onion,chicken seasoning,parsley,and salt and mix well.
2. Shape into 4 patties.
3. Cook at 360°F(180°C)for 11 minutes or until turkey is well done and juices run clear.
4. Top each burger with a slice of cheese and cook 2 minutes to melt.
5. Serve on buns with your favorite toppings.

Indian-inspired Chicken Skewers

Servings:4
Cooking Time:40 Minutes+Chilling Time
Ingredients:
- 1 lb boneless,skinless chicken thighs,cubed
- 1 red onion,diced
- 1 tbsp grated ginger
- 2 tbsp lime juice
- 1 cup canned coconut milk
- 2 tbsp tomato paste
- 2 tbsp olive oil
- 1 tbsp ground cumin
- 1 tbsp ground coriander
- 1 tsp cayenne pepper
- 1 tsp ground turmeric
- ½tsp red chili powder
- ¼tsp curry powder
- 2 tsp salt
- 2 tbsp chopped cilantro

Directions:
1. Toss red onion,ginger,lime juice,coconut milk,tomato paste,olive oil,cumin,coriander,cayenne pepper,turmeric,chili powder,curry powder,salt,and chicken until fully coated.Let chill in the fridge for 2 hours.
2. Preheat air fryer to 350ºF.Thread chicken onto 8 skewers and place them on a kebab rack.Place rack in the frying basket and Air Fry for 12 minutes.Discard marinade.Garnish with cilantro to serve.

Classic Chicken Cobb Salad

Servings:4
Cooking Time:30 Minutes
Ingredients:
- 4 oz cooked bacon,crumbled
- 2 chicken breasts,cubed
- 1 tbsp sesame oil
- Salt and pepper to taste
- 4 cups torn romaine lettuce
- 2 tbsp olive oil
- 1 tbsp white wine vinegar
- 2 hard-boiled eggs,sliced
- 2 tomatoes,diced
- 6 radishes,finely sliced
- ¼cup blue cheese crumbles
- ¼cup diced red onions
- 1 avocado,diced

Directions:
1. Preheat air fryer to 350ºF.Combine chicken cubes,sesame oil,salt,and black pepper in a bowl.Place chicken cubes in the frying basket and Air Fry for 9 minutes,flipping once.Reserve.In a bowl,combine the lettuce,olive oil,and vinegar.Divide between 4 bowls.Add in the cooked chicken,hard-boiled egg slices,bacon,tomato cubes,radishes,blue cheese,onion,and avocado cubes.Serve.

Satay Chicken Skewers

Servings:4
Cooking Time:35 Minutes
Ingredients:
- 2 chicken breasts,cut into strips
- 1½tbsp Thai red curry paste
- ¼cup peanut butter
- 1 tbsp maple syrup
- 1 tbsp tamari
- 1 tbsp lime juice
- 2 tsp chopped onions
- ¼tsp minced ginger
- 1 clove garlic,minced
- 1 cup coconut milk
- 1 tsp fish sauce
- 1 tbsp chopped cilantro

Directions:
1. Mix the peanut butter,maple syrup,tamari,lime juice,¼tsp of sriracha,onions,ginger,garlic,and 2 tbsp of water in a bowl.Reserve 1 tbsp of the sauce.Set aside.Combine the reserved peanut sauce,fish sauce,coconut milk,Thai red curry paste,cilantro and chicken strips in a bowl and let marinate in the fridge for 15 minutes.
2. Preheat air fryer at 350ºF.Thread chicken strips onto skewers and place them on a kebab rack.Place rack in the frying basket and Air Fry for 12 minutes.Serve with previously prepared peanut sauce on the side.

Spring Chicken Salad

Servings:4
Cooking Time:25 Minutes
Ingredients:
- 3 chicken breasts,cubed
- 1 small red onion,sliced
- 1 red bell pepper,sliced
- 1 cup green beans,sliced
- 2 tbsp ranch salad dressing
- 2 tbsp lemon juice
- ½tsp dried basil
- 10 oz spring mix

Directions:

1. Preheat air fryer to 400°F(205°C).Put the chicken,red onion,red bell pepper,and green beans in the frying basket and Roast for 10-13 minutes until the chicken is cooked through.Shake the basket at least once while cooking.As the chicken is cooking,combine the ranch dressing,lemon juice,and basil.When the chicken is done,remove it and along with the veggies to a bowl and pour the dressing over.Stir to coat.Serve with spring mix.

Jerk Chicken Drumsticks

Servings:2
Cooking Time:20 Minutes
Ingredients:
- 1 or 2 cloves garlic
- 1 inch of fresh ginger
- 2 serrano peppers,(with seeds if you like it spicy,seeds removed for less heat)
- 1 teaspoon ground allspice
- 1 teaspoon ground nutmeg
- 1 teaspoon chili powder
- ½teaspoon dried thyme
- ½teaspoon ground cinnamon
- ½teaspoon paprika
- 1 tablespoon brown sugar
- 1 teaspoon soy sauce
- 2 tablespoons vegetable oil
- 6 skinless chicken drumsticks

Directions:
1. Combine all the ingredients except the chicken in a small chopper or blender and blend to a paste.Make slashes into the meat of the chicken drumsticks and rub the spice blend all over the chicken(a pair of plastic gloves makes this really easy).Transfer the rubbed chicken to a non-reactive covered container and let the chicken marinate for at least 30 minutes or overnight in the refrigerator.
2. Preheat the air fryer to 400°F(205°C).
3. Transfer the drumsticks to the air fryer basket.Air-fry for 10 minutes.Turn the drumsticks over and air-fry for another 10 minutes.Serve warm with some rice and vegetables or a green salad.

Chicken Wings Al Ajillo

Servings:4
Cooking Time:35 Minutes
Ingredients:
- 2 lb chicken wings,split at the joint
- 2 tbsp melted butter
- 2 tbsp grated Cotija cheese
- 4 cloves garlic,minced
- ½tbsp hot paprika
- ¼tsp salt

Directions:
1. Preheat air fryer to 250ºF.Coat the chicken wings with 1 tbsp of butter.Place them in the basket and Air Fry for 12 minutes,tossing once.In another bowl,whisk 1 tbsp of

butter,Cotija cheese,garlic,hot paprika,and salt.Reserve.Increase temperature to 400ºF.Air Fry wings for 10 more minutes,tossing twice.Transfer them to the bowl with the sauce,and toss to coat.Serve immediately.

Boss Chicken Cobb Salad

Servings:2
Cooking Time:30 Minutes
Ingredients:
- 4 oz cooked bacon,crumbled
- ¼cup diced peeled red onion
- ½cup crumbled blue cheese
- 1 egg
- 1 tbsp honey
- 1 tbsp Dijon mustard
- ½tsp apple cider vinegar
- 2 chicken breasts,cubed
- 3/4 cup bread crumbs
- Salt and pepper to taste
- 3 cups torn iceberg lettuce
- 2 cups baby spinach
- ½cup ranch dressing
- ½avocado,diced
- 1 beefsteak tomato,diced
- 1 hard-boiled egg,diced
- 2 tbsp parsley

Directions:
1. Preheat air fryer at 350ºF.Mix the egg,honey,mustard,and vinegar in a bowl.Toss in chicken cubes to coat.Shake off excess marinade of chicken.In another bowl,combine breadcrumbs,salt,and pepper.Dredge chicken cubes in the mixture.Place chicken cubes in the greased frying basket.Air Fry for 8-10 minutes,tossing once.In a salad bowl,combine lettuce,baby spinach,and ranch dressing and toss to coat.Add in the cooked chicken and the remaining ingredients.Serve immediately.

Chicken Meatballs With A Surprise

Servings:4
Cooking Time:35 Minutes
Ingredients:
- 1/3 cup cottage cheese crumbles
- 1 lb ground chicken
- ½tsp onion powder
- ¼cup chopped basil
- ½cup bread crumbs
- ½tsp garlic powder

Directions:
1. Preheat air fryer to 350ºF.Combine the ground chicken,onion,basil,cottage cheese,bread crumbs,and garlic powder in a bowl.Form into 18 meatballs,about 2 tbsp each.Place the chicken meatballs in the greased frying basket and Air Fry for 12 minutes,shaking once.Serve.

Vegetarians Recipes

Ricotta Veggie Potpie

Servings:4
Cooking Time:30 Minutes
Ingredients:
- 1¼cup flour
- ¾cup ricotta cheese
- 1 tbsp olive oil
- 1 potato,peeled and diced
- ¼cup diced mushrooms
- ¼cup diced carrots
- ¼cup diced celery
- ¼cup diced yellow onion
- 1 garlic clove,minced
- 1 tbsp unsalted butter
- 1 cup milk
- ½tsp ground black pepper
- 1 tsp dried thyme
- 2 tbsp dill,chopped

Directions:
1. Preheat air fryer to 350°F(175°C).Combine 1 cup flour and ricotta cheese in a medium bowl and stir until the dough comes together.Heat oil over medium heat in a small skillet.Stir in potato,mushroom,carrots,dill,thyme,celery,onion,and garlic.Cook for 4-5 minutes,often stirring,until the onions are soft and translucent.
2. Add butter and melt,then stir in the rest of the flour.Slowly pour in the milk and keep stirring.Simmer for 5 minutes until the sauce has thickened,then stir in pepper and thyme.Spoon the vegetable mixture into four 6-ounce ramekins.Cut the dough into 4 equal sections and work it into rounds that fit over the size of the ramekins.Top the ramekins with the dough,then place the ramekins in the frying basket.Bake for 10 minutes until the crust is golden.Serve hot and enjoy.

Tacos

Servings:24
Cooking Time:8 Minutes Per Batch
Ingredients:
- 1 24-count package 4-inch corn tortillas
- 1½cups refried beans(about¾of a 15-ounce can)
- 4 ounces sharp Cheddar cheese,grated
- ½cup salsa
- oil for misting or cooking spray

Directions:
1. Preheat air fryer to 390°F(200°C).
2. Wrap refrigerated tortillas in damp paper towels and microwave for 30 to 60 seconds to warm.If necessary,rewarm tortillas as you go to keep them soft enough to fold without breaking.
3. Working with one tortilla at a time,top with 1 tablespoon of beans,1 tablespoon of grated cheese,and 1 teaspoon of salsa.Fold over and press down very gently on the center.Press edges firmly all around to seal.Spray both sides with oil or cooking spray.

4. Cooking in two batches,place half the tacos in the air fryer basket.To cook 12 at a time,you may need to stand them upright and lean some against the sides of basket.It's okay if they're crowded as long as you leave a little room for air to circulate around them.
5. Cook for 8 minutes or until golden brown and crispy.
6. Repeat steps 4 and 5 to cook remaining tacos.

Harissa Veggie Fries

Servings:4
Cooking Time:55 Minutes
Ingredients:
- 1 pound red potatoes,cut into rounds
- 1 onion,diced
- 1 green bell pepper,diced
- 1 red bell pepper,diced
- 2 tbsp olive oil
- Salt and pepper to taste
- ¾tsp garlic powder
- ¾tsp harissa seasoning

Directions:
1. Combine all ingredients in a large bowl and mix until potatoes are well coated and seasoned.Preheat air fryer to 350°F(175°C).Pour all of the contents in the bowl into the frying basket.Bake for 35 minutes,shaking every 10 minutes,until golden brown and soft.Serve hot.

Vegetarian Paella

Servings:3
Cooking Time:50 Minutes
Ingredients:
- ½cup chopped artichoke hearts
- ½sliced red bell peppers
- 4 mushrooms,thinly sliced
- ½cup canned diced tomatoes
- ½cup canned chickpeas
- 3 tbsp hot sauce
- 2 tbsp lemon juice
- 1 tbsp allspice
- 1 cup rice

Directions:
1. Preheat air fryer to 400°F(205°C).Combine the artichokes,peppers,mushrooms,tomatoes and their juices,chickpeas,hot sauce,lemon juice,and allspice in a baking pan.Roast for 10 minutes.Pour in rice and 2 cups of boiling water,cover with aluminum foil,and Roast for 22 minutes.Discard the foil and Roast for 3 minutes until the top is crisp.Let cool slightly before stirring.Serve.

Pineapple&Veggie Souvlaki

Servings:4
Cooking Time:35 Minutes
Ingredients:
- 1 can pineapple rings in pineapple juice
- 1 red bell pepper,stemmed and seeded
- 1/3 cup butter
- 2 tbsp apple cider vinegar
- 2 tbsp hot sauce

- 1 tbsp allspice
- 1 tsp ground nutmeg
- 16 oz feta cheese
- 1 red onion,peeled
- 8 mushrooms,quartered

Directions:
1. Preheat air fryer to 400°F(205°C).Whisk the butter,pineapple juice,apple vinegar,hot sauce,allspice,and nutmeg until smooth.Set aside.Slice feta cheese into 16 cubes,then the bell pepper into 16 chunks,and finally red onion into 8 wedges,separating each wedge into 2 pieces.
2. Cut pineapple ring into quarters.Place veggie cubes and feta into the butter bowl and toss to coat.Thread the veggies,tofu,and pineapple onto 8 skewers,alternating 16 pieces on each skewer.Grill for 15 minutes until golden brown and cooked.Serve warm.

Smoked Paprika Sweet Potato Fries

Servings:4
Cooking Time:35 Minutes
Ingredients:
- 2 sweet potatoes,peeled
- 1½tbsp cornstarch
- 1 tbsp canola oil
- 1 tbsp olive oil
- 1 tsp smoked paprika
- 1 tsp garlic powder
- Salt and pepper to taste
- 1 cup cocktail sauce

Directions:
1. Cut the potatoes lengthwise to form French fries.Put in a resealable plastic bag and add cornstarch.Seal and shake to coat the fries.Combine the canola oil,olive oil,paprika,garlic powder,salt,and pepper fries in a large bowl.Add the sweet potato fries and mix to combine.
2. Preheat air fryer to 380°F(195°C).Place fries in the greased basket and fry for 20-25 minutes,shaking the basket once until crisp.Drizzle with Cocktail sauce to serve.

Falafels

Servings:12
Cooking Time:10 Minutes
Ingredients:
- 1 pouch falafel mix
- 2–3 tablespoons plain breadcrumbs
- oil for misting or cooking spray

Directions:
1. Prepare falafel mix according to package directions.
2. Preheat air fryer to 390°F(200°C).
3. Place breadcrumbs in shallow dish or on wax paper.
4. Shape falafel mixture into 12 balls and flatten slightly.Roll in breadcrumbs to coat all sides and mist with oil or cooking spray.
5. Place falafels in air fryer basket in single layer and cook for 5minutes.Shake basket,and continue cooking for 5minutes,until they brown and are crispy.

Home-style Cinnamon Rolls

Servings:4
Cooking Time:40 Minutes
Ingredients:
- ½pizza dough
- 1/3 cup dark brown sugar
- ¼cup butter,softened
- ½tsp ground cinnamon

Directions:
1. Preheat air fryer to 360°F(180°C).Roll out the dough into a rectangle.Using a knife,spread the brown sugar and butter,covering all the edges,and sprinkle with cinnamon.Fold the long side of the dough into a log,then cut it into 8 equal pieces,avoiding compression.Place the rolls,spiral-side up,onto a parchment-lined sheet.Let rise for 20 minutes.Grease the rolls with cooking spray and Bake for 8 minutes until golden brown.Serve right away.

Crispy Apple Fries With Caramel Sauce

Servings:4
Cooking Time:15 Minutes
Ingredients:
- 4 medium apples,cored
- ¼tsp cinnamon
- ¼tsp nutmeg
- 1 cup caramel sauce

Directions:
1. Preheat air fryer to 350°F(175°C).Slice the apples to a 1/3-inch thickness for a crunchy chip.Place in a large bowl and sprinkle with cinnamon and nutmeg.Place the slices in the air fryer basket.Bake for 6 minutes.Shake the basket,then cook for another 4 minutes or until crunchy.Serve drizzled with caramel sauce and enjoy!

Roasted Veggie Bowls

Servings:4
Cooking Time:30 Minutes
Ingredients:
- 1 cup Brussels sprouts,trimmed and quartered
- ½onion,cut into half-moons
- ½cup green beans,chopped
- 1 cup broccoli florets
- 1 red bell pepper,sliced
- 1 yellow bell pepper,sliced
- 1 tbsp olive oil
- ½tsp chili powder
- ¼tsp ground cumin
- ¼tsp ground coriander

Directions:
1. Preheat air fryer to 350ºF.Combine all ingredients in a bowl.Place veggie mixture in the frying basket and Air Fry for 15 minutes,tossing every 5 minutes.Divide between 4 medium bowls and serve.

Cheesy Eggplant Rounds

Servings:4
Cooking Time:35 Minutes
Ingredients:
- 1 eggplant,peeled
- 2 eggs
- ½cup all-purpose flour
- ¾cup bread crumbs
- 2 tbsp grated Swiss cheese
- Salt and pepper to taste
- ¾cup tomato passata
- ½cup shredded Parmesan
- ½cup shredded mozzarella

Directions:
1. Preheat air fryer to 400°F(205°C).Slice the eggplant into½-inch rounds.Set aside.Set out three small bowls.In the first bowl,add flour.In the second bowl,beat the eggs.In the third bowl,mix the crumbs,2 tbsp of grated Swiss cheese,salt,and pepper.Dip each eggplant in the flour,then dredge in egg,then coat with bread crumb mixture.Arrange the eggplant rounds on the greased frying basket and spray with cooking oil.Bake for 7 minutes.Top each eggplant round with 1 tsp passata and½tbsp each of shredded Parmesan and mozzarella.Cook until the cheese melts,2-3 minutes.Serve warm and enjoy!

Fried Potatoes With Bell Peppers

Servings:4
Cooking Time:30 Minutes
Ingredients:
- 3 russet potatoes,cubed
- 1 tbsp canola oil
- 1 tbsp olive oil
- 1 tsp paprika
- Salt and pepper to taste
- 1 chopped shallot
- ½chopped red bell peppers
- ½diced yellow bell peppers

Directions:
1. Preheat air fryer to 370°F(185°C).Whisk the canola oil,olive oil,paprika,salt,and pepper in a bowl.Toss in the potatoes to coat.Place the potatoes in the air fryer and Bake for 20 minutes,shaking the basket periodically.Top the potatoes with shallot and bell peppers and cook for an additional 3-4 minutes or until the potatoes are cooked through and the peppers are soft.Serve warm.

Veggie Burgers

Servings:4
Cooking Time:15 Minutes
Ingredients:
- 2 cans black beans,rinsed and drained
- ½cup cooked quinoa
- ½cup shredded raw sweet potato
- ¼cup diced red onion
- 2 teaspoons ground cumin
- 1 teaspoon coriander powder
- ½teaspoon salt
- oil for misting or cooking spray

- 8 slices bread
- suggested toppings:lettuce,tomato,red onion,Pepper Jack cheese,guacamole

Directions:
1. In a medium bowl,mash the beans with a fork.
2. Add the quinoa,sweet potato,onion,cumin,coriander,and salt and mix well with the fork.
3. Shape into 4 patties,each¾-inch thick.
4. Mist both sides with oil or cooking spray and also mist the basket.
5. Cook at 390°F(200°C)for 15minutes.
6. Follow the recipe for Toast,Plain&Simple.
7. Pop the veggie burgers back in the air fryer for a minute or two to reheat if necessary.
8. Serve on the toast with your favorite burger toppings.

Easy Cheese&Spinach Lasagna

Servings:6
Cooking Time:50 Minutes
Ingredients:
- 1 zucchini,cut into strips
- 1 tbsp butter
- 4 garlic cloves,minced
- ½yellow onion,diced
- 1 tsp dried oregano
- ¼tsp red pepper flakes
- 1 can diced tomatoes
- 4 oz ricotta
- 3 tbsp grated mozzarella
- ½cup grated cheddar
- 3 tsp grated Parmesan cheese
- ⅛cup chopped basil
- 2 tbsp chopped parsley
- Salt and pepper to taste
- ¼tsp ground nutmeg

Directions:
1. Preheat air fryer to 375°F(190°C).Melt butter in a medium skillet over medium heat.Stir in half of the garlic and onion and cook for 2 minutes.Stir in oregano and red pepper flakes and cook for 1 minute.Reduce the heat to medium-low and pour in crushed tomatoes and their juices.Cover the skillet and simmer for 5 minutes.
2. Mix ricotta,mozzarella,cheddar cheese,rest of the garlic,basil,black pepper,and nutmeg in a large bowl.Arrange a layer of zucchini strips in the baking dish.Scoop 1/3 of the cheese mixture and spread evenly over the zucchini.Spread 1/3 of the tomato sauce over the cheese.Repeat the steps two more times,then top the lasagna with Parmesan cheese.Bake in the frying basket for 25 minutes until the mixture is bubbling and the mozzarella is melted.Allow sitting for 10 minutes before cutting.Serve warm sprinkled with parsley and enjoy!

Spinach And Cheese Calzone

Servings:2
Cooking Time:10 Minutes
Ingredients:
- ⅔cup frozen chopped spinach,thawed
- 1 cup grated mozzarella cheese
- 1 cup ricotta cheese

- ½teaspoon Italian seasoning
- ½teaspoon salt
- freshly ground black pepper
- 1 store-bought or homemade pizza dough*(about 12 to 16 ounces)
- 2 tablespoons olive oil
- pizza or marinara sauce(optional)

Directions:
1. Drain and squeeze all the water out of the thawed spinach and set it aside.Mix the mozzarella cheese,ricotta cheese,Italian seasoning,salt and freshly ground black pepper together in a bowl.Stir in the chopped spinach.
2. Divide the dough in half.With floured hands or on a floured surface,stretch or roll one half of the dough into a 10-inch circle.Spread half of the cheese and spinach mixture on half of the dough,leaving about one inch of dough empty around the edge.
3. Fold the other half of the dough over the cheese mixture,almost to the edge of the bottom dough to form a half moon.Fold the bottom edge of dough up over the top edge and crimp the dough around the edges in order to make the crust and seal the calzone.Brush the dough with olive oil.Repeat with the second half of dough to make the second calzone.
4. Preheat the air fryer to 360°F(180°C).
5. Brush or spray the air fryer basket with olive oil.Air-fry the calzones one at a time for 10 minutes,flipping the calzone over half way through.Serve with warm pizza or marinara sauce if desired.

Veggie-stuffed Bell Peppers

Servings:4
Cooking Time:40 Minutes
Ingredients:
- ½cup canned fire-roasted diced tomatoes,including juice
- 2 red bell peppers
- 4 tsp olive oil
- ½yellow onion,diced
- 1 zucchini,diced
- ¾cup chopped mushrooms
- ¼cup tomato sauce
- 2 tsp Italian seasoning
- ¼tsp smoked paprika
- Salt and pepper to taste

Directions:
1. Cut bell peppers in half from top to bottom and discard the seeds.Brush inside and tops of the bell peppers with some olive oil.Set aside.Warm the remaining olive oil in a skillet over medium heat.Stir-fry the onion,zucchini,and mushrooms for 5 minutes until the onions are tender.Combine tomatoes and their juice,tomato sauce,Italian seasoning,paprika,salt,and pepper in a bowl.
2. Preheat air fryer to 350ºF.Divide both mixtures between bell pepper halves.Place bell pepper halves in the frying basket and Air Fry for 8 minutes.Serve immediately.

Eggplant Parmesan

Servings:4
Cooking Time:8 Minutes Per Batch
Ingredients:
- 1 medium eggplant,6–8 inches long

- salt
- 1 large egg
- 1 tablespoon water
- ⅔cup panko breadcrumbs
- ⅓cup grated Parmesan cheese,plus more for serving
- 1 tablespoon Italian seasoning
- ¾teaspoon oregano
- oil for misting or cooking spray
- 1 24-ounce jar marinara sauce
- 8 ounces spaghetti,cooked
- pepper

Directions:
1. Preheat air fryer to 390°F(200°C).
2. Leaving peel intact,cut eggplant into 8 round slices about¾-inch thick.Salt to taste.
3. Beat egg and water in a shallow dish.
4. In another shallow dish,combine panko,Parmesan,Italian seasoning,and oregano.
5. Dip eggplant slices in egg wash and then crumbs,pressing lightly to coat.
6. Mist slices with oil or cooking spray.
7. Place 4 eggplant slices in air fryer basket and cook for 8 minutes,until brown and crispy.
8. While eggplant is cooking,heat marinara sauce.
9. Repeat step 7 to cook remaining eggplant slices.
10. To serve,place cooked spaghetti on plates and top with marinara and eggplant slices.At the table,pass extra Parmesan cheese and freshly ground black pepper.

Sesame Orange Tofu With Snow Peas

Servings:4
Cooking Time:40 Minutes
Ingredients:
- 14 oz tofu,cubed
- 1 tbsp tamari
- 1 tsp olive oil
- 1 tsp sesame oil
- 1½tbsp cornstarch,divided
- ½tsp salt
- ¼tsp garlic powder
- 1 cup snow peas
- ½cup orange juice
- ¼cup vegetable broth
- 1 orange,zested
- 1 garlic clove,minced
- ¼tsp ground ginger
- 2 scallions,chopped
- 1 tbsp sesame seeds
- 2 cups cooked jasmine rice
- 2 tbsp chopped parsley

Directions:
1. Preheat air fryer to 400°F(205°C).Combine tofu,tamari,olive oil,and sesame oil in a large bowl until tofu is coated.Add in 1 tablespoon cornstarch,salt,and garlic powder and toss.Arrange the tofu on the frying basket.Air Fry for 5 minutes,then shake the basket.Add snow peas and Air Fry for 5 minutes.Place tofu mixture in a bowl.

2. Bring the orange juice,vegetable broth,orange zest,garlic,and ginger to a boil over medium heat in a small saucepan.Whisk the rest of the cornstarch and 1 tablespoon water in a small bowl to make a slurry.Pour the slurry into the saucepan and constantly stir for 2 minutes until the sauce has thickened.Let off the heat for 2 minutes.Pour the orange sauce,scallions,and sesame seeds in the bowl with the tofu and stir to coat.Serve with jasmine rice sprinkled with parsley.Enjoy!

Vegetable Hand Pies

Servings:8
Cooking Time:10 Minutes Per Batch
Ingredients:
- ¾cup vegetable broth
- 8 ounces potatoes
- ¾cup frozen chopped broccoli,thawed
- ¼cup chopped mushrooms
- 1 tablespoon cornstarch
- 1 tablespoon milk
- 1 can organic flaky biscuits(8 large biscuits)
- oil for misting or cooking spray

Directions:
1. Place broth in medium saucepan over low heat.
2. While broth is heating,grate raw potato into a bowl of water to prevent browning.You will need¾cup grated potato.
3. Roughly chop the broccoli.
4. Drain potatoes and put them in the broth along with the broccoli and mushrooms.Cook on low for 5 minutes.
5. Dissolve cornstarch in milk,then stir the mixture into the broth.Cook about a minute,until mixture thickens a little.Remove from heat and cool slightly.
6. Separate each biscuit into 2 rounds.Divide vegetable mixture evenly over half the biscuit rounds,mounding filling in the center of each.
7. Top the four rounds with filling,then the other four rounds and crimp the edges together with a fork.
8. Spray both sides with oil or cooking spray and place 4 pies in a single layer in the air fryer basket.
9. Cook at 330°F(165°C)for approximately 10 minutes.
10. Repeat with the remaining biscuits.The second batch may cook more quickly because the fryer will be hot.

Veggie Fried Rice

Servings:4
Cooking Time:25 Minutes
Ingredients:
- 1 cup cooked brown rice
- ⅓cup chopped onion
- ½cup chopped carrots
- ½cup chopped bell peppers
- ½cup chopped broccoli florets
- 3 tablespoons low-sodium soy sauce
- 1 tablespoon sesame oil
- 1 teaspoon ground ginger
- 1 teaspoon ground garlic powder
- ½teaspoon black pepper
- ⅛teaspoon salt
- 2 large eggs

Directions:

1. Preheat the air fryer to 370°F(185°C).
2. In a large bowl,mix together the brown rice,onions,carrots,bell pepper,and broccoli.
3. In a small bowl,whisk together the soy sauce,sesame oil,ginger,garlic powder,pepper,salt,and eggs.
4. Pour the egg mixture into the rice and vegetable mixture and mix together.
5. Liberally spray a 7-inch springform pan(or compatible air fryer dish)with olive oil.Add the rice mixture to the pan and cover with aluminum foil.
6. Place a metal trivet into the air fryer basket and set the pan on top.Cook for 15 minutes.Carefully remove the pan from basket,discard the foil,and mix the rice.Return the rice to the air fryer basket,turning down the temperature to 350°F(175°C)and cooking another 10 minutes.
7. Remove and let cool 5 minutes.Serve warm.

Falafel

Servings:4
Cooking Time:10 Minutes
Ingredients:
- 1 cup dried chickpeas
- ½onion,chopped
- 1 clove garlic
- ¼cup fresh parsley leaves
- 1 teaspoon salt
- ¼teaspoon crushed red pepper flakes
- 1 teaspoon ground cumin
- ½teaspoon ground coriander
- 1 to 2 tablespoons flour
- olive oil
- Tomato Salad
- 2 tomatoes,seeds removed and diced
- ½cucumber,finely diced
- ¼red onion,finely diced and rinsed with water
- 1 teaspoon red wine vinegar
- 1 tablespoon olive oil
- salt and freshly ground black pepper
- 2 tablespoons chopped fresh parsley

Directions:
1. Cover the chickpeas with water and let them soak overnight on the counter.Then drain the chickpeas and put them in a food processor,along with the onion,garlic,parsley,spices and 1 tablespoon of flour.Pulse in the food processor until the mixture has broken down into a coarse paste consistency.The mixture should hold together when you pinch it.Add more flour as needed,until you get this consistency.
2. Scoop portions of the mixture(about 2 tablespoons in size)and shape into balls.Place the balls on a plate and refrigerate for at least 30 minutes.You should have between 12 and 14 balls.
3. Preheat the air fryer to 380°F(195°C).
4. Spray the falafel balls with oil and place them in the air fryer.Air-fry for 10 minutes,rolling them over and spraying them with oil again halfway through the cooking time so that they cook and brown evenly.
5. Serve with pita bread,hummus,cucumbers,hot peppers,tomatoes or any other fillings you might like.

Cauliflower Steaks Gratin

Servings:2
Cooking Time:13 Minutes
Ingredients:
- 1 head cauliflower
- 1 tablespoon olive oil
- salt and freshly ground black pepper
- ½teaspoon chopped fresh thyme leaves
- 3 tablespoons grated Parmigiano-Reggiano cheese
- 2 tablespoons panko breadcrumbs

Directions:
1. Preheat the air-fryer to 370°F(185°C).
2. Cut two steaks out of the center of the cauliflower.To do this,cut the cauliflower in half and then cut one slice about 1-inch thick off each half.The rest of the cauliflower will fall apart into florets,which you can roast on their own or save for another meal.
3. Brush both sides of the cauliflower steaks with olive oil and season with salt,freshly ground black pepper and fresh thyme.Place the cauliflower steaks into the air fryer basket and air-fry for 6 minutes.Turn the steaks over and air-fry for another 4 minutes.Combine the Parmesan cheese and panko breadcrumbs and sprinkle the mixture over the tops of both steaks and air-fry for another 3 minutes until the cheese has melted and the breadcrumbs have browned.Serve this with some sautéed bitter greens and air-fried blistered tomatoes.

Lentil Burritos With Cilantro Chutney

Servings:4
Cooking Time:30 Minutes
Ingredients:
- 1 cup cilantro chutney
- 1 lb cooked potatoes,mashed
- 2 tsp sunflower oil
- 3 garlic cloves,minced
- 1½tbsp fresh lime juice
- 1½tsp cumin powder
- 1 tsp onion powder
- 1 tsp coriander powder
- Salt to taste
- ½tsp turmeric
- ¼tsp cayenne powder
- 4 large flour tortillas
- 1 cup cooked lentils
- ½cup shredded cabbage
- ¼cup minced red onions

Directions:
1. Preheat air fryer to 390°F(200°C).Place the mashed potatoes,sunflower oil,garlic,lime,cumin,onion powder,coriander,salt,turmeric,and cayenne in a large bowl.Stir well until combined.Lay the tortillas out flat on the counter.In the middle of each,distribute the potato filling.Add some of the lentils,cabbage,and red onions on top of the potatoes.Close the wraps by folding the bottom of the tortillas up and over the filling,then folding the sides in,then roll the bottom up to form a burrito.Place the wraps in the greased frying basket,seam side down.Air Fry for 6-8 minutes,flipping once until golden and crispy.Serve topped with cilantro chutney.

Roasted Vegetable Thai Green Curry

Servings:4
Cooking Time:16 Minutes
Ingredients:
- 1(13-ounce)can coconut milk
- 3 tablespoons green curry paste
- 1 tablespoon soy sauce*
- 1 tablespoon rice wine vinegar
- 1 teaspoon sugar
- 1 teaspoon minced fresh ginger
- ½onion,chopped
- 3 carrots,sliced
- 1 red bell pepper,chopped
- olive oil
- 10 stalks of asparagus,cut into 2-inch pieces
- 3 cups broccoli florets
- basmati rice for serving
- fresh cilantro
- crushed red pepper flakes(optional)

Directions:
1. Combine the coconut milk,green curry paste,soy sauce,rice wine vinegar,sugar and ginger in a medium saucepan and bring to a boil on the stovetop.Reduce the heat and simmer for 20 minutes while you cook the vegetables.Set aside.
2. Preheat the air fryer to 400°F(205°C).
3. Toss the onion,carrots,and red pepper together with a little olive oil and transfer the vegetables to the air fryer basket.Air-fry at 400°F(205°C)for 10 minutes,shaking the basket a few times during the cooking process.Add the asparagus and broccoli florets and air-fry for an additional 6 minutes,again shaking the basket for even cooking.
4. When the vegetables are cooked to your liking,toss them with the green curry sauce and serve in bowls over basmati rice.Garnish with fresh chopped cilantro and crushed red pepper flakes.

Broccoli Cheddar Stuffed Potatoes

Servings:2
Cooking Time:42 Minutes
Ingredients:
- 2 large russet potatoes,scrubbed
- 1 tablespoon olive oil
- salt and freshly ground black pepper
- 2 tablespoons butter
- ¼cup sour cream
- 3 tablespoons half-and-half(or milk)
- 1¼cups grated Cheddar cheese,divided
- ¾teaspoon salt
- freshly ground black pepper
- 1 cup frozen baby broccoli florets,thawed and drained

Directions:
1. Preheat the air fryer to 400°F(205°C).
2. Rub the potatoes all over with olive oil and season generously with salt and freshly ground black pepper.Transfer the potatoes into the air fryer basket and air-

fry for 30 minutes,turning the potatoes over halfway through the cooking process.

3. Remove the potatoes from the air fryer and let them rest for 5 minutes.Cut a large oval out of the top of both potatoes.Leaving half an inch of potato flesh around the edge of the potato,scoop the inside of the potato out and into a large bowl to prepare the potato filling.Mash the scooped potato filling with a fork and add the butter,sour cream,half-and-half,1 cup of the grated Cheddar cheese,salt and pepper to taste.Mix well and then fold in the broccoli florets.

4. Stuff the hollowed out potato shells with the potato and broccoli mixture.Mound the filling high in the potatoes–you will have more filling than room in the potato shells.

5. Transfer the stuffed potatoes back to the air fryer basket and air-fry at 360°F(180°C)for 10 minutes.Sprinkle the remaining Cheddar cheese on top of each stuffed potato,lower the heat to 330°F(165°C)and air-fry for an additional minute or two to melt cheese.

Rigatoni With Roasted Onions,Fennel,Spinach And Lemon Pepper Ricotta

Servings:2
Cooking Time:13 Minutes
Ingredients:
- 1 red onion,rough chopped into large chunks
- 2 teaspoons olive oil,divided
- 1 bulb fennel,sliced¼-inch thick
- ¾cup ricotta cheese
- 1½teaspoons finely chopped lemon zest,plus more for garnish
- 1 teaspoon lemon juice
- salt and freshly ground black pepper
- 8 ounces(½pound)dried rigatoni pasta
- 3 cups baby spinach leaves

Directions:
1. Bring a large stockpot of salted water to a boil on the stovetop and Preheat the air fryer to 400°F(205°C).
2. While the water is coming to a boil,toss the chopped onion in 1 teaspoon of olive oil and transfer to the air fryer basket.Air-fry at 400°F(205°C)for 5 minutes.Toss the sliced fennel with 1 teaspoon of olive oil and add this to the air fryer basket with the onions.Continue to air-fry at 400°F(205°C)for 8 minutes,shaking the basket a few times during the cooking process.
3. Combine the ricotta cheese,lemon zest and juice,¼teaspoon of salt and freshly ground black pepper in a bowl and stir until smooth.
4. Add the dried rigatoni to the boiling water and cook according to the package directions.When the pasta is cooked al dente,reserve one cup of the pasta water and drain the pasta into a colander.
5. Place the spinach in a serving bowl and immediately transfer the hot pasta to the bowl,wilting the spinach.Add the roasted onions and fennel and toss together.Add a little pasta water to the dish if it needs moistening.Then,dollop the lemon pepper ricotta cheese on top and nestle it into the hot pasta.Garnish with more lemon zest if desired.

Hearty Salad

Servings:2

Cooking Time:15 Minutes
Ingredients:
- 5 oz cauliflower,cut into florets
- 2 grated carrots
- 1 tbsp olive oil
- 1 tbsp lemon juice
- 2 tbsp raisins
- 2 tbsp roasted pepitas
- 2 tbsp diced red onion
- ¼cup mayonnaise
- 1/8 tsp black pepper
- 1 tsp cumin
- ½tsp chia seeds
- ½tsp sesame seeds

Directions:
1. Preheat air fryer at 350ºF.Combine the cauliflower,cumin,olive oil,black pepper and lemon juice in a bowl,place it in the frying basket,and Bake for 5 minutes.Transfer it to a serving dish.Toss in the remaining ingredients.Let chill covered in the fridge until ready to use.Serve sprinkled with sesame and chia seeds.

Sweet Corn Bread

Servings:6
Cooking Time:35 Minutes
Ingredients:
- 2 eggs,beaten
- ½cup cornmeal
- ½cup pastry flour
- 1/3 cup sugar
- 1 tsp lemon zest
- ½tbsp baking powder
- ¼tsp salt
- ¼tsp baking soda
- ½tbsp lemon juice
- ½cup milk
- ¼cup sunflower oil

Directions:
1. Preheat air fryer to 350°F(175°C).Add the cornmeal,flour,sugar,lemon zest,baking powder,salt,and baking soda in a bowl.Stir with a whisk until combined.Add the eggs,lemon juice,milk,and oil to another bowl and stir well.Add the wet mixture to the dry mixture and stir gently until combined.Spray a baking pan with oil.Pour the batter in and Bake in the fryer for 25 minutes or until golden and a knife inserted in the center comes out clean.Cut into wedges and serve.

Easy Zucchini Lasagna Roll-ups

Servings:2
Cooking Time:40 Minutes
Ingredients:
- 2 medium zucchini
- 2 tbsp lemon juice
- 1½cups ricotta cheese
- 1 tbsp allspice
- 2 cups marinara sauce
- 1/3 cup mozzarella cheese

Directions:

1. Preheat air fryer to 400°F(205°C).Cut the ends of each zucchini,then slice into 1/4-inch thick pieces and drizzle with lemon juice.Roast for 5 minutes until slightly tender.Let cool slightly.Combine ricotta cheese and allspice in a bowl;set aside.Spread 2 tbsp of marinara sauce on the bottom of a baking pan.Spoon 1-2 tbsp of the ricotta mixture onto each slice,roll up each slice and place them spiral-side up in the pan.Scatter with the remaining ricotta mixture and drizzle with marinara sauce.Top with mozzarella cheese and Bake at 360°F for 20 minutes until the cheese is bubbly and golden brown.Serve warm.

Chive Potato Pierogi

Servings:4
Cooking Time:55 Minutes
Ingredients:
- 2 boiled potatoes,mashed
- Salt and pepper to taste
- 1 tsp cumin powder
- 2 tbsp sour cream
- ¼cup grated Parmesan
- 2 tbsp chopped chives
- 1 tbsp chopped parsley
- 1¼cups flour
- ¼tsp garlic powder
- ¾cup Greek yogurt
- 1 egg

Directions:
1. Combine the mashed potatoes along with sour cream,cumin,parsley,chives,pepper,and salt and stir until slightly chunky.Mix the flour,salt,and garlic powder in a large bowl.Stir in yogurt until it comes together as a sticky dough.Knead in the bowl for about 2-3 minutes to make it smooth.Whisk the egg and 1 teaspoon of water in a small bowl.Roll out the dough on a lightly floured work surface to¼-inch thickness.Cut out 12 circles with a cookie cutter.
2. Preheat air fryer to 350°F(175°C).Divide the potato mixture and Parmesan cheese between the dough circles.Brush the edges of them with the egg wash and fold the dough over the filling into half-moon shapes.Crimp the edges with a fork to seal.Arrange the on the greased frying basket and Air Fry for 8-10 minutes,turning the pierogies once,until the outside is golden.Serve warm.

Garlic Okra Chips

Servings:4
Cooking Time:20 Minutes
Ingredients:
- 2 cups okra,cut into rounds
- 1½tbsp.melted butter
- 1 garlic clove,minced
- 1 tsp powdered paprika
- Salt and pepper to taste

Directions:
1. Preheat air fryer to 350°F(175°C).Toss okra,melted butter,paprika,garlic,salt and pepper in a medium bowl until okra is coated.Place okra in the frying basket and Air Fry for 5 minutes.Shake the basket and Air Fry for another 5 minutes.Shake one more time and Air Fry for 2 minutes until crispy.Serve warm and enjoy.

Fennel Tofu Bites

Servings:4
Cooking Time:35 Minutes
Ingredients:
- 1/3 cup vegetable broth
- 2 tbsp tomato sauce
- 2 tsp soy sauce
- 1 tbsp nutritional yeast
- 1 tsp Italian seasoning
- 1 tsp granulated sugar
- 1 tsp ginger grated
- ½tsp fennel seeds
- ½tsp garlic powder
- Salt and pepper to taste
- 14 oz firm tofu,cubed
- 2/3 cup bread crumbs
- 1 tsp Italian seasoning
- 2 tsp toasted sesame seeds
- 1 cup marinara sauce,warm

Directions:
1. In a large bowl,whisk the vegetable broth,soy sauce,ginger,tomato sauce,nutritional yeast,Italian seasoning,sugar,fennel seeds,garlic powder,salt and black pepper.Toss in tofu to coat.Let marinate covered in the fridge for 30 minutes,tossing once.
2. Preheat air fryer at 350°F.Mix the breadcrumbs,Italian seasoning,and salt in a bowl.Strain marinade from tofu cubes and dredge them in the breadcrumb mixture.Place tofu cubes in the greased frying basket and Air Fry for 10 minutes,turning once.Serve sprinkled with sesame seeds and marinara sauce on the side.

Stuffed Zucchini Boats

Servings:2
Cooking Time:20 Minutes
Ingredients:
- olive oil
- ½cup onion,finely chopped
- 1 clove garlic,finely minced
- ½teaspoon dried oregano
- ¼teaspoon dried thyme
- ¾cup couscous
- 1½cups chicken stock,divided
- 1 tomato,seeds removed and finely chopped
- ½cup coarsely chopped Kalamata olives
- ½cup grated Romano cheese
- ¼cup pine nuts,toasted
- 1 tablespoon chopped fresh parsley
- 1 teaspoon salt
- freshly ground black pepper
- 1 egg,beaten
- 1 cup grated mozzarella cheese,divided
- 2 thick zucchini

Directions:
1. Preheat a sautépan on the stovetop over medium-high heat.Add the olive oil and sautéthe onion until it just starts to soften–about 4 minutes.Stir in the garlic,dried oregano and thyme.Add the couscous and sautéfor just a minute.Add 1¼cups of the chicken stock and simmer over low heat for 3

to 5 minutes,until liquid has been absorbed and the couscous is soft.Remove the pan from heat and set it aside to cool slightly.

2. Fluff the couscous and add the tomato,Kalamata olives,Romano cheese,pine nuts,parsley,salt and pepper.Mix well.Add the remaining chicken stock,the egg and½cup of the mozzarella cheese.Stir to ensure everything is combined.

3. Cut each zucchini in half lengthwise.Then,trim each half of the zucchini into four 5-inch lengths.(Save the trimmed ends of the zucchini for another use.)Use a spoon to scoop out the center of the zucchini,leaving some flesh around the sides.Brush both sides of the zucchini with olive oil and season the cut side with salt and pepper.

4. Preheat the air fryer to 380°F(195°C).

5. Divide the couscous filling between the four zucchini boats.Use your hands to press the filling together and fill the inside of the zucchini.The filling should be mounded into the boats and rounded on top.

6. Transfer the zucchini boats to the air fryer basket and drizzle the stuffed zucchini boats with olive oil.Air-fry for 19 minutes.Then,sprinkle the remaining mozzarella cheese on top of the zucchini,pressing it down onto the filling lightly to prevent it from blowing around in the air fryer.Air-fry for one more minute to melt the cheese.Transfer the finished zucchini boats to a serving platter and garnish with the chopped parsley.

Berbere Eggplant Dip

Servings:4
Cooking Time:35 Minutes
Ingredients:
- 1 eggplant,halved lengthwise
- 3 tsp olive oil
- 2 tsp pine nuts
- ¼cup tahini
- 1 tbsp lemon juice
- 2 cloves garlic,minced
- ¼tsp berbere seasoning
- ⅛tsp ground cumin
- Salt and pepper to taste
- 1 tbsp chopped parsley

Directions:
1. Preheat air fryer to 370ºF.Brush the eggplant with some olive oil.With a fork,pierce the eggplant flesh a few times.Place them,flat sides-down,in the frying basket.Air Fry for 25 minutes.Transfer the eggplant to a cutting board and let cool for 3 minutes until easy to handle.Place pine nuts in the frying basket and Air Fry for 2 minutes,shaking every 30 seconds.Set aside in a bowl.

2. Scoop out the eggplant flesh and add to a food processor.Add in tahini,lemon juice,garlic,berbere seasoning,cumin,salt,and black pepper and pulse until smooth.Transfer to a serving bowl.Scatter with toasted pine nuts,parsley,and the remaining olive oil.Serve immediately.

Cheese&Bean Burgers

Servings:2
Cooking Time:35 Minutes
Ingredients:
- 1 cup cooked black beans
- ½cup shredded cheddar

- 1 egg,beaten
- Salt and pepper to taste
- 1 cup bread crumbs
- ½cup grated carrots

Directions:
1. Preheat air fryer to 350°F(175°C).Mash the beans with a fork in a bowl.Mix in the cheese,salt,and pepper until evenly combined.Stir in half of the bread crumbs and egg.Shape the mixture into 2 patties.Coat each patty with the remaining bread crumbs and spray with cooking oil.Air Fry for 14-16 minutes,turning once.When ready,removeto a plate.Top with grated carrots and serve.

Creamy Broccoli&Mushroom Casserole

Servings:4
Cooking Time:30 Minutes
Ingredients:
- 4 cups broccoli florets,chopped
- 1 cup crushed cheddar cheese crisps
- ¼cup diced onion
- ¼tsp dried thyme
- ¼tsp dried marjoram
- ¼tsp dried oregano
- ½cup diced mushrooms
- 1 egg
- 2 tbsp sour cream
- ¼cup mayonnaise
- Salt and pepper to taste

Directions:
1. Preheat air fryer to 350ºF.Combine all ingredients,except for the cheese crisps,in a bowl.Spoon mixture into a round cake pan.Place cake pan in the frying basket and Bake for 14 minutes.Let sit for 10 minutes.Distribute crushed cheddar cheese crisps over the top and serve.

Garlicky Brussel Sprouts With Saffron Aioli

Servings:4
Cooking Time:20 Minutes
Ingredients:
- 1 lb Brussels sprouts,halved
- 1 tsp garlic powder
- Salt and pepper to taste
- ½cup mayonnaise
- ½tbsp olive oil
- 1 tbsp Dijon mustard
- 1 tsp minced garlic
- Salt and pepper to taste
- ½tsp liquid saffron

Directions:
1. Preheat air fryer to 380°F(195°C).Combine the Brussels sprouts,garlic powder,salt and pepper in a large bowl.Place in the fryer and spray with cooking oil.Bake for 12-14 minutes,shaking once,until just brown.

2. Meanwhile,in a small bowl,mix mayonnaise,olive oil,mustard,garlic,saffron,salt and pepper.When the Brussels sprouts are slightly cool,serve with aioli.Enjoy!

Mushroom-rice Stuffed Bell Peppers

Servings:4
Cooking Time:30 Minutes
Ingredients:
- 4 red bell peppers,tops sliced
- 1½cups cooked rice
- ¼cup chopped leeks
- ¼cup sliced mushrooms
- ¾cup tomato sauce
- Salt and pepper to taste
- ¾cup shredded mozzarella
- 2 tbsp parsley,chopped

Directions:
1. Fill a large pot of water and heat on high until it boils.Remove seeds and membranes from the peppers.Carefully place peppers into the boiling water for 5 minutes.Remove and set aside to cool.Mix together rice,leeks,mushrooms,tomato sauce,parsley,salt,and pepper in a large bowl.Stuff each pepper with the rice mixture.Top with mozzarella.
2. Preheat air fryer to 350°F(175°C).Arrange the peppers on the greased frying basket and Bake for 10 minutes.Serve.

Tortilla Pizza Margherita

Servings:1
Cooking Time:15 Minutes
Ingredients:
- 1 flour tortilla
- ¼cup tomato sauce
- 1/3 cup grated mozzarella
- 3 basil leaves

Directions:
1. Preheat air fryer to 350°F(175°C).Put the tortilla in the greased basket and pour the sauce in the center.Spread across the whole tortilla.Sprinkle with cheese and Bake for 8-10 minutes or until crisp.Remove carefully and top with basil leaves.Serve hot.

Mushroom Bolognese Casserole

Servings:4
Cooking Time:20 Minutes
Ingredients:
- 1 cup canned diced tomatoes
- 2 garlic cloves,minced
- 1 tsp onion powder
- ¾tsp dried basil
- ¾tsp dried oregano
- 1 cup chopped mushrooms
- 16 oz cooked spaghetti

Directions:
1. Preheat air fryer to 400°F(205°C).Whisk the tomatoes and their juices,garlic,onion powder,basil,oregano,and mushrooms in a baking pan.Cover with aluminum foil and Bake for 6 minutes.Slide out the pan and add the cooked spaghetti;stir to coat.Cover with aluminum foil and Bake for 3 minutes until and bubbly.Serve and enjoy!

Desserts And Sweets

Rich Blueberry Biscuit Shortcakes

Servings:4
Cooking Time:35 Minutes
Ingredients:
- 1 lb blueberries,halved
- ¼cup granulated sugar
- 1 tsp orange zest
- 1 cup heavy cream
- 1 tbsp orange juice
- 2 tbsp powdered sugar
- ¼tsp cinnamon
- ¼tsp nutmeg
- 2 cups flour
- 1 egg yolk
- 1 tbsp baking powder
- ½tsp baking soda
- ½tsp cornstarch
- ½tsp salt
- ½tsp vanilla extract
- ½tsp honey
- 4 tbsp cold butter,cubed
- 1¼cups buttermilk

Directions:
1. Combine blueberries,granulated sugar,and orange zest in a bowl.Let chill the topping covered in the fridge until ready to use.Beat heavy cream,orange juice,egg yolk,vanilla extract and powdered sugar in a metal bowl until peaks form.Let chill the whipped cream covered in the fridge until ready to use.
2. Preheat air fryer at 350ºF.Combine flour,cinnamon,nutmeg,baking powder,baking soda,cornstarch,honey,butter cubes,and buttermilk in a bowl until a sticky dough forms.Flour your hands and form dough into 8 balls.Place them on a lightly greased pizza pan.Place pizza pan in the frying basket and Air Fry for 8 minutes.Transfer biscuits to serving plates and cut them in half.Spread blueberry mixture to each biscuit bottom and place tops of biscuits.Garnish with whipped cream and serve.

Magic Giant Chocolate Cookies

Servings:2
Cooking Time:30 Minutes
Ingredients:
- 2 tbsp white chocolate chips
- ½cup flour
- 1/8 tsp baking soda
- ¼cup butter,melted
- ¼cup light brown sugar
- 2 tbsp granulated sugar
- 2 eggs
- 2 tbsp milk chocolate chips
- ¼cup chopped pecans
- ¼cup chopped hazelnuts
- ½tsp vanilla extract
- Salt to taste

Directions:

1. Preheat air fryer at 350ºF.In a bowl,combine the flour,baking soda,butter,brown sugar,granulated sugar,eggs,milk chocolate chips,white chocolate chips,pecans,hazelnuts,vanilla extract,and salt.Press cookie mixture onto a greased pizza pan.Place pizza pan in the frying basket and Bake for 10 minutes.Let cool completely for 10 minutes.Turn over on a plate and serve.

Roasted Pears

Servings:4
Cooking Time:10 Minutes
Ingredients:
- 2 Ripe pears,preferably Anjou,stemmed,peeled,halved lengthwise,and cored
- 2 tablespoons Butter,melted
- 2 teaspoons Granulated white sugar
- Grated nutmeg
- ¼cup Honey
- ½cup(about 1½ounces)Shaved Parmesan cheese

Directions:
1. Preheat the air fryer to 400°F(205°C).
2. Brush each pear half with about 1½teaspoons of the melted butter,then sprinkle their cut sides with½teaspoon sugar.Grate a pinch of nutmeg over each pear.
3. When the machine is at temperature,set the pear halves cut side up in the basket with as much air space between them as possible.Air-fry undisturbed for 10 minutes,or until hot and softened.
4. Use a nonstick-safe spatula,and perhaps a flatware tablespoon for balance,to transfer the pear halves to a serving platter or plates.Cool for a minute or two,then drizzle each pear half with 1 tablespoon of the honey.Lay about 2 tablespoons of shaved Parmesan over each half just before serving.

Holiday Peppermint Cake

Servings:4
Cooking Time:20 Minutes
Ingredients:
- 1½cups flour
- 3 eggs
- 1/3 cup molasses
- ½cup olive oil
- ½cup almond milk
- ½tsp vanilla extract
- ½tsp peppermint extract
- 1 tsp baking powder
- ½tsp salt

Directions:
1. Preheat air fryer to 380°F(195°C).Whisk the eggs and molasses in a bowl until smooth.Slowly mix in the olive oil,almond milk,and vanilla and peppermint extracts until combined.Sift the flour,baking powder,and salt in another bowl.Gradually incorporate the dry ingredients into the wet ingredients until combined.Pour the batter into a greased baking pan and place in the fryer.Bake for 12-15 minutes until a toothpick inserted in the center comes out clean.Serve and enjoy!

Greek Pumpkin Cheesecake

Servings:4
Cooking Time:35 Minutes+Chilling Time
Ingredients:
- 2 tbsp peanut butter
- ¼cup oat flour
- ½cup Greek yogurt
- 2 tbsp sugar
- ¼cup ricotta cheese
- ¼cup canned pumpkin
- 1 tbsp vanilla extract
- 2 tbsp cornstarch
- ¼tsp ground cinnamon

Directions:
1. Preheat air fryer to 320°F(160°C).For the crust:Whisk the peanut butter,oat flour,1 tbsp of Greek yogurt,and 1 tsp of sugar until you get a dough.Remove the dough onto a small cake pan and press down to get a½-inch thick crust.Set aside.Mix the ricotta cheese,pumpkin,vanilla extract,cornstarch,cinnamon,½cup of Greek yogurt,and 1 tbsp of sugar until smooth.Pour over the crust and Bake for 20 minutes until golden brown.Let cool completely and refrigerate for 1 hour before serving.

Giant Oatmeal - peanut Butter Cookie

Servings:4
Cooking Time:18 Minutes
Ingredients:
- 1 cup Rolled oats(not quick-cooking or steel-cut oats)
- ½cup All-purpose flour
- ½teaspoon Ground cinnamon
- ½teaspoon Baking soda
- ⅓cup Packed light brown sugar
- ¼cup Solid vegetable shortening
- 2 tablespoons Natural-style creamy peanut butter
- 3 tablespoons Granulated white sugar
- 2 tablespoons(or 1 small egg,well beaten)Pasteurized egg substitute,such as Egg Beaters
- ⅓cup Roasted,salted peanuts,chopped
- Baking spray

Directions:
1. Preheat the air fryer to 350°F(175°C).
2. Stir the oats,flour,cinnamon,and baking soda in a bowl until well combined.
3. Using an electric hand mixer at medium speed,beat the brown sugar,shortening,peanut butter,granulated white sugar,and egg substitute or egg(as applicable)until smooth and creamy,about 3 minutes,scraping down the inside of the bowl occasionally.
4. Scrape down and remove the beaters.Fold in the flour mixture and peanuts with a rubber spatula just until all the flour is moistened and the peanut bits are evenly distributed in the dough.
5. For a small air fryer,coat the inside of a 6-inch round cake pan with baking spray.For a medium air fryer,coat the inside of a 7-inch round cake pan with baking spray.And for a large air fryer,coat the inside of an 8-inch round cake pan with baking spray.Scrape and gently press the dough into the prepared pan,spreading it into an even layer to the perimeter.
6. Set the pan in the basket and air-fry undisturbed for 18 minutes,or until well browned.

7. Transfer the pan to a wire rack and cool for 15 minutes.Loosen the cookie from the perimeter with a spatula,then invert the pan onto a cutting board and let the cookie come free.Remove the pan and reinvert the cookie onto the wire rack.Cool for 5 minutes more before slicing into wedges to serve.

Fruity Oatmeal Crisp

Servings:6
Cooking Time:25 Minutes
Ingredients:
- 2 peeled nectarines,chopped
- 1 peeled apple,chopped
- 1/3 cup raisins
- 2 tbsp honey
- 1/3 cup brown sugar
- ¼cup flour
- ½cup oatmeal
- 3 tbsp softened butter

Directions:
1. Preheat air fryer to 380°F(195°C).Mix together nectarines,apple,raisins,and honey in a baking pan.Set aside.Mix brown sugar,flour,oatmeal and butter in a medium bowl until crumbly.Top the fruit in a greased pan with the crumble.Bake until bubbly and the topping is golden,10-12 minutes.Serve warm and top with vanilla ice cream if desired.

Orange Gooey Butter Cake

Servings:6
Cooking Time:85 Minutes
Ingredients:
- Crust Layer:
- ½cup flour
- ¼cup sugar
- ½teaspoon baking powder
- ⅛teaspoon salt
- 2 ounces(½stick)unsalted European style butter,melted
- 1 egg
- 1 teaspoon orange extract
- 2 tablespoons orange zest
- Gooey Butter Layer:
- 8 ounces cream cheese,softened
- 4 ounces(1 stick)unsalted European style butter,melted
- 2 eggs
- 2 teaspoons orange extract
- 2 tablespoons orange zest
- 4 cups powdered sugar
- Garnish:
- powdered sugar
- orange slices

Directions:
1. Preheat the air fryer to 350°F(175°C).
2. Grease a 7-inch cake pan and line the bottom with parchment paper.Combine the flour,sugar,baking powder and salt in a bowl.Add the melted butter,egg,orange extract and orange zest.Mix well and press this mixture into the bottom of the greased cake pan.Lower the pan into the basket using an aluminum foil sling(fold a piece of aluminum foil into a strip about 2-inches wide by 24-inches long).Fold the ends of the aluminum foil over the top of the dish before returning the basket to the air fryer.Air-fry uncovered for 8 minutes.

3. To make the gooey butter layer,beat the cream cheese,melted butter,eggs,orange extract and orange zest in a large bowl using an electric hand mixer.Add the powdered sugar in stages,beat until smooth with each addition.Pour this mixture on top of the baked crust in the cake pan.Wrap the pan with a piece of greased aluminum foil,tenting the top of the foil to leave a little room for the cake to rise.

4. Air-fry for 60 minutes at 350°F(175°C).Remove the aluminum foil and air-fry for an additional 17 minutes.

5. Let the cake cool inside the pan for at least 10 minutes.Then,run a butter knife around the cake and let the cake cool completely in the pan.When cooled,run the butter knife around the edges of the cake again and invert it onto a plate and then back onto a serving platter.Sprinkle the powdered sugar over the top of the cake and garnish with orange slices.

Lemon Pound Cake Bites

Servings:6
Cooking Time:20 Minutes
Ingredients:
- 1 pound cake,cubed
- 1/3 cup cinnamon sugar
- ½stick butter,melted
- 1 cup vanilla yogurt
- 3 tbsp brown sugar
- 1 tsp lemon zest

Directions:
1. Preheat the air fryer to 350°F(175°C).Drizzle the cake cubes with melted butter,then put them in the cinnamon sugar and toss until coated.Put them in a single layer in the frying basket and Air Fry for 4 minutes or until golden.Remove and place on a serving plate.Combine the yogurt,brown sugar,and lemon zest in a bowl.Serve with the cake bites.

One-bowl Chocolate Buttermilk Cake

Servings:6
Cooking Time:16-20 Minutes
Ingredients:
- ¾cup All-purpose flour
- ½cup Granulated white sugar
- 3 tablespoons Unsweetened cocoa powder
- ½teaspoon Baking soda
- ¼teaspoon Table salt
- ½cup Buttermilk
- 2 tablespoons Vegetable oil
- ¾teaspoon Vanilla extract
- Baking spray(see here)

Directions:
1. Preheat the air fryer to 325°F(160°C)(or 330°F(165°C),if that's the closest setting).
2. Stir the flour,sugar,cocoa powder,baking soda,and salt in a large bowl until well combined.Add the buttermilk,oil,and vanilla.Stir just until a thick,grainy batter forms.
3. Use the baking spray to generously coat the inside of a 6-inch round cake pan for a small batch,a 7-inch round cake pan for a medium batch,or an 8-inch round cake pan for a large batch.Scrape and spread the chocolate batter into this pan,smoothing the batter out to an even layer.
4. Set the pan in the basket and air-fry undisturbed for 16 minutes for a 6-inch layer,18 minutes for a 7-inch layer,or 20 minutes for an 8-inch layer,or until a toothpick or cake tester inserted into the center of the cake comes out clean.Start checking it at the 14-minute mark to know where you are.
5. Use hot pads or silicone baking mitts to transfer the cake pan to a wire rack.Cool for 5 minutes.To unmold,set a cutting board over the baking pan and invert both the board and the pan.Lift the still-warm pan off the cake layer.Set the wire rack on top of the cake layer and invert all of it with the cutting board so that the cake layer is now right side up on the wire rack.Remove the cutting board and continue cooling the cake for at least 10 minutes or to room temperature,about 30 minutes,before slicing into wedges.

Honey-pecan Yogurt Cake

Servings:6
Cooking Time:18-24 Minutes
Ingredients:
- 1 cup plus 3½tablespoons All-purpose flour
- ¼teaspoon Baking powder
- ¼teaspoon Baking soda
- ¼teaspoon Table salt
- 5 tablespoons Plain full-fat,low-fat,or fat-free Greek yogurt
- 5 tablespoons Honey
- 5 tablespoons Pasteurized egg substitute,such as Egg Beaters
- 2 teaspoons Vanilla extract
- ⅔cup Chopped pecans
- Baking spray(see here)

Directions:
1. Preheat the air fryer to 325°F(160°C)(or 330°F(165°C),if the closest setting).
2. Mix the flour,baking powder,baking soda,and salt in a small bowl until well combined.
3. Using an electric hand mixer at medium speed,beat the yogurt,honey,egg substitute or egg,and vanilla in a medium bowl until smooth,about 2 minutes,scraping down the inside of the bowl once or twice.
4. Turn off the mixer;scrape down and remove the beaters.Fold in the flour mixture with a rubber spatula,just until all of the flour has been moistened.Fold in the pecans until they are evenly distributed in the mixture.
5. Use the baking spray to generously coat the inside of a 6-inch round cake pan for a small batch,a 7-inch round cake pan for a medium batch,or an 8-inch round cake pan for a large batch.Scrape and spread the batter into the pan,smoothing the batter out to an even layer.
6. Set the pan in the basket and air-fry for 18 minutes for a 6-inch layer,22 minutes for a 7-inch layer,or 24 minutes for an 8-inch layer,or until a toothpick or cake tester inserted into the center of the cake comes out clean.Start checking it at the 15-minute mark to know where you are.
7. Use hot pads or silicone baking mitts to transfer the cake pan to a wire rack.Cool for 5 minutes.To unmold,set a cutting board over the baking pan and invert both the board and the pan.Lift the still-warm pan off the cake layer.Set the wire rack on top of that layer and invert all of it with the cutting board so that the cake layer is now right side up on the wire rack.Remove the cutting board and continue cooling the cake for at least 10 minutes or to room temperature,about 30 minutes,before slicing into wedges.

Peanut Butter S' mores

Servings:10
Cooking Time:1 Minute
Ingredients:
- 10 Graham crackers(full,double-square cookies as they come out of the package)
- 5 tablespoons Natural-style creamy or crunchy peanut butter
- ½cup Milk chocolate chips
- 10 Standard-size marshmallows(not minis and not jumbo campfire ones)

Directions:
1. Preheat the air fryer to 350°F(175°C).
2. Break the graham crackers in half widthwise at the marked place,so the rectangle is now in two squares.Set half of the squares flat side up on your work surface.Spread each with about 1½teaspoons peanut butter,then set 10 to 12 chocolate chips point side up into the peanut butter on each,pressing gently so the chips stick.
3. Flatten a marshmallow between your clean,dry hands and set it atop the chips.Do the same with the remaining marshmallows on the other coated graham crackers.Do not set the other half of the graham crackers on top of these coated graham crackers.
4. When the machine is at temperature,set the treats graham cracker side down in a single layer in the basket.They may touch,but even a fraction of an inch between them will provide better air flow.Air-fry undisturbed for 45 seconds.
5. Use a nonstick-safe spatula to transfer the topped graham crackers to a wire rack.Set the other graham cracker squares flat side down over the marshmallows.Cool for a couple of minutes before serving.

Chewy Coconut Cake

Servings:6
Cooking Time:18-22 Minutes
Ingredients:
- ¾cup plus 2½tablespoons All-purpose flour
- ¾teaspoon Baking powder
- ⅛teaspoon Table salt
- 7½tablespoons(1 stick minus½tablespoon)Butter,at room temperature
- ⅓cup plus 1 tablespoon Granulated white sugar
- 5 tablespoons Packed light brown sugar
- 5 tablespoons Pasteurized egg substitute,such as Egg Beaters
- 2 teaspoons Vanilla extract
- ½cup Unsweetened shredded coconut(see here)
- Baking spray

Directions:
1. Preheat the air fryer to 325°F(160°C)(or 330°F(165°C),if that's the closest setting).
2. Mix the flour,baking powder,and salt in a small bowl until well combined.
3. Using an electric hand mixer at medium speed,beat the butter,granulated white sugar,and brown sugar in a medium bowl until creamy and smooth,about 3 minutes,occasionally scraping down the inside of the bowl.Beat in the egg substitute or egg and vanilla until smooth.

4. Scrape down and remove the beaters.Fold in the flour mixture with a rubber spatula just until all the flour is moistened.Fold in the coconut until the mixture is a uniform color.
5. Use the baking spray to generously coat the inside of a 6-inch round cake pan for a small batch,a 7-inch round cake pan for a medium batch,or an 8-inch round cake pan for a large batch.Scrape and spread the batter into the pan,smoothing the batter out to an even layer.
6. Set the pan in the basket and air-fry for 18 minutes for a 6-inch layer,20 minutes for a 7-inch layer,or 22 minutes for an 8-inch layer,or until the cake is well browned and set even if there's a little soft give right at the center.Start checking it at the 16-minute mark to know where you are.
7. Use hot pads or silicone baking mitts to transfer the cake pan to a wire rack.Cool for at least 1 hour or up to 4 hours.Use a nonstick-safe knife to slice the cake into wedges right in the pan,lifting them out one by one.

Mango-chocolate Custard

Servings:4
Cooking Time:40 Minutes
Ingredients:
- 4 egg yolks
- 2 tbsp granulated sugar
- 1/8 tsp almond extract
- 1½cups half-and-half
- 3/4 cup chocolate chips
- 1 mango,pureed
- 1 mango,chopped
- 1 tsp fresh mint,chopped

Directions:
1. Beat the egg yolks,sugar,and almond extract in a bowl.Set aside.Place half-and-half in a saucepan over low heat and bring it to a low simmer.Whisk a spoonful of heated half-and-half into egg mixture,then slowly whisk egg mixture into saucepan.Stir in chocolate chips and mango purée for 10 minutes until chocolate melts.Divide between 4 ramekins.
2. Preheat air fryer at 350ºF.Place ramekins in the frying basket and Bake for 6-8 minutes.Let cool onto a cooling rack for 15 minutes,then let chill covered in the fridge for at least 2 hours or up to 2 days.Serve with chopped mangoes and mint on top.

Pear And Almond Biscotti Crumble

Servings:6
Cooking Time:65 Minutes
Ingredients:
- 7-inch cake pan or ceramic dish
- 3 pears,peeled,cored and sliced
- ½cup brown sugar
- ¼teaspoon ground ginger
- 1 teaspoon ground cinnamon
- ⅛teaspoon ground nutmeg
- 2 tablespoons cornstarch
- 1¼cups(4 to 5)almond biscotti,coarsely crushed
- ¼cup all-purpose flour
- ¼cup sliced almonds
- ¼cup butter,melted

Directions:

1. Combine the pears,brown sugar,ginger,cinnamon,nutmeg and cornstarch in a bowl.Toss to combine and then pour the pear mixture into a greased 7-inch cake pan or ceramic dish.
2. Combine the crushed biscotti,flour,almonds and melted butter in a medium bowl.Toss with a fork until the mixture resembles large crumbles.Sprinkle the biscotti crumble over the pears and cover the pan with aluminum foil.
3. Preheat the air fryer to 350°F(175°C).
4. Air-fry at 350°F(175°C)for 60 minutes.Remove the aluminum foil and air-fry for an additional 5 minutes to brown the crumble layer.
5. Serve warm.

Lemon Iced Donut Balls

Servings:6
Cooking Time:25 Minutes
Ingredients:

- 1 can jumbo biscuit dough
- 2 tsp lemon juice
- ½cup icing sugar,sifted

Directions:

1. Preheat air fryer to 360°F(180°C).Divide the biscuit dough into 16 equal portions.Roll the dough into balls of 1½inches thickness.Place the donut holes in the greased frying basket and Air Fry for 8 minutes,flipping once.Mix the icing sugar and lemon juice until smooth.Spread the icing over the top of the donuts.Leave to set a bit.Serve.

Caramel Blondies With Macadamia Nuts

Servings:4
Cooking Time:35 Minutes+Cooling Time
Ingredients:

- 1/3 cup ground macadamia
- ½cup unsalted butter
- 1 cup white sugar
- 1 tsp vanilla extract
- 2 eggs
- ½cup all-purpose flour
- ½cup caramel chips
- ¼tsp baking powder
- A pinch of salt

Directions:

1. Preheat air fryer to 340°F(170°C).Whisk the eggs in a bowl.Add the melted butter and vanilla extract and whip thoroughly until slightly fluffy.Combine the flour,sugar,ground macadamia,caramel chips,salt,and baking powder in another bowl.Slowly pour the dry ingredients into the wet ingredients,stirring until thoroughly blended and until there are no lumps in the batter.Spoon the batter into a greased cake pan.Place the pan in the air fryer.Bake for 20 minutes until a knife comes out dry and clean.Let cool for a few minutes before cutting and serving.

Donut Holes

Servings:13
Cooking Time:12 Minutes
Ingredients:

- 6 tablespoons Granulated white sugar
- 1½tablespoons Butter,melted and cooled

- 2 tablespoons(or 1 small egg,well beaten)Pasteurized egg substitute,such as Egg Beaters
- 6 tablespoons Regular or low-fat sour cream(not fat-free)
- ¾teaspoon Vanilla extract
- 1⅔cups All-purpose flour
- ¾teaspoon Baking powder
- ¼teaspoon Table salt
- Vegetable oil spray

Directions:

1. Preheat the air fryer to 350°F(175°C).
2. Whisk the sugar and melted butter in a medium bowl until well combined.Whisk in the egg substitute or egg,then the sour cream and vanilla until smooth.Remove the whisk and stir in the flour,baking powder,and salt with a wooden spoon just until a soft dough forms.
3. Use 2 tablespoons of this dough to create a ball between your clean palms.Set it aside and continue making balls:8 more for the small batch,12 more for the medium batch,or 17 more for the large one.
4. Coat the balls in the vegetable oil spray,then set them in the basket with as much air space between them as possible.Even a fraction of an inch will be enough,but they should not touch.Air-fry undisturbed for 12 minutes,or until browned and cooked through.A toothpick inserted into the center of a ball should come out clean.
5. Pour the contents of the basket onto a wire rack.Cool for at least 5 minutes before serving.

Fall Pumpkin Cake

Servings:6
Cooking Time:50 Minutes
Ingredients:

- 1/3 cup pecan pieces
- 5 gingersnap cookies
- 1/3 cup light brown sugar
- 6 tbsp butter,melted
- 3 eggs
- ½tsp vanilla extract
- 1 cup pumpkin purée
- 2 tbsp sour cream
- ½cup flour
- ¼cup tapioca flour
- ½tsp cornstarch
- ½cup granulated sugar
- ½tsp baking soda
- 1 tsp baking powder
- 1 tsp pumpkin pie spice
- 6 oz mascarpone cheese
- 1 1/3 cups powdered sugar
- 1 tsp cinnamon
- 2 tbsp butter,softened
- 1 tbsp milk
- 1 tbsp flaked almonds

Directions:

1. Blitz the pecans,gingersnap cookies,brown sugar,and 3 tbsp of melted butter in a food processor until combined.Press mixture into the bottom of a lightly greased cake pan.Preheat air fryer at 350ºF.In a bowl,whisk the eggs,remaining melted butter,½tsp of vanilla extract,pumpkin purée,and sour cream.In another bowl,combine the

flour,tapioca flour,cornstarch,granulated sugar,baking soda,baking powder,and pumpkin pie spice.Add wet ingredients to dry ingredients and combine.Do not overmix.Pour the batter into a cake pan and cover it with aluminum foil.Place cake pan in the frying basket and Bake for 30 minutes.Remove the foil and cook for another 5 minutes.Let cool onto a cooling rack for 10 minutes.Then,turn cake onto a large serving platter.In a small bowl,whisk the mascarpone cheese,powdered sugar,remaining vanilla extract,cinnamon,softened butter,and milk.Spread over cooled cake and cut into slices.Serve sprinkled with almonds and enjoy!

Giant Buttery Chocolate Chip Cookie

Servings:4
Cooking Time:16 Minutes
Ingredients:
- ⅔cup plus 1 tablespoon All-purpose flour
- ¼teaspoon Baking soda
- ¼teaspoon Table salt
- Baking spray(see the headnote)
- 4 tablespoons(¼cup/½stick)plus 1 teaspoon Butter,at room temperature
- ¼cup plus 1 teaspoon Packed dark brown sugar
- 3 tablespoons plus 1 teaspoon Granulated white sugar
- 2½tablespoons Pasteurized egg substitute,such as Egg Beaters
- ½teaspoon Vanilla extract
- ¾cup plus 1 tablespoon Semisweet or bittersweet chocolate chips

Directions:
1.   Preheat the air fryer to 350°F(175°C).
2.   Whisk the flour,baking soda,and salt in a bowl until well combined.
3.   For a small air fryer,coat the inside of a 6-inch round cake pan with baking spray.For a medium air fryer,coat the inside of a 7-inch round cake pan with baking spray.And for a large air fryer,coat the inside of an 8-inch round cake pan with baking spray.
4.   Using a hand electric mixer at medium speed,beat the butter,brown sugar,and granulated white sugar in a bowl until smooth and thick,about 3 minutes,scraping down the inside of the bowl several times.
5.   Beat in the pasteurized egg substitute or egg(as applicable)and vanilla until uniform.Scrape down and remove the beaters.Fold in the flour mixture and chocolate chips with a rubber spatula,just until combined.Scrape and gently press this dough into the prepared pan,getting it even across the pan to the perimeter.
6.   Set the pan in the basket and air-fry undisturbed for 16 minutes,or until the cookie is puffed,browned,and feels set to the touch.
7.   Transfer the pan to a wire rack and cool for 10 minutes.Loosen the cookie from the perimeter with a spatula,then invert the pan onto a cutting board and let the cookie come free.Remove the pan and reinvert the cookie onto the wire rack.Cool for 5 minutes more before slicing into wedges to serve.

Party S'mores

Servings:6
Cooking Time:15 Minutes
Ingredients:
- 2 dark chocolate bars,cut into 12 pieces
- 12 buttermilk biscuits
- 12 marshmallows

Directions:
1.   Preheat air fryer to 350°F(175°C).Place 6 biscuits in the air fryer.Top each square with a piece of dark chocolate.Bake for 2 minutes.Add a marshmallow to each piece of chocolate.Cook for another minute.Remove and top with another piece of biscuit.Serve warm.

Sea-salted Caramel Cookie Cups

Servings:12
Cooking Time:12 Minutes
Ingredients:
- ⅓cup butter
- ¼cup brown sugar
- 1 teaspoon vanilla extract
- 1 large egg
- 1 cup all-purpose flour
- ½cup old-fashioned oats
- ½teaspoon baking soda
- ¼teaspoon salt
- ⅓cup sea-salted caramel chips

Directions:
1.   Preheat the air fryer to 300°F(150°C).
2.   In a large bowl,cream the butter with the brown sugar and vanilla.Whisk in the egg and set aside.
3.   In a separate bowl,mix the flour,oats,baking soda,and salt.Then gently mix the dry ingredients into the wet.Fold in the caramel chips.
4.   Divide the batter into 12 silicon muffin liners.Place the cookie cups into the air fryer basket and cook for 12 minutes or until a toothpick inserted in the center comes out clean.
5.   Remove and let cool 5 minutes before serving.

Thumbprint Sugar Cookies

Servings:10
Cooking Time:8 Minutes
Ingredients:
- 2½tablespoons butter
- ⅓cup cane sugar
- 1 teaspoon pure vanilla extract
- 1 large egg
- 1 cup all-purpose flour
- ½teaspoon baking soda
- ¼teaspoon salt
- 10 chocolate kisses

Directions:
1.   Preheat the air fryer to 350°F(175°C).
2.   In a large bowl,cream the butter with the sugar and vanilla.Whisk in the egg and set aside.
3.   In a separate bowl,mix the flour,baking soda,and salt.Then gently mix the dry ingredients into the wet.Portion the dough into 10 balls;then press down on each with the bottom of a cup to create a flat cookie.

4. Liberally spray the metal trivet of an air fryer basket with olive oil mist.
5. Place the cookies in the air fryer basket on the trivet and cook for 8 minutes or until the tops begin to lightly brown.
6. Remove and immediately press the chocolate kisses into the tops of the cookies while still warm.
7. Let cool 5 minutes and then enjoy.

Dark Chocolate Peanut Butter S' mores

Servings:4
Cooking Time:6 Minutes
Ingredients:
- 4 graham cracker sheets
- 4 marshmallows
- 4 teaspoons chunky peanut butter
- 4 ounces dark chocolate
- ½teaspoon ground cinnamon

Directions:
1. Preheat the air fryer to 390°F(200°C).Break the graham crackers in half so you have 8 pieces.
2. Place 4 pieces of graham cracker on the bottom of the air fryer.Top each with one of the marshmallows and bake for 6 or 7 minutes,or until the marshmallows have a golden brown center.
3. While cooking,slather each of the remaining graham crackers with 1 teaspoon peanut butter.
4. When baking completes,carefully remove each of the graham crackers,add 1 ounce of dark chocolate on top of the marshmallow,and lightly sprinkle with cinnamon.Top with the remaining peanut butter graham cracker to make the sandwich.Serve immediately.

Keto Cheesecake Cups

Servings:6
Cooking Time:10 Minutes
Ingredients:
- 8 ounces cream cheese
- ¼cup plain whole-milk Greek yogurt
- 1 large egg
- 1 teaspoon pure vanilla extract
- 3 tablespoons monk fruit sweetencr
- ¼teaspoon salt
- ½cup walnuts,roughly chopped

Directions:
1. Preheat the air fryer to 315°F(155°C).
2. In a large bowl,use a hand mixer to beat the cream cheese together with the yogurt,egg,vanilla,sweetener,and salt.When combined,fold in the chopped walnuts.
3. Set 6 silicone muffin liners inside an air-fryer-safe pan.Note:This is to allow for an easier time getting the cheesecake bites in and out.If you don't have a pan,you can place them directly in the air fryer basket.
4. Evenly fill the cupcake liners with cheesecake batter.
5. Carefully place the pan into the air fryer basket and cook for about 10 minutes,or until the tops are lightly browned and firm.
6. Carefully remove the pan when done and place in the refrigerator for 3 hours to firm up before serving.

Fried Cannoli Wontons

Servings:10
Cooking Time:8 Minutes
Ingredients:
- 8 ounces Neufchâtel cream cheese
- ¼cup powdered sugar
- 1 teaspoon vanilla extract
- ¼teaspoon salt
- ¼cup mini chocolate chips
- 2 tablespoons chopped pecans(optional)
- 20 wonton wrappers
- ¼cup filtered water

Directions:
1. Preheat the air fryer to 370°F(185°C).
2. In a large bowl,use a hand mixer to combine the cream cheese with the powdered sugar,vanilla,and salt.Fold in the chocolate chips and pecans.Set aside.
3. Lay the wonton wrappers out on a flat,smooth surface and place a bowl with the filtered water next to them.
4. Use a teaspoon to evenly divide the cream cheese mixture among the 20 wonton wrappers,placing the batter in the center of the wontons.
5. Wet the tip of your index finger,and gently moisten the outer edges of the wrapper.Then fold each wrapper until it creates a secure pocket.
6. Liberally spray the air fryer basket with olive oil mist.
7. Place the wontons into the basket,and cook for 5 to 8 minutes.When the outer edges begin to brown,remove the wontons from the air fryer basket.Repeat cooking with remaining wontons.
8. Serve warm.

Ricotta Stuffed Apples

Servings:4
Cooking Time:25 Minutes
Ingredients:
- ½cup cheddar cheese
- ¼cup raisins
- 2 apples
- ½tsp ground cinnamon

Directions:
1. Preheat air fryer to 350°F(175°C).Combine cheddar cheese and raisins in a bowl and set aside.Chop apples lengthwise and discard the core and stem.Sprinkle each half with cinnamon and stuff each half with 1/4 of the cheddar mixture.Bake for 7 minutes,turn,and Bake for 13 minutes more until the apples are soft.Serve immediately.

Carrot Cake With Cream Cheese Icing

Servings:6
Cooking Time:55 Minutes
Ingredients:
- 1¼cups all-purpose flour
- 1 teaspoon baking powder
- ½teaspoon baking soda
- 1 teaspoon ground cinnamon
- ¼teaspoon ground nutmeg
- ¼teaspoon salt

- 2 cups grated carrot(about 3 to 4 medium carrots or 2 large)
- ¾cup granulated sugar
- ¼cup brown sugar
- 2 eggs
- ¾cup canola or vegetable oil
- For the icing:
- 8 ounces cream cheese,softened at room,Temperature:8 tablespoons butter(4 ounces or 1 stick),softened at room,Temperature:1 cup powdered sugar
- 1 teaspoon pure vanilla extract

Directions:
1. Grease a 7-inch cake pan.
2. Combine the flour,baking powder,baking soda,cinnamon,nutmeg and salt in a bowl.Add the grated carrots and toss well.In a separate bowl,beat the sugars and eggs together until light and frothy.Drizzle in the oil,beating constantly.Fold the egg mixture into the dry ingredients until everything is just combined and you no longer see any traces of flour.Pour the batter into the cake pan and wrap the pan completely in greased aluminum foil.
3. Preheat the air fryer to 350°F(175°C).
4. Lower the cake pan into the air fryer basket using a sling made of aluminum foil(fold a piece of aluminum foil into a strip about 2-inches wide by 24-inches long).Fold the ends of the aluminum foil into the air fryer,letting them rest on top of the cake.Air-fry for 40 minutes.Remove the aluminum foil cover and air-fry for an additional 15 minutes or until a skewer inserted into the center of the cake comes out clean and the top is nicely browned.
5. While the cake is cooking,beat the cream cheese,butter,powdered sugar and vanilla extract together using a hand mixer,stand mixer or food processor(or a lot of elbow grease!).
6. Remove the cake pan from the air fryer and let the cake cool in the cake pan for 10 minutes or so.Then remove the cake from the pan and let it continue to cool completely.Frost the cake with the cream cheese icing and serve.

Fluffy Orange Cake
Servings:6
Cooking Time:30 Minutes
Ingredients:
- 1/3 cup cornmeal
- 1¼cups flour
- ¾cup white sugar
- 1 tsp baking soda
- ¼cup safflower oil
- 1¼cups orange juice
- 1 tsp orange zest
- ¼cup powdered sugar

Directions:
1. Preheat air fryer to 340°F(170°C).Mix cornmeal,flour,sugar,baking soda,safflower oil,1 cup of orange juice,and orange zest in a medium bowl.Mix until combined.
2. Pour the batter into a greased baking pan and set into the air fryer.Bake until a toothpick in the center of the cake comes out clean.Remove the cake and place it on a cooling rack.Use the toothpick to make 20 holes in the

cake.Meanwhile,combine the rest of the juice with the powdered sugar in a small bowl.Drizzle the glaze over the hot cake and allow it to absorb.Leave to cool completely,then cut into pieces.Serve and enjoy!

Maple Cinnamon Cheesecake
Servings:4
Cooking Time:12 Minutes
Ingredients:
- 6 sheets of cinnamon graham crackers
- 2 tablespoons butter
- 8 ounces Neufchâtel cream cheese
- 3 tablespoons pure maple syrup
- 1 large egg
- ½teaspoon ground cinnamon
- ¼teaspoon salt

Directions:
1. Preheat the air fryer to 350°F(175°C).
2. Place the graham crackers in a food processor and process until crushed into a flour.Mix with the butter and press into a mini air-fryer-safe pan lined at the bottom with parchment paper.Place in the air fryer and cook for 4 minutes.
3. In a large bowl,place the cream cheese and maple syrup.Use a hand mixer or stand mixer and beat together until smooth.Add in the egg,cinnamon,and salt and mix on medium speed until combined.
4. Remove the graham cracker crust from the air fryer and pour the batter into the pan.
5. Place the pan back in the air fryer,adjusting the temperature to 315°F(155°C).Cook for 18 minutes.Carefully remove when cooking completes.The top should be lightly browned and firm.
6. Keep the cheesecake in the pan and place in the refrigerator for 3 or more hours to firm up before serving.

German Streusel-stuffed Baked Apples
Servings:4
Cooking Time:40 Minutes
Ingredients:
- 2 large apples
- 3 tbsp flour
- 3 tbsp light brown sugar
- ⅛tsp ground cinnamon
- 1 tsp vanilla extract
- 1 tsp chopped pecans
- 2 tbsp cold butter
- 2 tbsp salted caramel sauce

Directions:
1. Cut the apples in half through the stem and scoop out the core and seeds.Mix flour,brown sugar,vanilla,pecans and cinnamon in a bowl.Cut in the butter with a fork until it turns into crumbs.Top each apple half with 2½tbsp of the crumble mixture.
2. Preheat air fryer to 325°F(160°C).Put the apple halves in the greased frying basket.Cook until soft in the center and the crumble is golden,about 25-30 minutes.Serve warm topped with caramel sauce.

Coconut Cream Roll-ups

Servings:4
Cooking Time:20 Minutes
Ingredients:
- ½cup cream cheese,softened
- 1 cup fresh raspberries
- ¼cup brown sugar
- ¼cup coconut cream
- 1 egg
- 1 tsp corn starch
- 6 spring roll wrappers

Directions:
1. Preheat air fryer to 350°F(175°C).Add the cream cheese,brown sugar,coconut cream,cornstarch,and egg to a bowl and whisk until all ingredients are completely mixed and fluffy,thick and stiff.Spoon even amounts of the creamy filling into each spring roll wrapper,then top each dollop of filling with several raspberries.Roll up the wraps around the creamy raspberry filling,and seal the seams with a few dabs of water.
2. Place each roll on the foil-lined frying basket,seams facing down.Bake for 10 minutes,flipping them once until golden brown and perfect on the outside,while the raspberries and cream filling will have cooked together in a glorious fusion.Remove with tongs and serve hot or cold.Serve and enjoy!

Brownies With White Chocolate

Servings:6
Cooking Time:30 Minutes
Ingredients:
- ¼cup white chocolate chips
- ¼cup muscovado sugar
- 1 egg
- 2 tbsp white sugar
- 2 tbsp canola oil
- 1 tsp vanilla
- ¼cup cocoa powder
- 1/3 cup flour

Directions:
1. Preheat air fryer to 340°F(170°C).Beat the egg with muscovado sugar and white sugar in a bowl.Mix in the canola oil and vanilla.Next,stir in cocoa powder and flour until just combined.Gently fold in white chocolate chips.Spoon the batter into a lightly pan.Bake until the brownies are set when lightly touched on top,about 20 minutes.Let to cool completely before slicing.

Cherry Cheesecake Rolls

Servings:6
Cooking Time:30 Minutes
Ingredients:
- 1 can crescent rolls
- 4 oz cream cheese
- 1 tbsp cherry preserves
- 1/3 cup sliced fresh cherries

Directions:
1. Roll out the dough into a large rectangle on a flat work surface.Cut the dough into 12 rectangles by cutting 3 cuts across and 2 cuts down.In a microwave-safe bowl,soften cream cheese for 15 seconds.Stir together with cherry preserves.Mound 2 tsp of the cherries-cheese mix on each piece of dough.Carefully spread the mixture but not on the edges.Top with 2 tsp of cherries each.Roll each triangle to make a cylinder.
2. Preheat air fryer to 350°F(175°C).Place the first batch of the rolls in the greased air fryer.Spray the rolls with cooking oil and Bake for 8 minutes.Let cool in the air fryer for 2-3 minutes before removing.Serve.

Honey Apple-pear Crisp

Servings:4
Cooking Time:25 Minutes
Ingredients:
- 1 peeled apple,chopped
- 2 peeled pears,chopped
- 2 tbsp honey
- ½cup oatmeal
- 1/3 cup flour
- 3 tbsp sugar
- 2 tbsp butter,softened
- ½tsp ground cinnamon

Directions:
1. Preheat air fryer to 380°F(195°C).Combine the apple,pears,and honey in a baking pan.Mix the oatmeal,flour,sugar,butter,and cinnamon in a bowl.Note that this mix won't be smooth.Dust the mix over the fruit,then Bake for 10-12 minutes.Serve hot.

Sugared Pizza Dough Dippers With Raspberry Cream Cheese Dip

Servings:10
Cooking Time:8 Minutes
Ingredients:
- 1 pound pizza dough*
- ½cup butter,melted
- ¾to 1 cup sugar
- Raspberry Cream Cheese Dip
- 4 ounces cream cheese,softened
- 2 tablespoons powdered sugar
- ½teaspoon almond extract or almond paste
- 1½tablespoons milk
- ¼cup raspberry preserves
- fresh raspberries

Directions:
1. Cut the ingredients in half or save half of the dough for another recipe.
2. When you're ready to make your sugared dough dippers,remove your pizza dough from the refrigerator at least 1 hour prior to baking and let it sit on the counter,covered gently with plastic wrap.
3. Roll the dough into two 15-inch logs.Cut each log into 20 slices and roll each slice so that it is 3-to 3½-inches long.Cut each slice in half and twist the dough halves together 3 to 4 times.Place the twisted dough on a cookie sheet,brush with melted butter and sprinkle sugar over the dough twists.
4. Preheat the air fryer to 350°F(175°C).
5. Brush the bottom of the air fryer basket with a little melted butter.Air-fry the dough twists in batches.Place 8 to 12(depending on the size of your air fryer)in the air fryer basket.
6. Air-fry for 6 minutes.Turn the dough strips over and brush the other side with butter.Air-fry for an additional 2 minutes.

7. While the dough twists are cooking,make the cream cheese and raspberry dip.Whip the cream cheese with a hand mixer until fluffy.Add the powdered sugar,almond extract and milk,and beat until smooth.Fold in the raspberry preserves and transfer to a serving dish.

8. As the batches of dough twists are complete,place them into a shallow dish.Brush with more melted butter and generously coat with sugar,shaking the dish to cover both sides.Serve the sugared dough dippers warm with the raspberry cream cheese dip on the side.Garnish with fresh raspberries.

Apple Dumplings

Servings:4
Cooking Time:25 Minutes
Ingredients:
- 1 Basic Pie Dough(see the following recipe)
- 4 medium Granny Smith or Pink Lady apples,peeled and cored
- 4 tablespoons sugar
- 4 teaspoons cinnamon
- ½teaspoon ground nutmeg
- 4 tablespoons unsalted butter,melted
- 4 scoops ice cream,for serving

Directions:
1. Preheat the air fryer to 330°F(165°C).
2. Bring the pie crust recipe to room temperature.
3. Place the pie crust on a floured surface.Divide the dough into 4 equal pieces.Roll out each piece to¼-inch-thick rounds.Place an apple onto each dough round.Sprinkle 1 tablespoon of sugar in the core part of each apple;sprinkle 1 teaspoon cinnamon and⅛teaspoon nutmeg over each.Place 1 tablespoon of butter into the center of each.Fold up the sides and fully cover the cored apples.
4. Place the dumplings into the air fryer basket and spray with cooking spray.Cook for 25 minutes.Check after 14 minutes cooking;if they're getting too brown,reduce the heat to 320°F(160°C)and complete the cooking.
5. Serve hot apple dumplings with a scoop of ice cream.

Date Oat Cookies

Servings:6
Cooking Time:20 Minutes
Ingredients:
- ¼cup butter,softened
- 2½tbsp milk
- ½cup sugar
- ½tsp vanilla extract
- ½tsp lemon zest
- ½tsp ground cinnamon
- 3/4 cup flour
- ¼tsp salt
- ¾cup rolled oats
- ¼tsp baking soda
- ¼tsp baking powder
- 2 tbsp dates,chopped

Directions:
1. Use an electric beater to whip the butter until fluffy.Add the milk,sugar,lemon zest,and vanilla.Stir until well combined.Add the cinnamon,flour,salt,oats,baking soda,and baking powder in a separate bowl and stir.Add the dry mix to the wet mix and stir with a wooden spoon.Pour in the dates.

2. Preheat air fryer to 350°F(175°C).Drop tablespoonfuls of the batter onto a greased baking pan,leaving room in between each.Bake for 6 minutes or until light brown.Make all the cookies at once,or save the batter in the fridge for later.Let them cool and enjoy!

Midnight Nutella®Banana Sandwich

Servings:2
Cooking Time:8 Minutes
Ingredients:
- butter,softened
- 4 slices white bread*
- ¼cup chocolate hazelnut spread(Nutella®)
- 1 banana

Directions:
1. Preheat the air fryer to 370°F(185°C).
2. Spread the softened butter on one side of all the slices of bread and place the slices buttered side down on the counter.Spread the chocolate hazelnut spread on the other side of the bread slices.Cut the banana in half and then slice each half into three slices lengthwise.Place the banana slices on two slices of bread and top with the remaining slices of bread(buttered side up)to make two sandwiches.Cut the sandwiches in half(triangles or rectangles)–this will help them all fit in the air fryer at once.Transfer the sandwiches to the air fryer.
3. Air-fry at 370°F(185°C)for 5 minutes.Flip the sandwiches over and air-fry for another 2 to 3 minutes,or until the top bread slices are nicely browned.Pour yourself a glass of milk or a midnight nightcap while the sandwiches cool slightly and enjoy!

Mango Cobbler With Raspberries

Servings:4
Cooking Time:30 Minutes
Ingredients:
- 1½cups chopped mango
- 1 cup raspberries
- 1 tbsp brown sugar
- 2 tsp cornstarch
- 1 tsp lemon juice
- 2 tbsp sunflower oil
- 1 tbsp maple syrup
- 1 tsp vanilla
- ½cup rolled oats
- 1/3 cup flour
- 3 tbsp coconut sugar
- 1 tsp cinnamon
- ¼tsp nutmeg
- ⅛tsp salt

Directions:
1. Place the mango,raspberries,brown sugar,cornstarch,and lemon juice in a baking pan.Stir with a rubber spatula until combined.Set aside.
2. In a separate bowl,add the oil,maple syrup,and vanilla and stir well.Toss in the oats,flour,coconut sugar,cinnamon,nutmeg,and salt.Stir until combined.Sprinkle evenly over the mango-raspberry filling.Preheat air fryer to 320°F(160°C).Bake for 20 minutes or until the topping is crispy and golden.Enjoy warm.

RECIPE INDEX

Manufactured by Amazon.ca
Bolton, ON

35755118R00057